A PENGUIN SPECIAL

S174

GEOGRAPHY OF
WORLD AFFAIRS

J. P. COLE

There are, at the present time, two great nations in the world which see[m]
to tend toward the same end, although they started from different poin[ts].
I allude to the Russians and the Americans. Both of them have grown [up]
unnoticed; and while the attention of mankind was directed elsewhe[re]
they have suddenly assumed a most prominent place among the natio[ns],
and the world learned their existence and their greatness at almost th[e]
same time.

All other nations seem to have nearly reached their natural limit[s],
and only to be charged with the maintenance of their power; but these a[re]
still in the act of growth; all the others are stopped, or continue to advan[ce]
with extreme difficulty; these are proceeding with ease and with celeri[ty]
along a path to which the human eye can assign no term. The America[n]
struggles against the natural obstacles which oppose him; the adversari[es]
of the Russian are men; the former combats the wilderness and savag[e]
life; the latter, civilization with all its weapons and its arts: the conques[ts]
of the one are therefore gained by the ploughshare; those of the othe[r]
by the sword. The Anglo-American relies upon personal interest [to]
accomplish his ends, and gives free scope to the unguided exertions an[d]
common sense of the citizens; the Russian centres all the authority [of]
society in a single arm: the principal instrument of the former is freedom[,]
of the latter servitude. Their starting-point is different, and their course[s]
are not the same; yet each of them seems to be marked out by the will [of]
Heaven to sway the destinies of half the globe.

Extract from *Democracy in America* by Alexis de Tocqueville
First Published in 1835

To be more precise about international tension, it is obvious that every[-]
thing in the end revolves round the relationship between two countries –
the U.S.S.R. and the U.S.A. To illustrate this figuratively, one can say
that just as you would have to tear the leaves from a cabbage gradually[,]
one by one, to discover the heart, so if you were to remove one by one
all the various undecided or disputed questions among countries then the
heart of the matter would turn out to be the contradictions between our
two countries, the U.S.A. and the U.S.S.R.

Khrushchev on International Tension (*Pravda*, 10 May 1957)

CONTENTS

Contents

LIST OF FIGURES

List of Figures

FOREWORD

The reader is asked to bear in mind that the rapidity with which important developments are occurring in world affairs makes it impossible to be up to date with everything in this book. What is more, since many parts of the world lag behind in the publication of figures it has been impossible to obtain reasonably complete sets of figures for a year or two immediately preceding the period of writing, which means that some statistical data will be a few years old by the time the book is read. In most cases, the substitution of the latest figures would not appreciably alter the conclusions drawn from the material.

The author wishes to thank Professor K. C. Edwards, M.A., Ph.D., F.R.G.S., and his other colleagues in the Department of Geography, Nottingham University, for their many helpful suggestions during the preparation of this book. He has further been encouraged by the interest shown by the students of the Department in many of the questions discussed in it. He is most grateful, also, to his wife, Isabel Cole, for her comments as a non-geographer, to his father, Philip Cole, for careful checking of the text, and to Colonel J. Kowalewski for many ideas.

J. P. COLE

ABBREVIATIONS

Benelux	Belgium, Netherlands, Luxembourg
Br.	British
C.	Central
C. Afr. Fed.	Federation of Rhodesia and Nyasaland
ch.	chapter
E.	East
ECSC	European Coal and Steel Community: France, Italy, West Germany, Belgium, Netherlands, Luxembourg
fig.	figure
Fr.	French
I(s)	Island(s)
kwh.	kilowatt hours
m.	million
NATO	North Atlantic Treaty Organization
Neth.	Netherlands
N.	North
S.	South
SEATO	South East Asia Treaty Organization
sq. ml.	square mile
Un. of S. Africa	Union of South Africa
U.S.S.R.	Union of Soviet Socialist Republics, or Soviet Union
U.K.	United Kingdom of Great Britain and Northern Ireland
U.N.	United Nations
UNESCO	United Nations Educational, Scientific, and Cultural Organization
U.S.(A)	United States (of America)
W.	West

PART ONE

Part One is intended to provide a brief background of the world, against which the twelve regional studies in Part Two and the studies of the U.S.A., the Soviet Union, and the U.K. in Part Three are set. So great has been the influence of Europe on most of the rest of the world during the last few centuries that no consideration of world affairs can be complete without some appreciation of this. Then there is the question of choosing suitable regions for the regional studies of different parts of the world. Many people accept the traditional continents, but for some purposes a more suitable division of the world into major regions can be made. Finally, the distribution of population, resources, and production is dealt with briefly in ch. 4 and some resultant problems discussed. The difference in living standards between different parts of the world is stressed.

Chapter 1

INTRODUCTION

I. INTRODUCTORY

AMERICAN leaders sometimes give the impression that they attribute all the troubles in the world to communism, while Soviet leaders believe, or profess to believe, that all international questions are related to problems arising from the death throes of capitalism. It has never been difficult to blame some process or regime or individual for the usual deplorable state of world affairs. Early in the 16th century, Sir Thomas More could think of nothing more horrible on this earth than 'ye most terrible death that all the Turkes in Turkey could deuyse'. Some generations ago, Napoleon was the scourge of Europe (though not in French eyes). Less than a generation ago it was Hitler and the Nazis. Now we feel that if only there were no Russians everything would be perfect. But there *are* Russians, and, whether we like it or not, we have to take notice of what they say and do.

The American and Russian leaders can oversimplify matters as much as they wish. After all, they represent the two most powerful nations in the world today. Smaller and weaker nations have to take a more realistic view, and at least listen to the U.S.A. and the U.S.S.R., even if they do not agree with the views and aims of the leaders of these two nations. The smaller and weaker nations must also listen to one another. For these reasons, few British statesmen see matters as clearly as American and Russian statesmen do; nor, for that matter, as clearly as their own predecessors did a hundred years ago, when Britain was the leading industrial nation in the world, if not the most powerful nation militarily. Britain, like so many other countries that have had a greater influence in the world in the past than they have now, must be prepared to take a realistic view of international problems.

To appreciate the significance of problems and events in world affairs, the student of the subject, professional or amateur, must have some knowledge of the scope and content of a number of disciplines. In particular, he must know something about the history of different parts of the world, at least during the last few centuries, and of the geography of different parts of the world at the present day.

The mention of the word *geography* usually provokes either a shudder of horror or the happy recollection of lists of rivers and mountains and capitals in far-off school days. The reason appears to be that few people who have not been directly concerned with the subject since they left school are aware either of its general scope or of its particular importance as a background to the understanding of world problems. In the study of world affairs it is essential at least to know a few basic facts about the physical environment, the population, and the economic life of the more important countries. It is also essential to know where they are located in the world and what neighbours they have. Syria, for example, is in Southwest Asia; its neighbours include Turkey and Israel but not the U.S.S.R. and Egypt; it has about 3 m. inhabitants and most of its employed population is engaged in agriculture; it occupies an area of about 70,000 sq. mls (and is therefore somewhat larger than England and Wales), most of which, however, is too arid to be of more than slight use for farming. Who, without knowing fundamental facts such as these, is in a position to assess the significance of the events that took place in and around Syria in 1956–7?

Such facts can be obtained from many different sources. At one extreme are works of reference such as year books, in which the material is presented but rarely interpreted. At the other extreme are travel books and articles describing personal experiences and impressions of different parts of the world. These are often biased and rarely complete. Between these extremes fall numerous geographical publications of interest to the student of world affairs. Some are listed at the end of this book. Two, in particular, cover the geographical background to world problems in ample detail and should be consulted by the reader who wishes to go more deeply into the subject than is possible in the present book. They are *The Changing World*, edited by W. G. East and A. E. F. Moodie (London, 1956), which has twenty contributors (including the editors) and is about 1,000 pages in length, and

World Political Geography, by G. E. Pearcy, R. H. Fifield, and associates (New York, 1956), which is also by a team of experts.

The present book is intended to provide a brief geographical background to the study of world affairs for the reader who has no special training in geography and who might hesitate to refer to textbooks written by and prepared for trained geographers. Technical terms have therefore been avoided as much as possible and explained where indispensable. The amount of detail is, of course, limited by the space available, but an attempt has been made to keep a balance by devoting to each major problem and each region of the world the share of the space available that, in the opinion of the author, its particular significance merits.

Part One (chapters 1-4) is devoted to general considerations and deals with some terms and misconceptions, the spread of European influence over the world since the 15th century, the question of dividing the world into regions, and some aspects of population and production. Part Two (chapters 5-7) includes an outline of the physical environment, population, economic life, and main geographical problems of each of twelve regions into which the world has been divided for the purposes of this book. Part Three (chapters 8-10) has special chapters on the U.S.S.R. and the U.S.A. and a study of the position of the U.K. in the world today. Although the topics are arranged in a sequence, each part and even each chapter can be read independently of those preceding or following it.

The figures (maps and diagrams) are placed as near as possible to the page or pages they illustrate. They are a vital part of the book and should be consulted whenever they are referred to in the text, as they are intended to show processes, distributions, and viewpoints.

So numerous are the misconceptions and prejudices concerning world affairs that the remainder of this chapter has been devoted to a discussion of some of these.

II. PROJECTIONS AND MAPS

MOST people will agree that maps are useful in the study of world affairs for showing where places are. Not so many are aware either of the many advantages that may be derived from a fuller application of maps or of the snags that arise from representing the surface of the spherical globe on the flat surface of a map.

There are many ways in which a map can be useful in the study of world affairs. It is often important to know not only where a place is but also where it is located in relation to certain other places. Too often a map merely shows a country or a district, without indicating in which part of the world it is located or what neighbours it has. There is, too, a tendency to use maps merely for showing such features as boundaries, towns, and railways. The blank background on which these are mapped might be mountain or lowland, desert or forest, good cropland or poor pasture. Many important distributions can be shown by means of maps. In addition, a process or a viewpoint may be better understood by a glance at a map than by the study of many pages of text.

Turning now to the difficulties connected with the construction of maps and the representation of material on them, the reader should appreciate that on any map showing a sizeable part of the earth's surface (a continent, for example) there must be some distortion. Just as it is impossible to flatten a large piece of orange peel without tearing it or pulling it out of shape, so a part of the earth's surface, when represented on the flat surface of a map, becomes distorted, whatever projection (the method of converting) is used. Area, distance, shape, and direction – all, or some of these must be sacrificed. The distortion is negligible when an area like Cornwall or Caithness is shown on a map, but it becomes appreciable for an area the size of Europe, and enormous when the whole world is represented on a flat surface. On some projections area is shown correctly (a projection of this kind is called equal area), but for this to be done, shape must be distorted. On other projections shape is preserved (orthomorphic projections) but area must be sacrificed, and some places will be much larger than they should, which means that the scale will be reasonably true only for a part of the map.

Fig. 1a, Mercator's projection, shows a map of the world familiar to many people. On this projection, shape is represented correctly, but area is greatly exaggerated towards the poles,

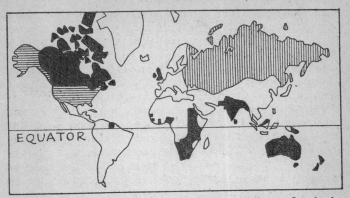

1a. The world on Mercator's projection. Key to shading on figs. 1a–1c. Black: British Empire in 1930s; horizontal lines: U.S.A. and Alaska; vertical lines: U.S.S.R.

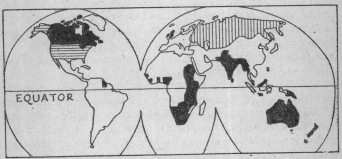

1b. The world on Interrupted Mollweide's homolographic projection.

because the scale increases away from the equator. Although Greenland appears to be as large as South America, in reality it is not much more than one-tenth the size. Fig. 1b shows the world on Interrupted Mollweide's homolographic projection. On this projection area is correct (compare Greenland and South America now) but shape is distorted, especially towards the poles.

19

On both these projections the equator is a straight line running across the map from one side to the other. A world map with the equator in this position is useful when the purpose of the map is to show how temperatures decrease away from the equator towards the poles. It also serves admirably to show how climate, vegetation, soils, agriculture, and even types of building and clothing are related to latitude, because all these are related to temperature. In the study of world affairs, however, it is often more important to know how various places are located in relation to one another than how they are located in relation to the equator. The best way of finding out this is to consult a globe. One of the worst ways is to refer to a projection of the kind shown in figs 1a and 1b. It is not possible to sell a collapsible globe with this book, but fortunately there are other projections of the world that are more useful for the study of world affairs than the type already discussed, though they are not so good as a globe. The globe, of course, is not without disadvantages, and one is that it is never possible to see more than part of the earth's surface on it at a time.

Fig. 1c illustrates Bartholomew's regional projection, which has been used for several world maps in this book. Neither the shape nor the scale of the continents is more than slightly distorted. The projection is constructed by 'peeling' the globe from the south pole and flattening the pieces produced. The oceans, of course, are hopelessly distorted, and Antarctica is divided into several parts. Another drawback of the projection is the fact that the Bering Strait (only about 50 miles wide at its narrowest), which separates the U.S. territory of Alaska from northeast U.S.S.R., has been stretched by the process of 'peeling'. In this book an attempt has been made to remedy this by showing the area twice on some maps. In spite of all these drawbacks the arrangement of the continents is much more realistic than it is on Mercator's projection or other projections of that kind.

The reader should appreciate that the world or parts of it can be shown on many different projections. Every projection is a compromise, but that does not mean that an attempt should not be made to find the most suitable compromise for any particular purpose. Familiar projections (such as Mercator's) are often used to illustrate such topics as world strategy when other projections would be far more suitable. There seems to be a widespread reluctance to make use of less-well-known projections, though some publications do from time to time make use of well-chosen if less familiar maps.

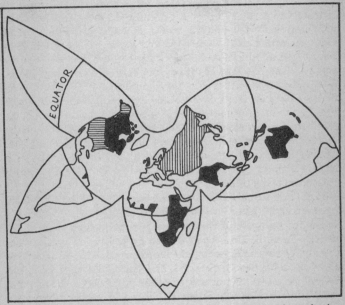

1c. The world on Bartholomew's regional projection (this projection is reproduced in various figures in chs. 1–4 with the kind permission of John Bartholomew and Son Ltd).

Just as we recognize the world, or large parts of it, only when we see them on certain projections, so also are we accustomed to seeing continents and countries only from a certain viewpoint. Doubtless the custom of putting north at the top of maps has advantages, though there is apparently no top and bottom to the universe and therefore no top and bottom to the world. We are accustomed to seeing north at the top and the Arctic Ocean the 'roof of the world', because when a globe is put on a stand, north, and not south (or any other point) is put near the top. We are erroneously applying our idea of gravity, or up and down in relation to the surface and centre of the earth, to the universe as a whole. At all events, N.–S. meridians (lines of longitude) and E.–W. parallels (lines of latitude) are used for the location of places on the earth's surface and, unless otherwise indicated, north is assumed to be at the top of a map. Obviously, it is pointless to put south or west-north-west or any other compass point at the top merely to be different. But as there is no rule about putting north at the top, there is no reason why another compass point should not be put there if a more useful map is produced by so doing. Sometimes, indeed, it is misleading to put north at the top.

One result of always putting north at the top of the map is that we tend to think of some countries and towns as being above others and of each country as having a right way up and a particular shape. This leads to what might be called north–south thinking. We are so accustomed to looking at various parts of the world in one particular way that we are unable to profit by the advantages that frequently occur, above all in political geography and the study of world affairs, from consulting maps that are not north–south.

A motorist travelling for the first time along A1 from London to York with the help of a road map will spread the map out in front of him to consult it. He will look north along the road he is following and north along the same road on the map. West will be to the left and east to the right. If the map shows a turning to the right leading to an inn or a castle the motorist knows that he will find the real turning to the right when he reaches the appropriate road junction. Supposing, now, he tries to use the same map to return from York to London. If he still spreads it out in front of him with north on the map farthest from him while, in reality, he is facing south, he will find all the features on the map the wrong way round. Among other things, he will find that east, not west, is now to the left on the ground, though west is still to the left on his map. If, on the other hand, he reorientates the map by turning it round and putting south

22

farthest from him, the lettering will be upside down but the features on the map will be correctly orientated in relation to those on the ground. Needless to say, special maps are available to enable motorists to follow routes in any direction, and north is only at the top when the traveller is actually heading in that direction.

Just as the route from London to York is most usefully represented on a map with north at the top, whereas the route from York to London should be shown on a map with south at the top, so, in the study of a larger part of the earth's surface, it may be helpful to look at a particular region from different angles. Consider the problem in relation to a larger area than part of England. An observer at a point several hundred miles (vertically) above northern Norway would (if he looked in the right direction) see Europe spread out before him like a map. But it would not be the familiar map of Europe. If he had a map with him, he would have to spread it out in front of him with south farthest away to make it recognizable as the country he was looking at below him.

If the question is now considered in terms of political geography the reader will grasp its significance in connexion with the study of world affairs. Take, for example, the Middle East. We may recognize it at once when we see the various lands and seas that belong to it, provided these are shown on a map with north at the top. But what happens if we try to think of the region in its true relationship to Britain? From a suitable map including both Britain and the Middle East we see that it lies beyond the continent of Europe and the eastern Mediterranean. We should come much nearer to appreciating it in this relationship by turning our map round and putting the southeast farthest from us. It would be better still to prepare a map with southeast at the top (compare figs 2a and 2b). And how does a Russian in Moscow look at the Middle East? It lies to the south of Russia. Looking at a familiar map of this part of the world we see that Russia is on top of the Middle East. Only a little imagination is necessary to visualize hordes of Russian troops pouring into the region, greatly assisted by gravity. But a realistic Russian who wanted to study the relationship of his country to the Middle East would prepare a map with south at the top (as, for example, in fig. 2c). An American, approaching it from the other side of the Atlantic aboard one of the ships of the 6th Fleet, would see it in yet another fashion.

It is hoped that from what has been said the reader will appreciate how we can obtain a more flexible and realistic outlook on world affairs if we remember that the choice of north as the top of the map is arbitrary and that there can be many viewpoints.

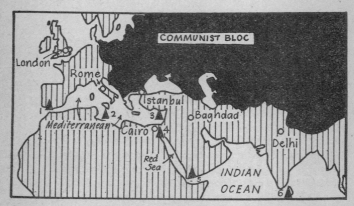

2a. The way we are accustomed to looking at England's position in relation to the Middle East. 1 Gibraltar, 2 Malta, 3 Cyprus, 4 Suez, 5 Aden, 6 Ceylon.

These viewpoints can be found more easily on a globe than in most atlases.

Incidentally, it should be appreciated that the northern and southern, eastern, and western hemispheres (half spheres) are not the only possible ones, and also that these and any other hemispheres (for example, the one with the most land in it) can be represented in various ways, not necessarily with north at the top.

III. VIEWPOINTS AND VIEWS

EACH individual who studies world affairs is bound to have his own viewpoint and views. The viewpoint is partially determined by the locality (in space) and the period (in time) in which he lives. His views are influenced by his environment, by the particular language he speaks, by the customs and traditions of his country and compatriots as well as by what he hears and reads. It is probable, however, that his own particular world outlook may not differ greatly from that of his contemporaries in the same part of the world. The British, for example, tend to have a collective, Anglocentric (or Britannocentric), outlook towards the world. Our outlook is bound to differ from that of the Mexicans or Persians or Australians. After living in another part of the world for some time, a person may of course begin to acquire a world outlook similar to that of the people among whom he is living.

2b. Another possible way of looking at England's position in relation to the Middle East. For explanation of numbers on map see caption to fig. 2a.

Not surprisingly, there is a tendency for people to feel that what they are accustomed to in their own district or country is normal and that everywhere else in the world there are only varying degrees of abnormality. But there is no justification for thinking that conditions in Britain (or anywhere else, of course) are any more normal than those in other parts of the world. Indeed, we should bear in mind that such a highly industrialized

2c. A Russian view of the Middle East.

and urbanized trading community as Britain is something very unusual both now and in the past.

The tendency for people to consider that what they are accustomed to is normal can easily be accompanied by another, more dangerous, tendency. This is for people to think that they, their compatriots, and their way of life are superior to others. They may base their claim to superiority on their superior

26

military strength, on the numbers of cars or telephones they have per hundred inhabitants, on the light colour of their skin, or on the fact that they belong to a certain religious faith or have a particular type of political organization.

The idea that one's own group is not merely different from all others, but also better, is widespread. It is reflected in the rivalry between individual communities and between tribes in simple societies, between towns and regions in civilized countries, and between nations and even continents on a world scale.

Owing to the strong influence that Europe has exerted on the rest of the world during the last few centuries, Europeans have developed a tendency to consider the world and world affairs with a collective or Europocentric viewpoint. Our thinking is consequently affected by various features of this viewpoint. In particular, the Europeans have imposed Europocentric place terms on the rest of the world. The *Near*, *Middle*, and *Far East* are only near, middle, and far in relation to Europe. The Far East is the centre of the world for the Chinese and Japanese. It is the Far West for people living in California and British Columbia. Likewise, the terms *Old World* and *New World* are misleading. If America was a new world for the European explorers who arrived there towards the end of the 15th century, it was the Old World for the tens of millions of people whose ancestors had already been living in the continent at least for a few thousand years. The terms *West*, *Western World*, and *Westernization* are also unfortunate. The West is a vague term widely used in world affairs, but we should remember that if it is west of the East, the East is also west of the West. If we must use these and other Europocentric terms we should not allow them to prejudice our thinking.[1]

There are as many viewpoints as individual viewers and as many collective viewpoints as groups of viewers with some collective interest and consciousness of their collectiveness. If we appreciate this fact we begin to be more critical of some of our

1. Other examples of the acceptance by all or much of the rest of the world of European place and time terms is the labelling of the meridian of Greenwich as 0 and the use of the Christian calendar (Sunday, of no significance in non-Christian countries, is still kept as a rest day).

own views and more sympathetic towards the views of others while remembering, of course, that these are just as biased as our own. Certainly we cannot afford to ignore what other people say and do, whether they are allies or enemies. Indeed, if they are more powerful, it often pays to do what they say.

Failure to consider the aims and aspirations of others leads to misunderstandings. Something might have been done to prevent the Second World War if certain countries had taken seriously what was said in others. What is more important, a third world war might be avoided if people in power spent more time trying to understand the views of others and less in broadcasting their own.

Failure to appreciate the impact on others of one's own statements and actions can also lead to misunderstandings. Politicians are frequently unable to anticipate reactions to their speeches and policies, because they have very little idea of what views other people are likely to hold. It is easy to build up a dream world about the history of one's own country and to be self-righteous about its actions and aspirations. It should be appreciated, however, that other countries do not necessarily agree. There is no better example than Britain itself. In the 1770s it unsuccessfully attempted to prevent its American colonies from gaining their independence. In the 1820s, on the other hand, it was helping the Spanish colonies to free themselves from Spanish colonial rule (one reason, no doubt, was because it could trade more easily with them when they were free). Throughout the 19th century, however, it was building up its empire in South Asia, and in the last decades of the century took part in the scramble for Africa. Yet by 1935, when the Italians set out to annex Abyssinia, the last large territory in Africa remaining outside European control, Britain had again changed its attitude towards colonialism, and opposed Mussolini. However brutal the Italians were towards the Abyssinians in this campaign it is hard to refute their claim that the British were hypocrites. It is easier to disclaim responsibility for the actions of our compatriots of one or a few generations ago than to explain, let alone justify, an inconsistent policy of this kind to others.

Excessive preoccupation with one's own views and viewpoints

can also lead to a misanthropic attitude in world affairs. The Soviet communists profess to sympathize with the workers of the world, yet their party newspaper, *Pravda*, is not the only Russian publication to include articles anticipating an economic depression and gloating over working days lost in strikes and high unemployment figures in capitalist countries, however much inconvenience and misery these bring to the workers themselves. Many U.S. publications are no less jubilant about bad harvests, shortfalls in industrial output, and rumours of unrest in the U.S.S.R., even if the ordinary Soviet citizens, rather than the members of the Communist Party, are likely to suffer the consequences. We in Britain have the misanthropic habit of lamenting industrial progress in Germany and Japan, yet this results in better conditions for the Germans and Japanese. After all, we can hardly blame the Germans for losing the war; they did their best to win it.

The large number of vague terms and terms that lend themselves to imprecise thinking and talking makes it easy to become hypocritical and misanthropic in connexion with world affairs. Terms like *the capitalist world* or *the free world* are vague and difficult to define. Then there are many partners, such as *information* and *hostile propaganda*, *partisan* and *terrorist*, *bandit* or *counter-revolutionary*. The *free world* of the U.S. press is everywhere outside the communist bloc, yet it includes countries governed by absolute monarchs and military dictators as well as colonies governed by European powers. The *capitalist powers* of the Soviet press include not only the U.S.A., where apart from defence and the Post Office almost nothing is nationalized, but also the U.K. and Italy, where many branches of the economy are state owned. Numerous other ill-defined terms confront the student of world affairs. Among them are democracy (but several countries with a communist regime style themselves democracies) and communism; aggression and justified armed intervention; satellite and ally; indoctrination and education.

We may blame politicians and journalists for introducing, distorting, and disseminating terms of this kind, but we too are responsible if we continue to use them, at least without endeavouring to decide what they really mean in any particular context.

Only when escape words of this kind are abandoned or defined, and personal views put aside, can world problems be studied with impartiality.

IV. RACE

SINCE the question of race is connected with so many world problems it seems fitting to conclude this chapter with a few notes on this important topic. Although numerous publications have been prepared on the subject for the non-specialist reader, many people with strong views on race, and particularly on skin colour, appear to be completely ignorant of the most elementary scientific principles concerning the classification of human beings.

For many people, racial groups coincide with cultural groups – political units or linguistic, religious, and other groups. If there are Swedish and Portuguese nations and languages there must be Swedish and Portuguese races. Certainly all the members of some nations (and of other groups of this kind) have many features in common, but it would be more difficult to be satisfied about a Swiss race than a Portuguese one, and the reader who hoped to prove the existence of an Indian or Brazilian or even a U.S. race would come across many difficulties.

Many other people are aware that race is generally accepted by scientists as referring to the measurable physical characteristics of human beings (e.g. height, type of hair) and not to cultural features (e.g. language, religion) nor even to mental capacity (ability in intelligence tests) which is, of course, quite different from volume of brain, a feature that can be measured. But they assume that skin colour (which depends largely on the quantity of the pigment melanin in the outer layers of the skin) is the most important distinguishing characteristic. Since much of the prejudice concerning race is based on this assumption or connected in some way with skin colour, this question deserves our consideration. Many Europeans and people of European origin assume that a darker skin is connected with inferior mental and moral standards. This assumption can easily lead to the argument that *if* people are dark skinned they must be inferior, and even a stage farther to the idea that *because* people are dark skinned they are bound to be inferior. But why do so many people attach much more importance to skin colour than to other characteristics?

The earliest attempt by Europeans to classify human beings into races, after they had explored most of the world in the 15th–17th centuries, was the classification (still at the back of many people's minds today) into white (European), yellow (East Asian), black (African), red (North American Indian), and brown. This early classification was probably based on skin colour for two main reasons. Firstly, before the long-distance movement over short periods of large numbers of people since the 16th century, skin colour was (with exceptions) reasonably uniform among all the inhabitants of large regions (e.g. the tropical Africans were all dark skinned by European standards, probably the result of millennia of natural selection) and it was therefore easy to associate a certain skin colour with a certain part of the world. Secondly, vision is in many ways the most powerful of our senses, and skin colour is one of the first features that strikes us, especially as it is a feature that affects the whole body, if only 'skin deeply'. One wonders if a blind person would attach such importance to skin colour as to some other characteristics. Perhaps dogs classify human beings by their smells.

At all events, it must be appreciated that skin colour is only one of many physical characteristics by which human beings can be classified, and is not necessarily any more useful in this respect than the others, which include type of hair (according to its cross section), shape of head (breadth measured against length, giving cephalic index), and type of blood (but not its colour, even if journalists and politicians talk of black and yellow blood). Whether or not any of the many inheritable physiological characteristics affect the mental capacity of individuals and groups and make them generally inferior or superior is not known. If any do, skin colour seems one of the least likely.

It remains to be proved scientifically, then, that the view held by many Europeans that light skin is connected with racial superiority is anything more than a tragic example of illogical inference. Certainly it is easy to point to the material advances made by Europeans during the last few centuries and to their present generally high living standards wherever they are scattered about the world today and to infer that light-skinned people must be superior at least in mental capacity, and perhaps even morally. Yet a thousand years ago most Europeans were living in agricultural communities differing little in their economic and social organization from those found in Africa a hundred years ago, and, presumably also to be found in Africa a thousand years ago. In contrast, China was then civilized (even though most of its inhabitants were rural dwellers). Were the Chinese therefore superior racially at that time?

Why such remarkable material advances have been made in Europe (and by Europeans outside Europe) in the last few centuries is a difficult matter to decide. Some argue that European 'stock' possesses special qualities. Others suggest that the physical environment of Europe, perhaps the changeable weather, stimulating mental activity, has been responsible. Both may be right – or neither. The development of the modern machine age in Europe may be nothing more than the result of a number of accidents producing a cumulative or snowball effect, each discovery and invention leading on to others. What matters most in world affairs is that some centuries ago Europeans emerged with the most effective way of demonstrating their racial superiority over the rest of the inhabitants of the world – the firearm.

Many current problems are a result of the reluctance of Europeans to mix with non-Europeans and of their reluctance even in the face of modern investigations regarding race to relinquish their superior position and their prejudices. Perhaps that is largely why there is a widespread idea that white people cannot perform physical work in the tropics (though Negroes work very well in cool climates). If they found they could, there would be less justification for relying on the natives.

In conclusion, two points should be considered by the reader. Firstly, when the general level of intelligence of members of different racial groups is compared (e.g. that of Negroes and whites in the U.S.A.) the tests suggest that differences in level may be entirely due to inequality of opportunity, particularly lack of educational facilities for the members of the underprivileged group or groups. Tests also suggest that where members of different races have been brought up in comparable living conditions, with similar educational facilities, their level of intelligence is also comparable. In other words, the generally poorer standard of intelligence and living conditions among non-Europeans in societies in which Europeans and non-Europeans live together results from their generally underprivileged social and economic position, not from their racial inferiority.

Secondly, in connexion with the mixing of races, and particularly of persons with different skin colour, many people consider that mixing produces degenerate half-castes. But perhaps the degeneration is psychological rather than physical, and the responsibility lies with the people still of pure race on both sides, but particularly on the European side, who maintain a prejudiced attitude towards mixing. And why object so strongly to the mixing of people with different skin colour without also objecting to the mixing of people with different shaped heads, different types of hair, or different types of blood? (Here, indeed, there is sometimes a good reason for advising against marriage.)

These problems are social rather than racial, but for various reasons it has been useful for politicians and others, even if aware of the findings of scientific investigations, to exploit the widespread ignorance of most people regarding race. The Nazis are one example, the Europeans in the Union of S. Africa another. The question is, even if it were proved conclusively that there is no such thing as racial superiority, would people change their attitude to the matter if it did not suit them to do so?

We might remember that at one extreme there is only one race of mankind – the human species (or, according to some anthropologists, human genus); at the other, there are as many races as individuals, for no two persons (not even 'identical' twins) are identical down to the last detail.

Chapter 2

THE SPREAD OF EUROPEAN
INFLUENCE

I. THE PROCESS OF EUROPEANIZATION

MANY current problems in world affairs are in some way related to the spread of European influence over the world in different forms and in varying degrees of intensity during the last five centuries. This process, which might be termed *europeanization* rather than *westernization*, has been accompanied since the War of American Independence (1775–83) by a parallel, but reverse, process of de-europeanization, by which European political influence has already been shaken off in some parts of the world.

Europe is the northwest corner of the great triangular-shaped land mass of Eurasia. It is broken into a number of peninsulas and islands by seas penetrating far towards the interior, while its continuity is further interrupted by high mountain ranges. The present generally accepted limits of the continent of Europe are the Ural Range and River Ural in the east, and the River Araks (in Transcaucasia), the Black Sea and the Mediterranean in the south. The limits of the Europa of the Ancient World and of Medieval Europe were certainly not so definite as this. Even so, what is important in a consideration of the effects of European influence on the rest of the world is the concept of a part of the world known as Europe, rather than the exact boundary of the region. The Empire of Alexander the Great, the Ottoman Empire (and now modern Turkey), and the Russian Empire (and now the U.S.S.R.) are three examples of empires which, according to the above definition of Europe, were or are partly inside and partly outside the present precise limits already mentioned.

The 15th century was a critical period for Europe in several ways. Three developments, in particular, greatly affected its subsequent relations with the rest of the world. Firstly, the Ottoman Empire, expanding from a small nucleus in Anatolia, was gaining control of the trade routes between South Europe and Asia and making it more and more difficult to import various commodities into Europe from South and East Asia, thus cutting Europe off from supplies of certain tropical plant products, such as spices, which could not be grown in Europe's climate, and from supplies of a number of luxury manufactures from the East. Secondly, in Europe itself, a number of sizeable states, some of which had already been in existence for a considerable time (e.g. England and Portugal) and some of which were just emerging (e.g. Spain), were developing a strong consciousness of their nationhood. In this respect, the introduction at this period of printing, which facilitated the dissemination of literature in national languages, must have been a powerful influence. Thirdly, it was becoming widely appreciated that the world is a sphere and, therefore, that its surface, the exact size of which was not of course known then, is finite in extent. This was believed for a time in the Ancient World, but not demonstrated by circumnavigation of the globe. The first globe was constructed in 1492, and in 1522 Magellan's expedition successfully completed the first voyage round the world, though Magellan himself died in the Philippines in 1521.

These three apparently disconnected developments together played a great part in starting off the process of europeanization. As a result of the expansion of the Ottoman Empire astride the old routes to the East, new ways of reaching South and East Asia were sought. Portuguese navigators were already exploring the western coast of Africa in the 15th century. Modern Spain, formed by the union of Aragon and Castile (which became effective in 1479) and by the final expulsion of the Moors (in 1492) started later, and, unable to challenge Portugal in Africa, backed the idea of a spherical world and supported Columbus and other explorers who set out westwards across the Atlantic to find Asia in that direction. Subsequently, England unsuccessfully sought yet other possible routes to the East, the northeast and northwest passages. During the 16th century, therefore, a number of European nations were already competing to extend their influence over the globe by exploring the oceans of the world. Portugal was the first modern European nation to penetrate by sea far beyond the limits of Europe, Spain the second. England, France, and later Holland, followed suit.

From eastern Europe another state, the Principality of Muscovy (Moscow), the nucleus of modern Russia, began to expand beyond the limits of the continent of Europe. But, unlike the nations of western Europe, it carried its influence by land, not by sea, and expanded across the great land mass of northern Asia. Whether or not the empire-building of Russia can be compared with that of the western European nations is a difficult and debatable question. In this book, Russia is considered to be one of the active participants in the process of the europeanization of the world during the last five centuries. Russia of the Tsars (and now the European part of the U.S.S.R.) is considered to be part of Europe. Appendix 1 contains some points connected with this question and the reader who does not accept the above remarks about Russia should refer to this. The matter has been put separately in order not to break the continuity of the main theme in this chapter. In this connexion, Turkey also occupies a doubtful position, a small part of modern Turkey being located in Europe, but most in Asia. In this book Turkey is considered not to be part of Europe. This question is also referred to in Appendix 1.

Returning now to the question of European influence on the rest of the world, it is important to bear in mind the great significance of the appreciation in the 15th and 16th centuries that the world is a sphere and its extent therefore measurable. Until it was established that the earth is a sphere and therefore finite, it was impossible to know where, if anywhere, the land and sea ended.

A few decades ago some European explorers discovered a group of about 300 Eskimos (the Polar Eskimos), living in the vicinity of Smith Sound, in the north of Greenland. These Eskimos believed themselves to be the only inhabitants of the universe. They had been isolated from other groups of Eskimos for some generations and knew of no other men except by legend.[1] Why, after all, should they be expected to know how large the earth is or what form it has? Similar in some ways, though it refers to a much larger group of people, is the story

1. See Weyer, E. M. *The Eskimos*, New Haven, 1932

of how Alexander the Great wept when he thought there was nowhere else for him to conquer. Even if he had heard of China, he certainly could not have known of the existence of civilizations in America or, for that matter, of America itself. The Incas, who built up a large Empire in the Andes of South America, had no evidence that their civilization was not the only one in the world. Genghis Khan's Empire covered an enormous part of Asia and Europe but still *terra incognita* lay beyond all its frontiers. For all these empire builders the world might have been any size and shape and (the problem was being debated in Europe in the Middle Ages) there might even have been other worlds like this one. When talking about the past we should think of the world not as we know it today, but as it was known or imagined to be by the inhabitants of the world at the particular period or periods to which we refer.

The situation changed completely around 1500. In 1494 (two years after the first voyage of Columbus to America) it was established by the Treaty of Tordesillas that Portugal should have any lands it acquired to the east, and Spain any to the west, of a meridian passing 370 leagues west of the Cape Verde Islands (this meridian, near 50° W., happens to pass close to the mouth of the Amazon). Some decades later, by the Treaty of Saragossa in 1529, a demarcation line was drawn on the other side of the world (about 145° E.). In this way the whole world was for the first time (but not the last) divided between two powers. Not much of it had of course actually been visited by Europeans at that time. Nevertheless, some decades after this, in 1581–1640, when Spain and Portugal were temporarily united, Spain did control most of South and Central America, as well as much of the coast of Africa and South Asia, thus encircling the globe with its possessions and their spheres of influence. What is important in world affairs is the fact that since the 16th century, any power or group of powers preparing to dominate the whole world or finding itself doing so unintentionally, whether militarily or economically, or in any other way, has been able to know the limits of the world.

Hardly a corner of the world has not by now felt the influence of Europeans in some way. Some regions, like Australia and the

U.S.A., have been transformed by them; other regions, such as the Belgian Congo and India, have merely been modified by their occupation; while such countries as China, Tibet, and the Yemen have until very recently hardly felt the impact of European culture at all.

In the 16th century the Europeans already had certain advantages over the rest of the world. Most important by far was the development by this period of reasonably effective firearms, which, as in the conquest of the Aztec and Inca Empires, helped small numbers of Europeans to overcome and control large numbers of non-Europeans. The cannon was being developed in Europe in the 14th and 15th centuries and hand weapons, the pistol and the musket, were also being developed, although with greater difficulty. Another instrument, which was vital in navigation in oceans, as opposed to seas, was the magnetic compass. This, also, was being used in Europe in the later Middle Ages. Printing, gunpowder, and the magnetic compass were, ironically, used in East Asia before they were used in Europe.[1]

The rivalry between European nations, both in Europe itself and elsewhere, acted as a further stimulus to explore the world and to acquire territories. Colonial territories became a matter of prestige as well as a source of wealth. The rivalry was strengthened by the Reformation and the desire of the different religious groups in 16th-century Europe to Christianize non-Europeans in their own particular ways.

The process of europeanization did not follow the same pattern everywhere. Each nation had its own approach, which itself changed with time. Broadly speaking, however, the following process took place. Explorers and traders set up footholds on the coasts of newly discovered areas (or in the case of the Russian land empire in Siberia, at the meeting-place of natural routes, such as rivers). If and when the footholds were consolidated and expanded by the annexation of appreciable pieces of territory, soldiers and administrators, including some representative of the crown (such as a Viceroy) followed, and forts were set up. With

1. The magnetic compass, and gunpowder for military purposes, in China in the 12th century, and the first book in moveable type in Korea in the early 15th century.

these came men of religion to maintain their creed among Europeans and, frequently, to convert the non-Europeans. In the colonies of Spain and Portugal, a class of land-hungry Iberians (inhabitants of Spain and Portugal) made up of the original conquerors, as well as of later settlers, were given large estates in conquered lands. In many parts of the world the Europeans came to form a ruling class dependent for its existence on the non-Europeans it ruled, a superstructure of largely non-productive members of the community.

In complete contrast were the settlers who left Europe to undertake some form of manual work in colonial territories. Some of the earliest of these were religious minorities persecuted in Europe, who went to North America. Not until the 18th century did appreciable numbers of Europeans of this kind settle outside Europe, and the great migration of settlers, when hundreds of thousands of emigrants left Europe each year, began only in the 19th century, with the introduction of the steamship and the development of railways.

Yet another type of settler, though not a voluntary one, was the non-European forced to move from his own homeland to another part of the world. Africa was the main source of slaves and America the destination of most who survived the journey there.

More recently, European influence has been extended, especially during the period of the Industrial Revolution, by the adoption by non-Europeans of European techniques and institutions. Japan, for example, was never a colony of a European power and never received European settlers, yet it has voluntarily adopted many features of European culture. China is now doing the same, modelling itself at present mainly on the U.S.S.R.

The participants in the process of europeanization over the last five centuries include Portugal, Spain, Russia, England, and France, all of which were active from the 15th or 16th centuries; Holland, which began early in the 17th; Germany, Italy, and Belgium, which started in the 19th century; and Denmark and Norway, which, however, only played a small part. Modern empire builders outside Europe include the U.S.A. and Japan, the former inhabited largely by people of European origin and the latter with industries run on modern European lines.

Fig. 3a shows the world in about 1500. Europe has hardly yet started to influence the rest of the world. The Ottoman Empire is pushing northwest towards the heart of the continent, and peoples of recent Asiatic origin inhabit the southern and eastern parts of what is now European U.S.S.R. Outside Europe there are extensive parts of the world which may also be called civilized because urban life is developed and empires and other large administrative units are to be found. Elsewhere there are thinly peopled lands inhabited by simple societies. These depend in some areas on plough or hoe cultivation, in other areas on the herding of domesticated animals, while in parts of the world they still maintain a precarious existence by hunting or gathering what is offered by nature. The distribution of the simple types of economy in fig. 3a is based on a map in Prof. C. Daryll Forde's very interesting book *Habitat, Economy and Society*.

Fig. 3b shows where European influence has extended after about two centuries. Spain and Portugal have concentrated on the tropics and between them hold almost all of South and Central America (though by no means all has been explored) as well as many coastal areas in Africa and South and Southeast Asia. Russia, in contrast, has colonized lands lying in cool temperate latitudes, some of them even within the Arctic Circle (see section I in ch. 8 for a more detailed account of the growth of the Russian Empire). England, France, and Holland nowhere hold such extensive territories, though France controls the important Mississippi–St Lawrence axis, dominating the interior of North America, while Holland, following in the footsteps of the weakest European empire builder, Portugal, has established a formidable chain of trading stations and forts between Europe and the East Indies. Little impression has yet been made by Europeans on Africa, and no impression on Australasia, while Russia has been the only European power to acquire more than a foothold on the mainland of Asia.

Before the 18th century, relatively few emigrants left Europe to settle in non-European lands. In 1700, for example, the English colonies in North America had fewer than 300,000 British settlers. Lima, the most important Spanish colonial town in South America at that date, had only about 20,000 people of

3a. The world in 1500. The distribution of simple subsistence economies is based, with the kind permission of the author, on a map *World distribution of dominant economies* in Prof. C. Daryll Forde's work *Habitat, Economy and Society*, London, 1934.

EUROPE

E = ENGLAND   F = FRANCE
M = PRINCIPALITY OF MOSCOW
P = PORTUGAL   S = SPAIN

A=AZTEC EMPIRE   C=CHINA   I=INCA EMPIRE   O=OTTOMAN EMPIRE

AREAS OUTSIDE EUROPE WITH SOME URBAN LIFE AND LARGE ADMINISTRATIVE UNITS.

SIMPLE SUBSISTENCE ECONOMIES

MAINLY CULTIVATORS

MAINLY PASTORALISTS

CULTIVATORS AND PASTORALISTS

HUNTERS AND FOOD GATHERERS

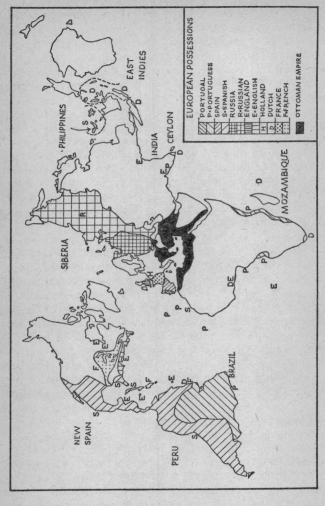

3b. The world in 1700, showing the extent of European influence.

EUROPEAN POSSESSIONS

PORTUGAL
P=PORTUGUESE
SPAIN
S=SPANISH
RUSSIA
R=RUSSIAN
ENGLAND
E=ENGLISH
HOLLAND
D=DUTCH
FRANCE
F=FRENCH

OTTOMAN EMPIRE

SIBERIA

PHILIPPINES

EAST
INDIES

INDIA
CEYLON

MOZAMBIQUE

NEW
SPAIN

PERU

BRAZIL

The Spread of European Influence

Spanish origin. The trade between the European colonial powers and their various possessions was in goods that were of high value in relation to their weight. Obviously the limited cargo-carrying capacity and speed of vessels restricted the amount of trade that could be carried on. Among the products entering Europe from the colonies were precious metals and stones, furs, spices, tobacco, dyes, and special types of wood, and, most important of all by 1700, sugar and sugar products. Cane sugar cannot be cultivated economically in Europe, and beet sugar was not cultivated commercially until the 19th century. Many of the slaves taken from Africa to America worked in the sugar plantations of Northeast Brazil and the West Indies. Neither perishable goods, such as tropical fruits and dairy produce, nor bulky goods such as cereals and coal, could be transported economically over long distances until the 19th century, when steamships were developed.

Much less territory was acquired by European powers outside Europe in the 18th century than in the preceding two centuries. Spain, France, and England spent much of their energy in frequent wars with one another, and Russia, seeking footholds on the Baltic and Black Seas, was more concerned with expansion in Europe itself than with pushing south from Siberia into Central and East Asia. During the 18th century the Russian Empire did, however, expand across the Bering Strait into North America, Holland extended its control over the East Indies, and the English possession of eastern North America and India was assured, while the first European (English) colony was established in Australia in 1788. On the eve of the French Revolution the French Empire consisted only of Haiti and some smaller islands and trading posts.

Between the 1780s and 1820s a reverse process, that of de-europeanization, took place in America, when most of the English colonies in North America and almost all of the Iberian colonies in Latin America gained their independence from Europe. In America, therefore, only Canada (English), Alaska (Russian), Cuba and Puerto Rico (Spanish), and some less important islands in the West Indies and footholds in Central and South America remained under European control. This did not mean, of course, that the cultural or economic influence of Europe was everywhere weakened. Britain, France, and other European nations merely replaced Spain and Portugal in the trade with Latin America. The U.S.A., on the other hand, soon rose to the rank of a major world power. The former ties between America and Europe were maintained by the migration of many millions of people from all parts of Europe to the new daughter states. The result was that each of the former colonies began to be influenced by several European nations instead of merely by the particular power that had previously held it as a possession. It is significant that it was the people of European origin and not the indigenous population (the American Indians) who were largely responsible for shaking off the control of Europe.

Towards the middle of the 19th century there began a second great period of empire building by European powers. This time Spain and Holland took very little part, but three younger nations, Belgium, Italy, and Germany, participated.

A comparison of figs 3b and 3c shows the areas colonized by Europeans between about 1700 and 1914 as well as the areas in which political, if not economic and cultural, influence was lost during this period. Almost all Africa was occupied during the second half of the 19th century, and most of the leading European powers of the time carved out a share. British colonization proceeded in Canada, Australia, and New Zealand. In Asia, Russia pushed south across the Caucasus into the northern lands of the Ottoman Empire, southeast into Central Asia and into the Lower Amur Valley, while in South Asia Britain further strengthened its hold on the Indian Empire, and France annexed part of South-East Asia (Indo-China). By 1914, therefore, only two main areas had not been colonized by Europeans: East Asia, where the Chinese Empire and Japan had resisted European territorial expansion, and Southwest Asia, where the Ottoman Empire had retained its hold after losing its African and most of its European territories to European powers.

That is not the end of the process of europeanization. Being on the losing side in the 1914–18 war, the Ottoman Empire was dispossessed of almost all its territories in Southwest Asia outside the heartland of Turkey itself, and Britain and France were able

EUROPEAN NATIONS
COLONIES OF EUROPE
BRITISH DOMINIONS
FORMER COLONIES OF EUROPE
LANDS NEVER HELD BY EUROPEANS IN THE LAST 500 YEARS EXCEPT IN SMALL LOCALITIES

1 TURKEY
2 PERSIA
3 AFGHANISTAN
4 ARABIA
5 SIAM

NEW ZEALAND
AUSTRALIA
PHILIPPINES
JAPAN
CHINA
INDIA
RUSSIAN EMPIRE
ABYSSINIA
Ital. Prot.
1889-96
UNION OF SOUTH AFRICA
LIBERIA
Africa
ALASKA
CANADA
U.S.A.
REPUBLICS OF LATIN AMERICA

3c. The world in 1914, showing the extent of European influence.

45

to make Southwest Asia their sphere of influence. In 1935, Italy invaded Abyssinia, the only extensive area in Africa by then still free from European colonization.

In addition, two nations outside Europe, the U.S.A. and Japan, began to expand towards the end of the 19th century. Japan was able to annex and dominate extensive densely populated territories in East Asia through having evolved its own version of the European Industrial Revolution.

Turkey (since the 1920s) and more recently China (only seriously in the last decade) have followed the example of Japan and adopted many features of European culture. In this way, very few parts of the world have escaped some form of European influence. Indeed, we are now witnessing what may turn out to be the last scramble for territory, at least on this planet, the exploration of Antarctica, with no permanent inhabitants, and no temporary inhabitants until a few years ago.

Finally, since 1945 a further stage has begun in the process of de-europeanization. Colonies held by Europeans but inhabited by non-Europeans (as opposed to people of European origin) have been granted or are still striving to achieve political independence. India, Indonesia, and Nigeria are examples.

II. THE RESULTS OF EUROPEANIZATION

FIG. 3d is an attempt to represent the broad outlines of the complex end product of more than four centuries of europeanization. The intensity of shading varies according to the intensity of europeanization. Apart from Europe itself (shaded black) there are lands such as Northeast U.S.A., Argentina, and Australia where the indigenous population has been reduced (in some cases by a deliberate policy of extermination, in others by the large numbers of European immigrants) to an insignificant proportion of the total population. Secondly, there are parts of the world where Europeans or people of European origin live alongside non-Europeans, and where one or the other group forms a significant minority. Examples are Southeast U.S.A. and the Un. of S. Africa. Thirdly, there are colonies such as Nigeria and Mozambique, held by European powers, but with only an

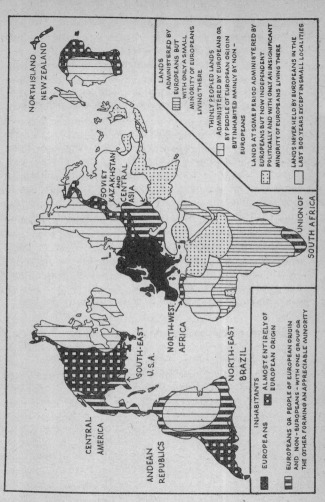

NORTH ISLAND
NEW ZEALAND

LANDS
ADMINISTERED BY
EUROPEANS BUT
WITH ONLY A SMALL
MINORITY OF EUROPEANS
LIVING THERE

THINLY PEOPLED LANDS
ADMINISTERED BY EUROPEANS OR
BY PEOPLE OF EUROPEAN ORIGIN
BUT INHABITED MAINLY BY NON-
EUROPEANS

LANDS AT SOME PERIOD ADMINISTERED BY
EUROPEANS BUT NOW INDEPENDENT
POLITICALLY AND WITH ONLY AN INSIGNIFICANT
MINORITY OF EUROPEANS LIVING THERE

LANDS NEVER HELD BY EUROPEANS IN THE
LAST 500 YEARS EXCEPT IN SMALL LOCALITIES

SOVIET
KAZAKHSTAN
AND
CENTRAL
ASIA

UNION OF
SOUTH AFRICA

NORTH-WEST
AFRICA

SOUTH-EAST
U.S.A.

NORTH-EAST
BRAZIL

CENTRAL
AMERICA

ANDEAN
REPUBLICS

INHABITANTS
EUROPEANS OR PEOPLE OF EUROPEAN ORIGIN

EUROPEANS OR PEOPLE OF EUROPEAN ORIGIN
AND NON-EUROPEANS – WITH ONE GROUP OR
THE OTHER FORMING AN APPRECIABLE MINORITY

3d. The world in 1957, showing the results of europeanization.

47

insignificant proportion of Europeans living there – a super-structure of administrators, teachers, doctors, and so on. Fourthly, there are independent countries, such as India and Indonesia in Asia, and the Sudan and Ghana in Africa, which have been European colonies for some time but which have not been settled by Europeans. Finally, there are countries that have never been possessions of Europe. Some, such as Japan and Turkey, have adopted many features of European culture, while others, such as the Yemen and Tibet, have until very recently attempted with almost complete success to keep Europeans and European ideas out of their countries.

What are the results of European influence on the rest of the world, and how do they affect present-day world problems? Firstly, there are the past actions of Europeans against non-Europeans. Contemporary Europeans may try to forget these or disclaim responsibility, but the memory cannot be wiped out in a few generations. Secondly, there are the present problem areas where Europeans and non-Europeans live in the same regions and where the non-Europeans are politically under-privileged and economically in an inferior position.

It is a mistake to think that some European nations have behaved better than others towards non-Europeans. It is a mistake also to think that Europeans have treated non-Europeans more harshly than they themselves have been treated in the past by non-Europeans. Another point to remember is that European nations have also treated each other just as harshly as they have treated non-Europeans. Finally, it should not be forgotten that Europeans have, on many occasions, brought benefits to non-Europeans. All this does not prevent most non-Europeans from harbouring resentment of some kind or other at unpleasant treatment received from Europeans, and understandably, too, for on the whole the story of europeanization is a dismal one. The key to it is the possession by Europeans of superior arms, assuring them of military superiority in other parts of the world.

Spain completely disorganized the economic and social structure of the Aztec and Inca Empires. It has been estimated[1] that

1. Mariátegui, J. C. *Siete Ensayos de Interpretación de la Realidad Peruana*, Lima, 1952, p. 55.

in three centuries of Spanish domination of the former Inca Empire the indigenous population decreased from 10 m. to 1 m. Even if this decrease is an exaggeration it is a grim reflection of the way in which the complex economic life of a remarkable civilization was slowly broken up. The Spaniards and Portuguese virtually enslaved the American Indians, and when and where there were too few of these to work for their conquerors they imported or purchased from other European traders Negro slaves from Africa. The Portuguese were the first modern Europeans to take slaves from Africa, but when in the 17th and 18th centuries a large-scale trade in African slaves was established it was the English who had the largest share most of the time. The French, Dutch, Spaniards, Portuguese, and, in the 18th century, also the Danes, all participated. The slaves were sold and used in America by the Spanish, Portuguese, English, and French colonists.

In the 19th century many primitive tribes in different parts of the world were exterminated or reduced in numbers and relegated to the poorest lands by the large number of settlers emigrating from Europe. In North America, Argentina, and Australasia there were conflicts in which the indigenous population was greatly reduced in numbers or even systematically exterminated, as in the campaign against the American Indians in the Argentinian pampa (1878–83) or in Tasmania, where the few thousand natives, who were living in Old Stone Age conditions, have disappeared. The last stages of the process by which the Europeans (mainly British) in North America reduced the American Indians from at least several million before they discovered the continent to their present number of a few hundred thousand have been immortalized in the Western films so popular in Europe and America. During the same period there were cruel wars of conquest in Africa by several European powers and in Central Asia by the Russians. During the rubber boom in the Amazon basin, people of European (mainly Portuguese) origin brutally exploited the primitive tribes of South American Indians, and in the Congo the same was done to the Africans.

During the present century the Soviet Communists 'collectivized' or 'denomadized' the Kazakhs and other nomadic tribes in Central Asia; the Italian Fascists invaded Abyssinia, using modern arms, including gas, against Africans with primitive arms, and the Nazi Germans endeavoured to exterminate the largest group of non-Europeans in Europe – the Jews.[1]

These are but a few examples from the tragic and squalid record of europeanization. Nothing would be more wrong than to say that all Europeans have treated all non-Europeans badly. For example, already during the 16th century Spanish and Portuguese men of religion were preoccupied with the material well-being, as well as the souls, of the American Indians, and ever since, Christian missionaries of many denominations have striven to help non-Europeans. In the 19th century it was the English, for whom until then the slave trade had been very profitable, who objected to it and began to take measures to suppress it.

The European attitude to non-Europeans has undoubtedly been improving since the Second World War ; the great social and economic advances made by the Belgians for the Africans of the Congo and the granting of self-government to a number of former British colonies are examples. Nevertheless, there are still uneasy regions in the world, and relations are most strained in the areas named in fig. 4d, where Europeans and non-Europeans live in the same regions. A note follows on each of the more important of these problem areas.

In the U.S.A. in 1950 there were some 15 m. Negroes out of a total population of 151 m. In 1800 the proportion of Negroes was higher: 1 m. out of 5 m. About two-thirds of the Negroes now live in Southeast U.S.A. (the old 'South'), and in one state here (Mississippi) they are almost as numerous as the whites, while in several other states they form between about one-third and two-fifths of the total population. The Negroes in states outside Southeast U.S.A. live mostly in urban areas. The average U.S. Negro is economically much poorer than the average white. Most of the states with the lowest per capita income have the highest percentage of Negroes,[2] as the figures for sample states suggest:

1. See *The Scourge of the Swastika*, by Lord Russell of Liverpool, London, 1954.

2. See *Statistical Abstract of the United States 1954*, p. 38 and p. 291. There are, of course, states such as Kentucky and Tennessee where the whites are also much poorer than the whites in more prosperous states.

TABLE 1

	Annual per capita income (in dollars, 1952)	Per cent Negro (in 1950)
U.S.A.	1709	10
Mississippi	834	45
S. Carolina	1095	39
Louisiana	1249	33
Illinois	2088	7
Wyoming	1650	1

An even better idea of the difference in income between the average Negro and average white is shown by the following data (which refer only to persons earning an income, not to all inhabitants, as the above figures do). More than 50 per cent of the Negroes receiving an income earned less than $1000 in 1949 and only about 0·5 per cent more than $5000. The median income for Negroes was $952. In the U.S.A. as a whole about 20 per cent of the working population earned less than $1000 and approximately 14 per cent more than $5000. The median income was $2619. It should be pointed out, of course, that most of the Negroes do unskilled work and belong to the lower income groups. Even though the Negroes belong mainly to the lower income groups in the U.S.A., however, they are far better off economically than the Negroes of Africa itself.

As well as being mostly in the poorer classes, the Negroes in Southeast U.S.A. are politically underprivileged and socially segregated. Although almost a hundred years have elapsed since the Civil War, the Negroes in the southern states are still not fairly represented in the U.S. government. Moreover, educational facilities have not generally been so good for Negroes as for whites, which is one reason why so few occupy well-paid posts. Finally, the persecution of Negroes still continues in certain forms. When 10 per cent of its population is thus underprivileged, the U.S.A. can hardly expect its teaching of democracy, equality of opportunity, and freedom of the individual to have the appeal it might otherwise have among non-Europeans. What is more, there appears to be no answer to the problem of the Negro in the U.S.A. The difference in colour between the people of European origin and the Negroes is much more marked than in most other parts of the world where people of European origin live alongside non-Europeans. It is hard to agree with the title of a report from *Time*, distributed by the U.S. Information Service: *The U.S. Negro, 1953 ... the greatest success story the world has ever known.* Even so, some attempt is at last being made to improve the position of the U.S. Negro, and it is a mistake to pick on isolated examples of the persecution of Negroes and imply that they are typical.

In the republics and the colonies of tropical Latin America there is almost everywhere a mixture of races. In some areas (e.g. Argentina), people of European origin predominate; in other areas (e.g. much of Mexico and the Andes), American Indians are in the majority; while in some parts (e.g. Haiti, Jamaica, and parts of Northeast Brazil) Negroes are the predominant element. The Europeans (Spaniards and Portuguese) who settled in tropical Latin America are generally darker-skinned than the northern Europeans who predominate in North America and the American Indians are mostly somewhere between the Europeans and the Negroes in skin colour. The sharp distinction drawn in the U.S.A. between non-white and white does not exist, therefore, but there is a distinction between varying degrees of darkness of skin colour. Although it is difficult to assess (as can be done with reasonable precision in the U.S.A.) the difference in living standards, privileges, and opportunity between the different races, it is safe to say that the landowning and professional classes, and the office workers of Latin America are generally of European origin. This, of course, is not true in a country such as Haiti, where very few Europeans settled. Here, however, the lighter-skinned people, with some admixture of European characteristics, dominate the pure or almost pure Negroes. In countries such as Mexico, Ecuador, and Bolivia, where the inhabitants are mainly American Indians, Spanish or mixed, the agricultural workers, miners, and more recently the factory workers, are mainly American Indian or mixed, while the more wealthy citizens are mainly Spanish or mixed. Everywhere in Latin America, as, indeed, also in the U.S.A., there are exceptions to the generalizations so far made. A work worth consulting on race problems in Latin America is the UNESCO publication (Paris, 1952) edited by C. Wagley: *Race and Class in Rural Brazil*.

In the Un. of S. Africa the situation is different again, for here the Negroes (Bantus) are in the majority and the Europeans in the minority, whereas there is no state in the U.S.A. with more Negroes than whites. The situation is further complicated by the fact that although most of the people of European origin are from Holland, an appreciable minority is English. In addition, there are settlers from Asia (mainly India) as well as the Cape coloured, who are mixed African and European. Whereas the federal government in the U.S.A. is endeavouring to bring the status of the Negro closer to that of the white settler, the present government in the Un. of S. Africa appears to be doing the opposite. The Negroes here are mostly farm workers and miners. Their standard of living is far below that of the people of European origin. They are underprivileged and their educational facilities are inferior to those of whites. Admittedly, their living conditions are in certain ways superior to those of most African natives living outside the Union. This is a doubtful compensation for being virtually the slaves of a prosperous European minority.

In certain other parts of Africa there are also problems connected with European settlement. In Southern Rhodesia there is an appreciable minority of people of English origin, and even in Kenya, where the Europeans form less than 1 per cent of the population, racial problems occur. In these parts of Africa the Europeans include permanent settlers owning land as well as temporary residents engaged in various kinds of professional duties.

In North Island, New Zealand, there are areas in which the indigenous population (Maoris) live alongside European (almost entirely British) settlers. The Maoris are in the minority, but although they undoubtedly suffered as a consequence of the impact of European civilization, and had lands confiscated, their economic and social position in New Zealand is now more favourable than that of almost any other non-European minority living among people of European origin anywhere in the world.

In Algeria, and to a lesser extent in Tunisia and Morocco, European settlers form a small but influential minority – more than 10 per cent in Algeria, but less than this in Morocco and Tunisia. While the latter countries are now independent from

France, trends in 1958 make it appear that France intends to keep some kind of permanent control over Algeria. The problem here is not so closely connected with differences in physical characteristics between two races as between the generally poor North Africans, and the Europeans who have far more than their share of the good farmland of the country – they took this by force during the gradual French occupation of Algeria between 1830 and the end of the century. Although they make up only one-ninth of the total population, the French and other settlers of European origin have about one-third of all the cultivated land.

Tension between the French settlers and Muslim Algerians has been growing since 1945, and has resulted in one of the bitterest struggles the world has seen between Europeans and non-Europeans because successive French governments have failed to make any significant concessions to the underprivileged majority of non-Europeans.[1] 'In three years of conflict (1954–7) at least 75,000 French and Muslims, including civilians, have been killed and wounded'.[2] An English translation of Jean-Paul Sartre's bitter attack on French policy appears in the *Observer*, 9 Mar. 1958.

In the U.S.S.R. about 80 per cent of the total population consists of Russians, Ukrainians, Belorussians, and other smaller European groups (e.g. Latvians). The remainder of the population is Asian (Transcaucasia being considered as non-European by many Russians, if not by the Transcaucasians themselves). The original inhabitants of most of Siberia were few in number, considering the great size of this territory, and their economic and social organizations were mainly simple. There appears to have been relatively little friction here between these peoples and the Russian and Ukrainian settlers who moved out in large numbers along the Trans-Siberian Railway after about 1900. In contrast, in Transcaucasia and Central Asia (lands that have been civilized longer than Russia itself) many social problems have arisen since the Russians conquered them in the last century. Before 1917 the Russians settled these territories in relatively small numbers and largely constituted a class of administrators

1. See the *Observer*, 11, 18, and 25 Aug. 1957.
2. See the *Sunday Times*, 3 Nov. 1957.

and professional workers. These colonies were important
principally as a source of raw materials, particularly cotton.
During the Soviet period, the intensity of Russian influence has
increased greatly. Republics have been formed round the more
important peoples (really language groups), but their independence is theoretical and they are dominated politically by the
Communist Party and economically by Soviet all-union planning.
Russians now make up about 20 per cent of the population of
the Kazakh Republic and 15 per cent of that of the Central Asian
Republics, according to one recent Soviet geographical publication.[1] While the way of life of these Asian subjects of Russia was
little modified before 1917, the Soviet policy has been to transform it in many ways. In agriculture, for example, nomadism has
been suppressed and the pastoralist farmers collectivized. The
language and traditions have been respected, but the Muslim
religion is discouraged, and the Russian language, the only
language in which many publications on technical matters are
available, is widely taught. The Russians in these Republics are
mainly urban dwellers, which suggests that they are still a privileged class, but it appears that many Russians and Ukrainians have
been settling here, particularly in Kazakhstan, as farmers. Some
idea of the Russian influence on these Asian colonies is given
by the fact that out of some 70,000 teachers in the Kazakh
Republic only 23,000 are Kazakhs.[2] The Soviet policy may well
be to 'russify' the Asians of the U.S.S.R. by settling a certain
proportion of Russians in every region and by eventually replacing the native language by Russian (see also ch. 8).

It will be appreciated from the foregoing examples that the
racial and social problems resulting from the presence of Europeans and non-Europeans in the same area differ from region to
region. It might be suggested that the greatest hatred arises where
the skin colour contrasts are greatest and miscegenation prohi-
bited or discouraged. This occurs where people of north European
origin (Scandinavians, Dutch, Germans, and British in particular)
live in the same area as dark-skinned people (especially Negroes).
Fortunately, many of the worst aspects of europeanization, such

1. N. I. Lyalikov and others, *Geografiya SSSR*, Moscow, 1955.
2. *Ekonomicheskaya Geografiya SSSR,* Moscow, 1957, p. 236.

as slave trade and the deliberate extermination of primitive peoples, no longer exist. Even so, Europeans or their descendants are a privileged section of the community in many regions of the world. It should be remembered that their claim to this privilege rests largely on their initial military superiority, and that to this day the French in Algeria, the Russians in Central Asia, and, for that matter, the British in all their dependent territories maintain themselves at their own invitation. Rarely in the last five centuries have Europeans been invited by the indigenous population to annex, colonize, and govern their lands. It is therefore a compliment to Britain that, except for Burma and Eire, all of the former possessions to which it has granted self-government have agreed to remain within the British Commonwealth. In contrast, the Indonesians have done everything possible to show their hatred of their former Dutch masters (and undoubtedly the Indonesian leaders have used this to keep the minds of the mass of the population off internal problems) while even the most stubborn French politician can hardly imagine that the opposition in Algeria comes merely from a handful of terrorists.

III. THE SHIFT OF POWER IN EUROPE

To conclude this examination of some of the main features of European colonization there follows a brief study of events in Europe during the last five centuries. The competition to colonize different parts of the world to some extent reflected the struggle for power within Europe itself. While the process of europeanization outside Europe was in progress a process was taking place in Europe by which the centre of power gradually shifted eastwards across the continent.

In the 16th century Spain was undoubtedly a powerful nation in Europe, although the data necessary to measure its strength with any precision are lacking. After its union with Portugal in 1581, it had territories in the Netherlands, Central Europe, and the Mediterranean, as well as almost all of Central and South America and numerous footholds in Africa and Southeast Asia. The defeat of the Armada in 1588 and the secession of Portugal in 1640 were setbacks for Spain in Europe and overseas, for the

Portuguese colonial possessions, like their mother country, were lost to Spain in 1640.

While the economic basis of Spain's power weakened in the 17th century, France, agriculturally a more prosperous country, was challenging the strength of Spain. After a series of wars in the 18th century in which Spain, France, and England were frequently involved, France emerged the strongest land power in Europe, and was not conclusively defeated until 1814–15, when England, Prussia, and Russia had all taken a hand in assuring its downfall. At this stage Russia, with its superiority in manpower and in the production of arms, might have taken over the role of dominant military power in Europe. By this time, however, it was behind western Europe technologically, and in the 19th century most of its leaders were unwilling to consider any of the social changes necessary to modify the antiquated economy of the country. Serfdom was at this time undoubtedly a great obstacle to progress, and Russia fared badly compared with Western Europe, where the French Revolution and subsequent wars had caused many changes. At this point, Britain, where many of the innovations of the Industrial Revolution had been applied for the first time, was gaining a powerful position in the world, and between about 1850 and 1870 was producing about half of the world's pig iron, a useful measure of its great industrial expansion. The final emergence of the German Empire in 1871 and its decisive defeat of France established Germany as the strongest single land power in Europe, larger in population than Britain or France and by then well in advance of Russia industrially. The final shift of power followed the defeat of the German armies in the U.S.S.R. in 1943–5 and resulted in the final emergence of that country as the leading land power in Europe.

The centre of power has thus shifted gradually from Spain, at the height of its power, perhaps, in the 1580s, to France, which controlled much of Europe around 1810, and then to Germany, which in 1942 held even more of Europe than France had done at the beginning of the previous century, and finally to the U.S.S.R. which itself occupies half of Europe and, in communist East Europe, controls another tenth.

Although the U.S.S.R. had become the leading land power of

Europe by 1945, the U.S.A. was already the leading world power from both a military and an economic point of view. The tension and rivalry between so-called West and East is no more than a continuation of the struggle for power between European nations. The U.S.A. is an offshoot of Europe now backing Western Europe against the U.S.S.R., the strongest single power on the continent.

During this period of conflict between the nations of Europe, England's role in European affairs has been to oppose the leading land power. Indeed, the part it has played in bringing about in turn the decline of Spain, France, and Germany has by no means been insignificant (though frequently magnified in British history books). Surely the next step for Britain and its former rivals is to collaborate in some form of union more solid and lasting than the North Atlantic Treaty Organization to balance the growing economic and military strength of the U.S.S.R.

Chapter 3

A REGIONAL DIVISION OF THE WORLD

SEVERAL reasons may be suggested why the traditional division of the land areas of the world into a number of continents is in many ways unsatisfactory and misleading in the study of world affairs. One is that the distribution of European settlers and the intensity of European influence outside Europe itself (see fig. 3d, ch. 2) bear little relationship to the continents as we know them, and vary greatly from one region to another within them. Another reason is that the U.S.S.R. and Turkey, each of which is a political and economic unit, lie partly in Europe, partly in Asia, and would have to be artificially divided to keep the two continents intact. Yet another reason is that there is a tendency for us to assume that countries in the same continent must have something in common. But such areas as Siberia, Syria, Indonesia, and Japan, all of which happen to be in Asia, differ so greatly both in their physical conditions and in their economic life that it would be difficult to find four more different areas anywhere in the world. More important still, the fact that they are all 'Asian' does not appear to have any real significance at all, though it has fostered the creation of the Asian part of the Afro-Asian bloc.

Perhaps the most important reason why the present major divisions of the land areas of the world are unsatisfactory for many purposes is the fact that the continents are improvised and arbitrary. Whether the reader recognizes only five continents or prefers to divide America into North and South or even raises Antarctica[1] to the rank of a continent, he should appreciate

1. Recent exploration in Antarctica suggests that parts of the Antarctic ice-cap (which covers almost all of the 'continent') may reach below sea-level and therefore be resting not, technically, on land, but on the sea bed. There may therefore be no compact land mass in Antarctica, but a land broken by many inlets, or even an archipelago. See, e.g. the *Geographical Journal* June 1954, p. 193. The most recent contribution to the exploration of Antarctica, the findings of the British Trans-Antarctic Expedition, appear to confirm, however, that Antarctica is in fact a continuous land mass.

that the names of some of the continents are of relatively recent origin, while others were only used vaguely before the world was explored by Europeans in the 15th and 16th centuries. The word Europe was employed in Ancient Greece, and both Asia and Africa were in use in the Ancient World. Asia referred to an undefined part of the world split up more precisely into such areas as Arabia and India, while Africa was merely the name of a small part of the Roman Empire in what is now North Africa and what was then Libya. The word America did not come into use until about 1500, while the island of New Holland only became Australia after British settlement began there in 1788. The terms Australasia (literally South Asia) and Oceania, alternatives for the Australian continent and the islands of the Southwest Pacific, are of even more recent origin. The application of the term Africa to the whole of the African land mass is also a relatively modern development.[1]

It is not surprising, therefore, that although most textbooks on regional geography still deal with the traditional continents, many geographers and other students of the world and world affairs regard these as over-simplified. That is why the world has, of course, frequently been divided for various purposes into groups of countries bearing little or no relationship to the traditional continents. One interesting example is the choice of cultural divisions in *Culture Worlds*, by R. J. Russell and F. B. Kniffen (New York, 1951). Their 'worlds' (subdivided into realms) are: Polar, European, Dry, African, Oriental, Pacific, and American. For the purpose of breaking down statistics the world has also been divided in many ways.[2] Fig. 4a shows the five continents and figs. 4b and 4c show two different divisions of the land areas of the world for certain purposes.

1. In this connexion, the following lines from *A Compendious Geographical Dictionary, etc* ... (London, 1795, p. 28) are interesting: 'Geographers generally reckon four continents, or very large portions of land, each containing many countries; namely Europe, Asia, Africa, and America; and also the continents near the poles.'

2. A useful breakdown into eleven areas is made, for example, by Francis Williams, C.B.E. in 'Geography and the News', an article in *The Geographical Magazine*, Oct. 1953.

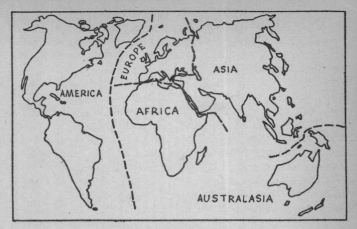

4a. The five continents.

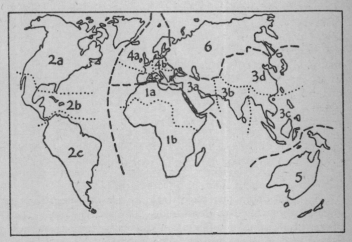

4b. The world divided into fourteen groups of countries for the purposes of the *Demographic Yearbook of the United Nations, 1955*. See text for explanation of numbers on map.

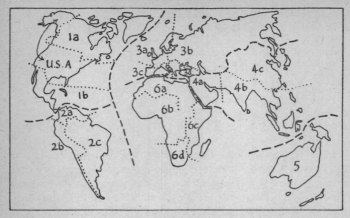

4c. The world divided into eighteen countries or groups of countries for the representation of the direction of United States foreign trade in *Statistical Abstract of the United States, 1955*. See text for explanation of numbers on map.

Seven divisions are frequently used in publications of the United Nations (Africa, N. America, S. America, Asia, Europe, Oceania, U.S.S.R.), but fig. 4b shows a more complicated set of fourteen regions used in one United Nations publication.[1] The divisions and sub-divisions are as follows (the numbers will be found in fig. 4b):

1a Northern Africa, 1b Tropical and Southern Africa; 2a Northern America, 2b Middle America, 2c South America; 3a South West Asia, 3b South Central Asia, 3c South East Asia, 3d East Asia; 4a Northern and Western Europe, 4b Central Europe, 4c Southern Europe; 5 Oceania; 6 U.S.S.R.

Fig. 4c shows another set of regions, this time used for the representation of data concerning U.S. foreign trade.[2] The following divisions, in addition, of course, to the U.S.A. itself, are used (the numbers will be found in fig. 4c):

1. See *Demographic Yearbook of the United Nations, 1955*, p. 115, and p. 12 for explanation.
2. See *Statistical Abstract of the United States, 1955*, pp. 916–21.

A Regional Division of the World

1 NORTH AMERICA: 1a Northern Area, 1b Southern Area.
2 SOUTH AMERICA: 2a Northern Area, 2b Western Area, 2c Eastern Area.
3 EUROPE: 3a Northwestern and Central Area, 3b Northeastern Area (includes all U.S.S.R.), 3c Southwestern Area, 3d Southeastern Area.
4 ASIA: 4a Western Area, 4b Southern and Southeastern Area, 4c Eastern Area.
5 AUSTRALIA and OCEANIA.
6 AFRICA: 6a Northern Area, 6b Western Area, 6c Eastern Area, 6d Southern Area.

Fig. 4d shows twelve regions of the world chosen for use in the present book in the consideration of world population and resources, and for descriptions of different parts of the world. The regions are shown again in fig. 5, this time on the projection, mentioned in ch. 1, which gives a better idea than the more familiar world projection in fig. 4d of the relationship of the land masses to one another. Once again the reader is reminded that a globe should constantly be consulted by students of world affairs.

There are obviously too many individual political units in the world for each to be considered separately, while at the other extreme, the five continents are too few. For the purposes of this book, therefore, the world has been divided into twelve regions. The regions have been chosen with the following considerations in mind: to respect as far as possible the limits of the five existing continents; to respect *de facto* political boundaries (one reason why this is essential is that often statistics are available only for whole countries, not for parts of them); and to produce compact groups of countries with no detached portions in other regions (the British Commonwealth could not therefore be a region). Although the countries in each region may have certain features and problems in common, it is not suggested that the regional boundaries are the only possible ones or that the regions have any particular geopolitical unity or significance. It was very difficult to decide in which region certain countries could best be included. Moreover, boundaries can be altered at any time as the result of political changes, while the regions themselves can be subdivided or grouped together for different purposes.

The reader who is familiar with the concepts of the late Sir Halford J. Mackinder regarding world geopolitical problems and the pivot area (later the Heartland) will find some familiar features in the present division.[1] For the purposes of the present book three main divisions are suggested. They are based on the

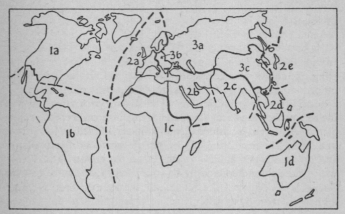

4d. The twelve regions into which the world is divided for the purposes of this book. See fig. 5 for details, and text for explanation of numbers.

fact that the communist bloc (or 'socialist camp' in Soviet publications) is a geopolitical fact and that it occupies much of Eurasia, the most extensive continuous land area in the world. The main divisions chosen are:

(1) An *outer zone* of large land masses and oceans separated, except in the Arctic Ocean area, from (3) the *communist bloc* by (2) an *inner zone* of peninsulas, islands, and seas. The two zones encircling the communist bloc are only 'inner' and 'outer' in relation to Eurasia.

1. The reader will find much of interest in Mackinder's paper: 'The Geographical Pivot of History' in the *Geographical Journal*, April 1904, Vol. XXIII, No. 4. Although so many political and technological changes have taken place since the paper was published, some of the ideas are still worth consideration. Later ideas of Mackinder will be found in *Democratic Ideals and Reality*, first published London, 1919.

A Regional Division of the World

The three main divisions are broken into the following twelve regions (Antarctica might be considered a thirteenth), numbered in fig. 4d and named in fig. 5:

1a *Anglo-America*.[1] This comprises America north of the Republic and Gulf of Mexico, Greenland, and the various U.S. islands of the North Pacific. Some unity is given to the region by the fact that English (hence Anglo-) is spoken by almost all the inhabitants.

1b *Latin America*. This region is the rest of America, including twenty republics and a number of small colonial territories. Here Spanish or Portuguese (languages of Latin origin) is the official language of all the more important countries.

1c *Africa except the Northwest and Northeast*. Africa south of the Sahara differs greatly from the Northwest, which is at present closely connected economically (and in part politically) to Europe, and from the Northeast, where Egypt and the northern part of the Sudan have much in common with the countries of Southwest Asia, which lie across the narrow Red Sea. The rest of the Sudan, Ethiopia, and the Somalilands have also been included with Southwest Asia.

1d *Australasia*. The large island of Australia and numerous smaller islands of various sizes is the fourth region. Here it might be argued that the island of New Guinea, as well as some smaller islands, should be included with Southeast Asia. At present, however, New Guinea is shared by Australia (eastern half) and the Netherlands (but the Netherlands part is claimed by Indonesia).

2a *Non-communist Europe and Northwest Africa*. This includes all the countries of Europe not under a communist regime and those parts of North Africa (Morocco, Algeria, Tunisia, and Libya) most closely associated with Europe. More precisely (but this would mean dividing a political unit) the western part of Libya (Tripolitania) might go here, and the eastern part (Cyrenaica) with Egypt, in Southwest Asia.

1. There is some confusion over the use of Anglo-America(n). In the sense of U.K.–U.S. relations it should be Anglo-U.S. (or more precisely U.K.-U.S.). Anglo-America(n) is then left to serve for the *English-speaking part* of America. For the Spaniards and Portuguese, América means South America, and a citizen of the U.S.A. is *norteamericano*.

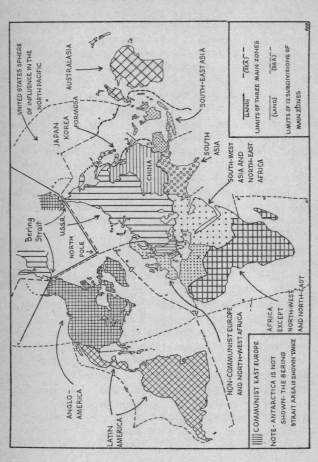

United States Sphere of Influence in the North Pacific

Australasia

South-East Asia

Japan
Korea
Formosa

China

South-West Asia and North-East Africa

South Asia

Bering Strait

U.S.S.R.

North Pole

Non-Communist Europe and North-West Africa

Africa except North-West and North-East

Anglo-America

Latin America

‖‖‖ COMMUNIST EAST EUROPE

NOTE - ANTARCTICA IS NOT SHOWN. THE BERING STRAIT AREA IS SHOWN TWICE

(LAND) — — (SEA) —
LIMITS OF THREE MAIN ZONES

(LAND) — — (SEA) —
LIMITS OF 12 SUBDIVISIONS OF MAIN ZONES

5. The twelve regions into which the world is divided for the purposes of this book. See text for explanation. Projection: Bartholomew's regional.

A Regional Division of the World

2b *Southwest Asia and Northeast Africa*. This region, still commonly known as the Near and Middle East, coincides approximately with the area usefully referred to as the land of the five seas plus the Nile basin. Afghanistan is included here rather than with South Asia because its economy and interests are in many respects closer to those of Southwest Asia.

2c *South Asia*. The former British Empire of South Asia, now India, Pakistan, Burma, and Ceylon, with Nepal and Bhutan. Burma might equally well be put with Southeast Asia.

2d *Southeast Asia*. A number of peninsulas and islands, most of which have at one time been European colonies. North Viet-Nam, now part of the communist bloc, has been included with Southeast Asia for convenience.

2e *Japan, Korea, and Formosa*. These are grouped together because (with the exception of North Korea) they are the only parts of East Asia still outside the communist bloc, and might even therefore be called non-communist East Asia. They have one feature in common – the great dependence on U.S. aid for the maintenance of their economies (see ch. 9).

3a *The U.S.S.R. and the Mongolian People's Republic*. The latter is a Soviet sphere of influence, formerly Outer Mongolia.

3b *East Europe*. The eight countries with communist regimes, lying between the U.S.S.R. and non-communist Europe.

3c *Communist China*. This region includes territories such as Tibet recently occupied by Chinese communist forces.

These twelve regions, several of which, unfortunately, have unwieldy titles, are used in chs 4–7 in various maps, diagrams and descriptions. Other regions may also be referred to – for example, South America as opposed to the whole of Latin America, or Southwest Asia, instead of Southwest Asia with Northeast Africa.

An interesting tendency may be noted in connexion with the regions chosen (or, for that matter, with any division of the world of this kind). A crisis in any country immediately affects neighbouring countries in the same region (or in an adjoining region just across a regional boundary), soon arouses interest in adjoining regions, and only more slowly attracts attention in regions that do not adjoin it. The Israeli invasion of Egypt in

October 1956, is an example. This attack immediately brought reactions from such neighbours as Syria and Jordan, and from the U.K. with its vital interests in the Suez Canal and a foothold (Cyprus) in the region. Neighbouring regions, the U.S.S.R., South Asia, and non-communist Europe were quick to issue threats or to offer opinions on the matter. Reactions were slower in more distant regions. U.S. diplomats were taken by surprise, China finally offered to send military aid to Egypt, while in Latin America, particularly in Venezuela, oil exploration was gradually speeded up and production boosted as a result of the closure of the canal, an event that demonstrated the vulnerability of the supply of Southwest Asian oil for Europe.

In a similar way the uprising in Hungary brought the most immediate and violent reaction from the two adjoining regions, the U.S.S.R. and non-communist Europe, whereas the conflict in remote Korea left most Europeans indifferent.

In these examples the event had repercussions in many parts of the world. As the world 'shrinks' with the improvement of communications, so news, politicians, troops, and supplies can be carried more and more quickly over great distances. As time goes on, then, each significant event will surely tend to have stronger and stronger repercussions all over the world, a tendency already appreciated by H. J. Mackinder more than fifty years ago: 'From the present time forth (1904) ... we shall ... have to deal with a closed political system and ... it will be one of world-wide scope. Every explosion of social forces ... will be sharply re-echoed from the far side of the globe, and weak elements in the political and economic organism of the world will be shattered in consequence.' (*op. cit.*, footnote p. 64.)

A student of world affairs may specialize in the study of a certain part of the world and he may not be interested in other parts. But he must know a little about every region of the world to understand the full significance and consequences of major world events, wherever they occur. The world is like a jig-saw puzzle, the pieces of which can be carefully studied without revealing much until all have been fitted together to give a complete picture.

Chapter 4

WORLD POPULATION AND
PRODUCTION

I. ON THE USE OF STATISTICS

IN this and in subsequent chapters a large number of population, production, and other figures are quoted. As far as possible statistics are for the years 1954–6. The principal source has been the *Statistical Abstract of the United Nations*, 1955 and 1956. Many other publications have also been consulted, and a few are listed among the selected references at the end of the book. Although most of the figures will be two or three years old by the time this book is published they will not usually differ significantly from current figures.

Statistical material varies greatly in its reliability. Some countries have already for some decades been publishing figures that are accurate or reliable to within only a small margin of error. Others have few or no facilities for collecting accurate statistical data, and many parts of the world have never even been covered by a census of population. Errors may occur during the collection and preparation of any material for publication, and in more popular publications one or two noughts may even be inadvertently (or deliberately) omitted or added without anyone noticing. But although it is difficult for these reasons to trace population and production changes from past periods up to the present and often impossible even to make accurate comparisons between different parts of the world at the present day, world problems can only be appreciated if there is some quantitative basis, however approximate it is, from which conclusions may be drawn.

Throughout this book round numbers have been used. When most numbers are only approximate anyway, it seems pointless to put such a precise figure as 150,697,361, the population of the U.S.A. on 1 June 1950, according to the census of that year, alongside such a vague figure as approximately 20 m., the estimated population of Ethiopia. For most purposes it is sufficient to know that the population of the U.S.A. was about 150 m. in 1950. By 1957 it had risen to 170 m. anyway.

Figures are often presented in such a way that their significance is difficult to appreciate. Frequently absolute figures are given where comparative figures would mean much more. To know that China has about 600 m. inhabitants is less useful than to know that it has about twelve times as many people as the U.K., or between one-fifth and one-quarter of the total population of the world. Unless something is provided against which absolute figures can be measured they may mean nothing at all to us. It has been estimated that some £40,000 m. will be spent during the next decade by world oil companies (outside the communist bloc) on expansion, but very few people would stop and question £4,000 m. or even £400 m. if one of these had been given as the result of a misprint.

In this book an attempt has been made to present figures so that they may be measured against others. In this way the significance of absolute figures may more readily be appreciated. Not infrequently figures are shown for production per inhabitant (*per caput*). In 1957, China and Belgium each produced about 5 m. tons of steel, but China has more than sixty times as many inhabitants as Belgium, which means that whereas *per caput* output in Belgium is about 500 kilograms, in China it is only about 8 kilograms.

II. AREA AND POPULATION

MORE than seven-tenths of the surface of the world is covered by water. Of the remainder, part, including Antarctica, Greenland, and many smaller areas, is permanently (or at least has been for thousands of years) covered with snow or ice. Without Antarctica, which occupies about 5 m. square miles and may not all be land anyway, the earth's land surface occupies roughly one-quarter of the total surface area and amounts to somewhat more than 52 m. sq. mls. Anglo-America, Latin America, and the U.S.S.R., the three largest regions suggested in ch. 3, each account for slightly less than one-sixth of this, while Africa and Australasia together cover more than one-quarter. Europe and

World Population and Production

Asia, excluding the U.S.S.R., occupy the remaining one-fifth, but together have considerably more than two-thirds of the total population of the world.

The political divisions of the world vary enormously in area. In addition to the U.S.S.R., which is more than $8\frac{1}{2}$ m. sq. mls in area, Canada, China, Brazil, the U.S.A., and Australia each cover 3 m.–4 m. sq. mls. Countries such as France (213,000 sq. mls) or New Zealand (140,000 sq. mls) are very small by comparison yet still far larger than minute but administratively separate (and, in their own particular ways, by no means insignificant) units such as Monaco, the Vatican City State, or Bermuda (the first two measured in acres rather than square miles). The great difference in area between the largest and the smallest political divisions of the world is one of several reasons why it is difficult to compare countries.

When we are assessing the importance of different countries we have to bear in mind not only their area but also their population. Owing to the very uneven distribution of the world's population over the habitable land, the density of population[1] varies greatly from one part to another. Although Australia is nearly 15 times the size of France, France has more than four times as many inhabitants. In Australia there are about 3 persons per square mile, in France about 200. The extremes of density are much farther apart. In Greenland there are about 40 square miles per person, while England and Wales have 760 inhabitants per square mile, and many urban areas in different parts of the world, of course, have tens of thousands of persons per square mile in the more crowded sections.

The great difference in the number of inhabitants between the most populous and the least populous political divisions of the world is a second reason why it is difficult to compare countries. The largest countries are not necessarily the ones with the most people. In table 2 the ten largest and the ten most populous countries are listed separately in order of importance.

1. The average number of persons per unit of area – a square mile, for example.

TABLE 2

Area	Per cent of Total World Land Area*	Population	Per cent of World Total
1 U.S.S.R.	16·3	China	22·4
2 Canada	7·4	India	14·1
3 China	7·3	U.S.S.R.	7·5
4 Brazil	6·3	U.S.A.	6·0
5 U.S.A.	5·8	Japan	3·3
6 Australia	5·7	Indonesia	3·0
7 French W. Africa	3·5	Pakistan	3·0
8 India	2·4	All Germany	2·6
9 Argentina	2·1	Brazil	2·2
10 Fr. Equat. Africa	1·9	U.K.	1·9

* Excluding Antarctica.

Only five countries appear in both columns. Certain countries with large populations, such as Japan, Germany, and the U.K., would come far down on the list of countries arranged in order of area, if it were continued, while Canada and Australia would be low on the population list. Two important points should be borne in mind in connexion with the density of population. Firstly, countries with a high density are not necessarily over-populated. Secondly, within countries, especially the larger ones, there are great variations in density from one part to another, just as there are over the world as a whole. In both Australia and Brazil, for example, more than four-fifths of the total population is concentrated in less than one-fifth of the total area.

Fig. 6 shows the main features of the distribution of population over the world. Each dot stands for approximately 10 million inhabitants and in most cases, of course, represents 10 m. people living in a much larger area than that actually covered by the dot itself.[1] The fact that Madagascar, for instance, has no dot, does not imply that it is uninhabited. The dot on the mainland opposite represents the $4\frac{1}{2}$ m. inhabitants of Madagascar, as well as $5\frac{1}{2}$ m. of the inhabitants of Africa itself.

It is obvious from the map that there are three main concentrations of population in the world: East Asia, South Asia, and

1. The dot is placed as near as possible to the 'centre of gravity' of the 10 m. people it represents.

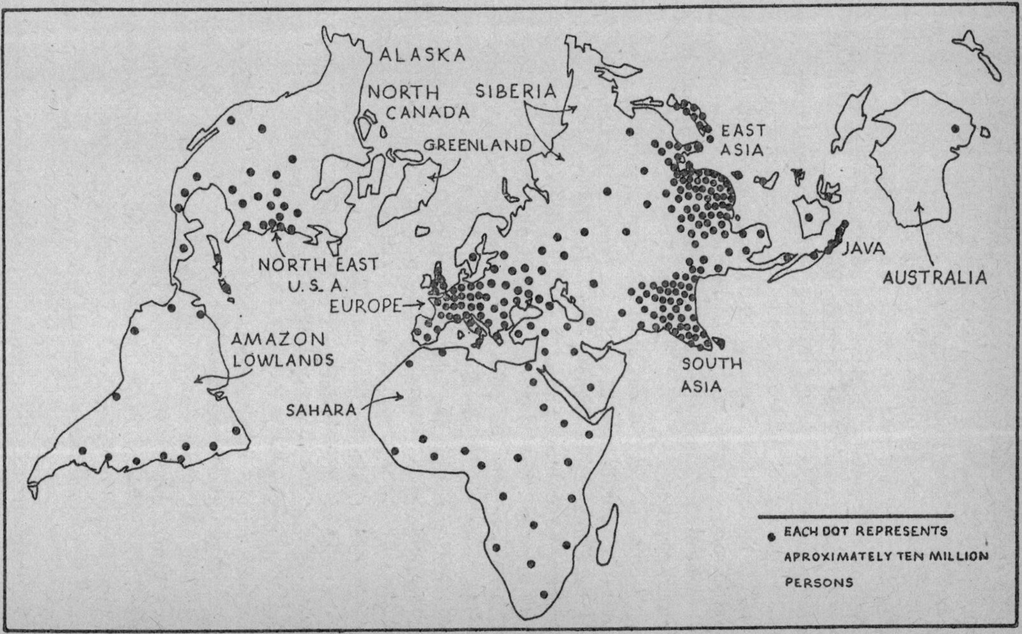

6. World population.

EACH DOT REPRESENTS
APROXIMATELY TEN MILLION
PERSONS

AUSTRALIA
JAVA
EAST
ASIA
SOUTH
ASIA
ALASKA
NORTH SIBERIA
CANADA
GREENLAND
EUROPE
NORTH EAST
U.S.A.
AMAZON
LOWLANDS
SAHARA

Europe. Two smaller concentrations stand out: Northeast (or industrial) U.S.A., and Java. In contrast, vast areas are clearly uninhabited or only thinly populated. They are: the coldest parts of the northern hemisphere, including Alaska, Greenland, most of Canada, and Siberia; the driest parts of the world, including the Sahara, the interior of Asia, and much of Australia; and the dense tropical forest of the Amazon lowlands..

East Asia (China, Japan, Korea, Formosa) has rather more than one quarter of the world's population, South and Southeast Asia, slightly less than a quarter, and Europe, including European U.S.S.R., about a quarter. At the other extreme, the more empty half of the world's land area accounts for less than 2 per cent of the total population.

To appreciate world problems it is necessary to consider changes of population as well as present distribution. The number of inhabitants in any given part of the world is constantly changing. We tend to think of the change only in terms of population increase, and there is some justification for this, for Ireland is probably the only country in the world of any size that has fewer inhabitants now than 150 years ago. On the other hand, although before the last 200 years or so there were fluctuations in different parts of the world, with increases in one area, decreases in another, there was probably never an increase everywhere at the same time. At present, on the contrary, there is an almost world-wide increase of population, although small areas, as, for example, parts of the French Alps, have lost population in recent decades.

To have a reasonably accurate idea of population changes, all that need be considered are the number of live births and of deaths and the number of people immigrating and emigrating during a given period. If a country had 1,000,000 inhabitants at the end of 1955 and 1,020,000 at the end of 1956 its population must have increased by 2 per cent during 1956. In many parts of the world today population is increasing at about this rate.

What happens to a population of 1,000,000 people in 1955 if it continues to increase annually by 2 per cent for some decades? The increase is 20,000 in the first year, bringing the total to

1,020,000. The increase in the next year is 2 per cent of 1,020,000, which is 20,400, not 20,000. 20,400 is added to 1,020,000, and the next figure is 2 per cent of 1,040,400. Instead of increasing at simple interest rate, which would be by 2 per cent of the original 1,000,000 per year, the increase takes place at compound interest rate and the effect is cumulative. The country of 1,000,000 would double its population not in 50 years but in less than 35 years. That is what has happened in Costa Rica. In 1920 this country had 420,000 inhabitants; in 1952, 850,000. This increase was not brought about by any appreciable immigration into the country. As a result of the natural increase (excess of live births over deaths) it doubled in little more than 30 years. If it doubles again during the same length of time, Costa Rica will have 1,700,000 people by 1985 – that is, *four* times as many as in 1920. This is not bound to happen, of course; on the other hand, there is nothing at present to suggest that the trend will alter.

It has been estimated that the population of the world increased by 43 million (more than the total population of France) in 1956. That is a rate of increase of 1·6 per cent per annum. If this continues, the total population of the world will be about 5,000 m. in the year 2000 – three times what it was in 1900 and nearly twice what it is now.

The rate of increase of population varies considerably from one country to another (and even within countries from one region to another). In certain European countries, particularly those with the highest standard of living and the highest proportion of urban dwellers, the increase is very slight. In contrast, the population is increasing rapidly in most Latin American countries and in many parts of Africa and Asia. In addition, both the U.S.S.R. (203 m. in 1957) and the U.S.A. (170 m. in 1957) gain some 3 m. inhabitants per year, the U.S.A. partly as a result of immigration. In Canada, Australia, Argentina, and Southern Brazil, immigration is relatively more significant even than in the U.S.A., and, of course, it is mainly the countries of Western Europe that provide the immigrants.

How can this world-wide increase of population be explained? Obviously it can only take place if more and more food and other items of consumption become available as well. During the last 150 years or so the world production of food has increased for two main reasons. Firstly, new lands have been brought into use for farming for the first time (mainly by people of European origin) and secondly, new techniques (e.g. the widespread use of chemical fertilizer) have made it possible to obtain higher yields in existing farming areas. At the same time the development of various branches of science, and in particular medical science, has helped to eliminate or lessen the effects of many diseases, to reduce the proportion of stillbirths, and to enable more babies to survive into childhood and more adults to reach old age.

Merely to maintain present living standards production must be raised to satisfy the needs of more than 40 million additional people each year. For more than 150 years now there have been gloomy forecasts that eventually population will increase more rapidly than production.[1] At the same time the opposite idea of material progress and constantly improving living standards has become the theme of economic development and the election promise of many political parties in almost every region of the world.

The example of the British Isles shows that the forecast of the pessimists has already come true in one part of the world. With some 20 m. inhabitants, it was more or less self-supporting in food and raw materials 150 years ago. As the number of inhabitants increased in the 19th century, home-produced food became sufficient to feed only part of the population. The pressure of population on the land in Ireland was relieved largely by emigration to North America. Population continued to increase in the rest of the British Isles, and the pressure on resources here was relieved largely by the expansion of manufacturing, which has enabled Britain to import from overseas an appreciable proportion of the raw materials and food it consumes, although, as from Ireland, millions have emigrated as well. Emigration and the export of manufactures to buy food and raw materials are satisfactory measures to deal with overpopulation as long as other parts of the world are prepared to receive immigrants

1. See, for example, the work of T. R. Malthus, *Essay on the Principle of Population*, 1798.

or have surpluses of food and raw materials that they wish to exchange for manufactures.

Clearly, only a limited number of countries can rely on the export of manufactures to import raw materials and food. At present Japan and most countries of non-communist Europe do so. Both the U.S.A. and the U.S.S.R. are doing the same thing, though at present foreign trade is less vital to their economies than it is to the smaller industrial countries. It seems improbable that India, China, and other overpopulated countries of Asia will be able to solve their demographic problems by exporting manufactures, while it is very unlikely that other parts of the world will be prepared to absorb more than a very small proportion of their constantly increasing populations. Other ways must be found.

In spite of its precarious economic position we might be reluctant to consider the U.K. as overpopulated, even if its density of population is very high. This is largely because the U.K. has important trading connexions with English-speaking parts of the world. Similarly, although living standards are low, for example, in Bolivia or Thailand, we should again hesitate to call countries such as these overpopulated. There may be pressure on present farmland, but both countries have areas in which cultivation and grazing can be extended and both could obtain higher yields in existing farming areas. On the other hand, there are countries such as Egypt and Haiti in which the possibilities of increasing food production are much more limited, yet population is increasing rapidly. Mexico is another interesting example. This country has about 30 m. inhabitants. It already imports some food, but manages with great effort at present to increase its food output to cater for the 1 m. new people each year. In twenty years' time, if the present rate of increase of population continues, there will be far more than 1 m. new people to feed each year, yet it is becoming more and more difficult and costly to raise food output because all the better quality farmland is already in use. Perhaps Mexico is a better example than Britain of the forecasts of the pessimists.

Broadly speaking, there are two ways in which the problem can be, and is being, solved. It is possible to slow down the rate of increase of population,[1] and it is possible to raise production by developing new resources and techniques. We may ask why the rate of increase of population has already been reduced in some parts of the world (and more in some sections of the community than in others). There are many different ways of doing this, ranging from outright infanticide and the deliberate neglect of weaker babies to more refined methods of prevention of birth and to the custom of marrying only a considerable length of time after reaching the age of puberty. In most societies, shortage of food has in the past been a formidable means of causing and regulating population changes. The practice of having small families so that each child can benefit from a large share of the family budget seems to have become widespread mainly in the industrial countries of the world, which, at the same time, are the countries with the highest living standards and the largest proportion of urban dwellers. In these countries it may not have been government practice to encourage the spread of knowledge about birth control methods, but usually no serious obstacles have been put in the way. On the other hand, in poorer countries with large rural populations there are several reasons why modern methods of birth control can be applied only with great difficulty. Apart from governmental and religious objections there are the enormous problems of manufacturing contraceptives, distributing them, explaining their application (and to be effective they must be properly applied, for a miss is as good as a mile). Then there is the question of persuading and enabling people who have not enough money to buy food or who receive no true wages, to purchase or acquire them at all. These conditions prevail, perhaps, among three-quarters of the population of the world. It may well be a matter of decades before modern birth control methods could be universally adopted. Even then it is unlikely, and indeed, hardly desirable, that there will be any compulsory limitation of the size of families. In the mean-

1. Incidentally, the idea that modern wars have greatly affected population changes is a misconception. In the six years of the Second World War, between 20 and 30 million people lost their lives as a direct result of the conflict. That represents less than one year's increase of the world's population.

time, it is of great importance to ensure that production is increased, particularly in the poorer countries.[1] To appreciate the possibilities of achieving increased production it is essential to have some idea of the world distribution of resources and their utilization.

III. PLANT AND ANIMAL PRODUCTS

WHEN considering the resources of the world and their utilization it is useful to have in mind a broad twofold division of raw materials into plant and animal on the one hand and mineral on the other. While most of the world's land surface, as well as extensive sea areas, are put to some use for farming, forestry, and fishing purposes, the distribution of economic minerals (any minerals utilized by man) is much more limited, and their extraction is usually confined to small districts. The contrast is further emphasized when it is remembered that whereas good conditions for farming and suitable conditions for forest growth are to a considerable extent confined to areas with certain types of climate, the distribution of minerals bears (with a few exceptions) no relationship at all to present-day climatic conditions.

Farming is by far the most important single form of employment in most countries of the world, but good-quality farmland, like population, is very unevenly scattered over the earth's land surface. In certain favoured land areas of the world, such as the plain of the Ganges in India and the Middlewest maize belt of the U.S.A., enough food can be produced on one square mile of land to feed several hundred people. In contrast, many millions of square miles produce no food at all. In fig. 7 an attempt has been made to show which parts of the world are most intensively used for farming and which are of little or no use, or are little used at present. Three categories are distinguished:

A. Lands that are used relatively intensively for cultivation or grazing. Not by any means all the area shaded black is intensively farmed, but on this scale little detail can be shown. For example,

1. The terms backward and underdeveloped mean more or less the same, but underdeveloped implies, rightly or wrongly, that it is only a matter of time before these countries enter a new era of prosperity.

7. World land use.

the Alps and Pyrenees could not easily be distinguished as areas only partially used for farming.

B. Lands that for various reasons are only partly used for farming. This includes the grazing of comparatively small numbers of animals on large areas and the cultivation of small, scattered zones, in some cases intensively (for example, the sugar plantations of Queensland, Australia).

C. Lands that at present are used for farming very little or not at all. This category includes very small cultivated clearings in the Amazon and Siberian forests, the reindeer herds that are grazed in northern Siberia, and the livestock grazed in small numbers in arid areas.

Without doubt there are or will be possibilities of increasing agricultural output in all three types of land. In the black regions the possibilities of extending the area of farmland are not great, but in many parts yields could be increased appreciably In the shaded regions there is greater opportunity for extending cultivation, while many areas could be utilized much more intensively than they are at present. In the white regions it will be difficult to extend cultivation and grazing until considerable advances have been made in agronomy and other branches of science.

In any consideration of the possibilities of increasing farm production, the following limitations, set by natural conditions, should not be forgotten. Firstly, many mountain areas are too rugged to be utilized without great difficulty. Slopes are steep and soil, where it forms, is easily removed. Secondly, owing to low rainfall (or, more precisely, precipitation) many parts of the world are too arid for plant growth without irrigation.[1] Thirdly, there are extensive regions in which temperatures are too low for the growth of vegetation or in which the shortness of the growing season greatly limits the range of plants that can be cultivated. These regions include most of the northern hemisphere north of latitude 60° and high mountain areas closer to the equator than this.[2] Finally, there are large tracts of tropical

1. The effectiveness of a given amount of rainfall increases, of course, away from the equator, with the reduction of evaporation.

2. Because temperature decreases with altitude as well as towards the poles.

forest which, at present, anyway, can be cleared only with great difficulty.

About 20–25 per cent of England is arable land and much of the remainder is good or moderate quality grazing land. For anyone accustomed to seeing an intensively utilized farming landscape of this kind it is difficult to appreciate how different most of the rest of the world is from Britain. In Brazil, for example, only about 2 per cent of the total area is cropland, while it has been estimated that only a few hundred square miles out of more than one million in the Brazilian Amazon region are cultivated. Only 1 per cent of the total area of Australia is cropland, though much of the remainder is used for grazing. Even in such a populous country as China, only a small part of the total area is farmed intensively.

Clearly, the amount of farmland available per inhabitant is far greater in some countries than in others. The U.S.A., for example, can produce enough food to provide each inhabitant with an average of 3000–3200 calories per day and could produce even more.[1] India only grows enough food to supply each Indian with little more than half that number of calories daily. Total farm production in the two countries is therefore roughly comparable in quantity, because India has more than twice as many people. In the U.K., Japan, and other small densely populated countries the amount of farmland available per inhabitant is very limited.

At the risk of oversimplifying matters it is useful to classify the countries of the world into three groups with regard to food production. The first group consists of those in which home-produced food is abundant and some food is even available for export. It includes the U.S.A., Canada, Australia, New Zealand, Argentina. The second group covers countries which could produce all the food they require, but in which, for various reasons, some shortage occurs. In this category are most of the other countries of Latin America, many African countries, Southeast Asia, and the U.S.S.R. (but if Mr Khrushchev's

1. It does, of course, import certain foodstuffs and beverages, which it cannot produce at home because it lies outside the tropics. On the other hand, it exports cotton, cereals, and other farm products.

forecasts prove to be correct, the U.S.S.R. will very shortly be in the first group). The third group comprises countries such as the U.K. and Switzerland which provide only part of the food they need, but which can afford to import food without difficulty, and countries such as China and India in which by any standards the bulk of the population is underfed, but which are unable to import large enough quantities of foodstuffs to increase food supplies substantially.

The world production of food and agricultural raw materials can be increased in two main ways. Higher yields can be obtained in existing areas of cultivation and grazing, or new areas can be farmed for the first time.

Higher yields can be obtained in existing farming areas by many different methods. Chemical fertilizers, at present available in abundance only in a limited number of countries, might be manufactured and used much more widely. The widespread application of trace elements[1] where these are deficient offers great possibilities to farmers. Sometimes the introduction of new types of plant or new breeds of animal into a region helps to raise yields there; in particular, there is room for experimentation with pasture grasses and other fodder plants for livestock in many parts of the world. Improved strains of plants and breeds of animals are constantly being evolved. Many weeds and insect pests may eventually be eliminated. There is good reason to be optimistic about the possibilities of producing more food in existing farming areas.

The introduction of farm machinery, and in particular, of tractors, does not necessarily result in higher yields in areas of intensive cultivation, but machinery does release farm workers from the land and enable them to take up other occupations. It may also become economical with tractors to plough extensive tracts of country where natural conditions make high yields unlikely. This has been done in parts of the U.S.A. and Australia but, as a result, soil has been blown or washed away and land rendered useless. The same thing is now being done in the U.S.S.R.

1. In many regions the application in small quantities of one element which is deficient in the soil (it may be, for example, cobalt or copper) can greatly improve the fertility of the land.

and China where poor steppe lands and even semi-desert areas are being ploughed by machinery in an attempt to grow more grain.

The expansion of agriculture into lands that are not at present utilized for farming brings with it many problems and risks. The tropical forest lands of South America, much of Africa, and many of the islands of Southeast Asia, have so far hardly been utilized at all for farming. One problem here is the difficulty of clearing the trees, together with their stumps and roots; another is the danger of soil erosion and loss of soil fertility. Once the forest has been cleared, however, there seems little danger of soil erosion if suitable pasture plants are grown and the land grazed, and, of course, provided suitable types of live-stock (probably cattle) are available. The coniferous forests, which cover much of Canada and Siberia, present another set of problems. In many areas the water in the subsoil is permanently frozen and only the uppermost layer thaws during the short warm season. The topsoil formed in these coniferous forests is usually deficient in plant foods and frequently rests on a hard layer, which cannot be penetrated by the roots of smaller plants. There are farms in clearings in the coniferous forest zone of Canada and Siberia, but they occupy only an insignificant fraction of the total area, and the soil requires the application of fertilizer to be productive.

In semi-arid and arid areas further problems occur. Special drought-resisting plants have been evolved for use in semi-arid areas where the rainfall is not very effective but does allow some plant growth, while dry farming methods, which enable the crops to make the best possible use of the moisture available, are practised. There is a tendency at present for cultivation to retreat from some semi-arid areas of the world. In Australia, for example, the wheat acreage now tends to be smaller than it was in the 1930s, though yields are higher. The rainfall in semi-arid areas is often unreliable, varying greatly in amount from year to year, and there is the constant danger that winds may remove soil from areas exposed by the plough.

Both in semi-arid and in arid zones in certain parts of the world there are possibilities of extending the irrigated area. This depends at present largely on the availability of water carried by rivers with their headwaters in more humid regions (usually mountainous). Irrigated land can be extended in certain parts of the U.S.S.R., Australia, Egypt, Iraq, Peru, and elsewhere. Expensive works of construction, including dams and channels, are generally necessary. It is possible that in the not very distant future it may not be too costly to pump distilled sea water from any coast into nearby areas of semi-desert and desert where soils are suitable for cultivation but rainfall inadequate.

Two other activities relating to plant and animal resources, forestry and fishing, although, strictly speaking, not farming, have many features in common with cultivation and grazing.

Although the forests of the world have hitherto largely been exploited without being replanted, there is a growing tendency in different countries for land that has been cleared for its timber to be reafforested. The cultivation of trees, or silviculture, is becoming a branch of farming. In many parts of the world, including most European countries, the U.S.A., the U.S.S.R., Japan, Brazil, and New Zealand, extensive acreages have been planted with various species of tree.

The U.S.S.R. and Canada have the most extensive reserves of softwood in the world, while most of the hardwood forest is in South America, Central Africa, and Southeast Asia. For various reasons softwood forest is usually easier to exploit, and its timber has a greater number of uses, than hardwood forest. Countries that have small stands of forest in relation to their total population include China, Japan, and most countries of Southwest Asia, as well as the U.K. and certain other industrial countries of Europe. *Per caput* consumption is so high in the U.S.A. that although that country still has considerable reserves, timber products now form a large item of import.

Commercial fishing is largely confined at present to a limited number of relatively shallow sea areas in temperate and even cold latitudes. This generalization does not, of course, take into account the locally important fishing industry in many lakes and rivers as well as in certain tropical seas, nor the whaling industry in the oceans of the southern hemisphere. Fish is a significant item of diet only in a few countries, including Japan, where it is the principal form of protein food, Norway, and the U.K.

At present, fishing is comparable rather with the hunting of wild land animals than with the grazing of domesticated ones. So far, only small-scale attempts have been made to breed and rear fishes, but it is possible that, in the future, shallow sea areas may be isolated and used for raising fish. Meanwhile, with a few exceptions, the seas and oceans of the world remain little utilized but possibly a vast potential source of food.

IV. MINERAL PRODUCTS

ECONOMIC minerals, like good-quality farmland (but mainly for different reasons), are very unevenly distributed over the earth's surface and, what is more, the minerals in some areas have already been extracted or heavily worked, whereas those in other parts have not been touched. Most of the land area of the world, including, of course, Antarctica, as well as much of Africa, South America, and Asia, has not yet been explored systematically for economic minerals. An illustration of the uneven distribution over the world of production of minerals is the fact that the U.S.A., with little more than one-twentieth of the total land area of the world, has about one-half of its oil production.

Broadly speaking, minerals are either sources of fuel and power or raw materials to be manufactured into something. The division is not, of course, rigid. Coal, for example, is largely used as a source of fuel and power, but many materials are made from it as well. At present, three minerals are of outstanding importance in the economy of all important industrial countries: coal, oil, and iron. Many others, including for example aluminium, copper, manganese, and tin, are no less vital, though they are used in small quantities. One important feature of the utilization of minerals is the fact that most are consumed today almost entirely by a limited number of industrial countries.

Of the minerals that are used as sources of fuel and power, coal and oil are by far the most important. World coal consumption has always been higher than world oil consumption even when the greater calorific value of a ton of oil is taken into consideration, but world oil output is now expanding more rapidly than coal output. Other sources of fuel and power, not all, of course, mineral, include nuclear fuels, natural gas, peat, wood, and dung, as well as wind, falling water, and animal and human energy. It should be appreciated that most of the electricity produced in the world is generated by coal, oil, and other fuels and not by water, although in certain countries, including Japan, Italy, Canada, and Brazil, more hydro-electricity than thermal electricity is generated. At all events, it is probably best to think of electricity as a means of distributing energy, rather than a source.

Coal[1] is still the basis of many branches of modern industry in the leading industrial countries of the world. One of its main uses is the smelting or refining of metallic ores. In particular, most of the world's pig iron is produced by the smelting of iron ore by certain types of coal that can be made into coke. The U.S.A. and the U.S.S.R. have the largest reserves of coal in the world. The reserves in Germany, China, the U.K., Poland, the Un. of S. Africa, Canada, and Colombia are satisfactory, and many other countries have enough to last at least some decades at present rates of production. Proved deposits are small or insignificant in most parts of Latin America, Africa, Southwest and Southeast Asia, which is one reason, though not everywhere the most important one, why there has been little industrial development in these parts of the world.

The international trade in coal is less important both relatively and absolutely than it was earlier in the present century. The main reasons appear to be the greater ease with which oil can be transported, and its higher calorific value, which makes a ton of oil worth more than a ton of coal. This means that most of the coal mined in the world is consumed in the countries in which it is extracted, while much of the oil produced in certain countries is consumed elsewhere. Another feature of the coal industry is the decline in absolute production over the last two or three decades in certain countries. The decline is most marked in the U.S.A. In many respects this is the most advanced country

1. This includes brown coal, or lignite, which is much lower in heating value than ordinary types of coal. Where figures are given for coal production and consumption, allowance has been made for this fact by reducing lignite to its coal equivalent.

industrially, and oil and other sources of power are now replacing coal in many branches of industry.

A striking feature of the oil industry is the fact that a considerable proportion of the oil produced enters world trade. Several of the world's leading producing countries consume only a small part of their output. There are four main oil-producing areas in the world (figures, millions of metric tons, are for 1955):

TABLE 3

1. U.S.A. and Canada, 380 m.
2. Southwest Asia, 161 m.
3. Venezuela, Mexico, Colombia, and Trinidad, 136 m.
4. U.S.S.R., 70 m.

These together accounted for 747 m. out of a world total of 795 m., that is, 94 per cent. In the U.S.A., Canada, the U.S.S.R., and Mexico, consumption is close to production, although the U.S.A. imports some 60 m. tons annually to supplement its own output of around 360 m. tons. In contrast, Venezuela exports almost all of its production of more than 100 m. tons (113 m. in 1955), as do Kuwait (55 m. tons), Saudi Arabia (47 m. tons), Iraq (34 m. tons), and other countries of Southwest Asia.

In most other countries of the world the output of oil is small or insignificant. Many industrial countries, including the U.K., Germany, France, Italy, and Japan, are large importers. India, Pakistan, and China are only small producers, but import very little. At present, oil plays an insignificant part in the economic life of countries such as these.

In addition to the main oil-producing areas of the world, listed above, there are many regions in which it is thought that extensive oil deposits may be found. These include Algeria, interior China, and the interior of the Amazon lowlands in South America.

Although other sources of fuel and power may be of great significance locally, only sources of atomic energy seem likely to rival coal and oil in importance in the future. It is difficult to say at present which countries have the best reserves of nuclear fuels. Producers include the U.S.A. and Canada, Australia, the Belgian Congo, East Germany, Czechoslovakia, and the U.S.S.R.

The second group of minerals, those which are not sources of fuel and power, is much more numerous than the first. It includes iron ore and the ores of various ferro-alloys such as manganese, chrome, and tungsten, which are associated with steel production; important non-ferrous metal ores, such as copper and aluminium, lead and zinc; silver, gold, platinum, and precious stones; minerals such as phosphates, nitrates, and potash, which form the basis of fertilizers; limestone for the smelting of iron ore and the manufacture of cement; and hundreds of others of varying degrees of importance. With advances in technology fresh uses are constantly being found for minerals, and new minerals are being used for the first time.

Almost always, minerals have to be processed in some way before they are of commercial use. The processes are rarely simple and the necessary equipment is often costly to install and complicated to run, while large amounts of power are frequently required. For these reasons it is the older and larger industrial countries that possess most of the installed capacity for the smelting and processing of minerals, either at home or in non-industrial countries where they have set up processing establishments.

Many minerals occur in large quantities only in a very limited number of localities. Not surprisingly, therefore, the production of a certain minerals in commercial quantities may be confined to a few countries only. Tin is an example. It is produced in small quantities in many countries, but outside the communist bloc Malaya accounts for more than one-third of the world's production, Indonesia and Bolivia each for about one-sixth. Most of the remainder comes from the Belgian Congo, Thailand, and Nigeria. It is the industrial countries, however, which consume most of the minerals produced in non-industrial countries, even if these countries buy back their own minerals later in some manufactured form. Chile, for example, exports almost all its copper, Venezuela its iron ore as well as its oil, and Indonesia its tin.

One mineral, iron ore, has been of outstanding importance throughout the period of modern industrial development and, indeed, throughout the Iron Age, which has lasted much longer. The absolute production of pig iron (almost all of which is made into steel) or of steel in a country is a good measure of its significance as a world power, while the amount of steel consumed per inhabitant in any country over a given period is a useful though very approximate indication of the standard of living there. At present, only a few countries produce more than 2–3 per cent of the world's steel, as the following table (1955 figures) shows:

TABLE 4

	Millions of Tons	Per cent of World Total	Per cent of World Population
World	266	–	–
U.S.A.	106	40	6
U.S.S.R.	45	17	7
W. Germany	21	8	2
U.K.	20	8	2
France and Saar	16	6	2
Japan	9	4	3
Belgium and Luxembourg	9	4	0·4

Millions of tons: Italy, $5\frac{1}{2}$; Czechoslovakia, Poland, $4\frac{1}{2}$ each; Canada, 4; China, 3; Australia, Sweden, Austria, India, 2 each.

Steel output in the U.S.A. fluctuates considerably from year to year but in recent years has not been far from 40 per cent of the world's total (266 m. tons in 1955). During the last decade the proportion produced by the U.S.S.R. has been rising slowly but steadily, but there are signs that this trend is changing. Although together they have more than one-third of the world's population, China and India turn out only a few million tons of steel between them.

Since countries with large populations, such as China and India, produce very little steel, and many others produce none at all, the *per caput* consumption varies enormously in different parts of the world (see table 7, page 101).

V. INDUSTRY

FIG. 8 is intended to summarize the main features of the world shareout of area and population, coal, steel, and oil output, railways and motor vehicles. Each column represents the world total of one of these, whether it is $52\frac{1}{2}$ m. square miles of land[1] or 270 m. tons of steel. Space does not permit the representation on the diagram of the share of each of the twelve regions suggested in chapter 3. Some are therefore grouped together. The main purpose is to bring out the share of the three main concentrations of industry in the world, Anglo-America, Western Europe, and the U.S.S.R. Take Anglo-America, the first division on each column, as an example. It has approximately 15 per cent of the total land surface of the world and therefore occupies fifteen-hundredths of the first column. Its share of the world's population is much smaller – about 6 per cent, and it therefore only takes up six-hundredths of the second. Since Anglo-America produces nearly 50 per cent of the world's oil, it occupies almost half of the oil column (last but one). The percentages are, of course, derived from absolute figures. In 1954, the total oil production of the world was 709 m. tons. Anglo-America's large share (about 49 per cent) of the oil column means that its absolute production was 49 per cent of 709 m., that is 351 m. tons.

No figures should be accepted without some consideration of their significance. In fig. 8 the shareout of coal (and lignite reduced to its equivalent in coal), crude oil (which, however, varies somewhat in quality and constitution from one region to another), and steel (which, again, is of many different grades), is reasonably straightforward. The railway mileage and motor vehicles are based on less satisfactory figures. Railway route mileage does not discriminate between single, double, and multiple track, nor between branch lines (or even main lines) that carry only a few trains a day (or even a week) and main lines along which many trains may pass in one hour. An average mile of railway is much more heavily used, for example, in the U.S.S.R. than in Australia or Africa. The motor vehicles in circulation include private cars and commercial vehicles. In Anglo-America the ratio of the former to the latter was about 5 to 1. In Japan and U.S.S.R. there are considerably more lorries, buses, and taxis than private cars. The average commercial vehicle is larger and is used much more intensively than the average private car.

1. Antarctica is not taken into consideration in the area column.

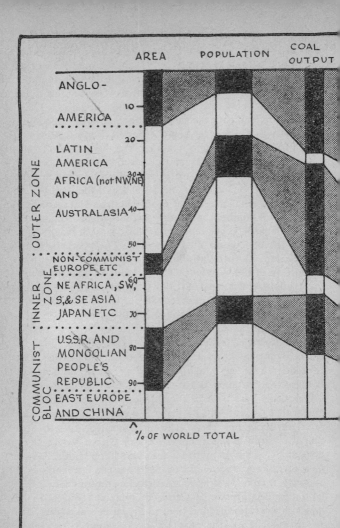

8. World shareout in the 1950s

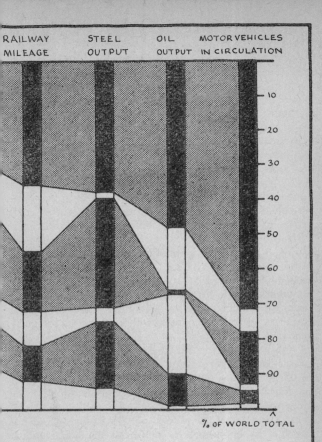

RAILWAY
MILEAGE   STEEL
OUTPUT   OIL
OUTPUT   MOTOR VEHICLES
IN CIRCULATION

10

20

30

40

50

60

70

80

90

% OF WORLD TOTAL

For explanation see text.

Although there are bound to be shortcomings in almost any set of figures, some important points emerge from fig. 8. If everything were shared out evenly among the different regions, divisions in each column would be the same size as the divisions in the population column. This, of course, is not so. For example, non-communist Europe, South Asia, and China have the largest divisions in the population column but produce between them only a very small amount of oil. What is of particular significance is the fact that only Anglo-America and the U.S.S.R. are reasonably well represented in all seven columns. If the oil column showed consumption, not production, non-communist Europe would also be represented all through, because it consumes most of the oil from the division below it, Southwest Asia. The diagram helps to bring out an important difference between Anglo-America and the U.S.S.R. The former has a greater share of the world's oil and motor vehicles than it has of coal and railways. The reverse is true of the U.S.S.R. The reason is that although large-scale modern industrial expansion is more recent in the U.S.S.R. than in Anglo-America, the policy there has been to concentrate on building up a basis of heavy industry and an efficient railway system, comparable with that existing for many decades already in the U.S.A.

In any study of industrial development in the modern world some knowledge of the main features of distribution, production, and movement of raw materials is essential. In this chapter attention has been concentrated on the consideration of the availability of farmland and on three of the basic ingredients of industry and trade, coal, oil, and steel. The reader should not underestimate the importance of numerous plant and animal products, textile fibres (such as cotton and wool), hides, vegetable oils, wood, and so on; nor the role of numerous minerals, which are of ever-increasing necessity to the expansion of industry. In particular, the *per caput* output of cement serves as a useful guide to the capacity of the building industry of a country, while the *per caput* output of such products as superphosphates and nitrogenous fertilizers is an indication of the progress made in obtaining higher yields in agriculture. No less important are questions of technical education and skilled labour, the organization of industrial establishments, government policy towards trade and economic planning, and many others.

It is by no means easy to assess precisely the industrial capacity of a country. Owing to great variations in the size, population, resources, and production, as well as in the level of education and consumption in different parts of the world, it is even less easy to compare the industrial strength of two or more countries. Take Switzerland and Italy as an example. In value (but the meaning of this is misleading as a result of complications and contradictions in exchange rates) Italy's industrial production is several times as high as Switzerland's. On the other hand, there are ten times as many people in Italy. Italy turns out about a quarter of a million cars and lorries per year; Switzerland has no motor-vehicles industry. On the other hand, Switzerland makes many precision instruments and machine tools not produced in Italy. Both produce manufactured goods for export, but the export market is much more vital to Switzerland than to Italy because it has to import half its food while Italy produces most of its food requirements at home. These are just a few of the complications that make comparison difficult. A comparison of the U.S.S.R. with the U.S.A. is even less easy to make owing to the different economic systems in capitalist and communist countries.

In a study of the distribution and development of industry it is useful to distinguish two main types.[1] The first type is heavy industry, producing capital goods such as girders, factory machinery, and railway locomotives, used for construction, for the manufacture of other goods, for transport purposes, and so on. The second type is light industry, producing consumer goods such as clothing, furniture, and household appliances. It is of course impossible to make the division rigid. In the U.S.A. private cars are regarded as consumer goods, while in the U.S.S.R. all motor vehicles except motor-cycles are classified as capital goods (Group 'A').

This twofold division of manufacturing industry into heavy and light helps us to classify the countries of the world into three

1. This applies to industry in the more limited sense of *manufacturing* industry, but does not cover industry in a broader sense, which can include processing, mining, and even farming, fishing, and forestry.

groups, according to their industrial development and production. Some, of course, are on the borderline between one group and another.[1] The countries of the world fall into the three groups as follows:

1. Those that produce both capital and consumer goods and are therefore in a position to expand their own industries with relatively little outside help. This includes the U.S.A. and the U.S.S.R., which are probably the most independent of all; the U.K., Germany, France, Italy, and other manufacturing countries of non-communist Europe; Poland and Czechoslovakia in communist East Europe; and Japan. Even these countries depend on each other for some capital goods. The U.K., for example, imports various kinds of machinery and equipment from the U.S.A. and Germany, but exports textile machinery and other equipment to many industrial countries.

2. Those that satisfy most of their consumer goods requirements but produce few or no capital goods and therefore depend on countries in the first group for their machinery and equipment as well as for technical assistance in the running of factories. China and India come into this category. So do Brazil, Canada, and Australia. All these countries are beginning to produce capital goods in appreciable quantities.

3. Those that have little or no modern industry at all. These are the smaller republics of Latin America, most European colonies in Africa, and countries such as Afghanistan, Pakistan, and Indonesia in Asia.

The extent to which a country can be industrialized on modern lines depends on many factors, including the resources of the country and the size[2] and standard of living of its population.

1. It should be remembered that, strictly speaking, each country would have to be placed in a class of its own, so numerous are the variables that have to be considered in an assessment of industrial capacity.

2. Only in countries with a large population can certain industries be run economically. Switzerland is without a motor-vehicle works not because it lacks the technicians, nor even the capital, to establish one, but because its internal market of $4\frac{1}{2}$ m. people is too small to make one worth while and because it can make other things more profitably.

Undoubtedly, industrial capacity is at present distributed over the world much more unevenly than food production. Obviously, a given number of people require a certain number of calories, without which they would perish, whereas almost all manufactured goods are luxuries rather than necessities, at least by the lowest standards. Nevertheless, in almost every country of the world today efforts are being made to establish and expand at least some branches of manufacturing on modern lines, and the production of many manufactured articles is much less the monopoly of a few countries than it was a hundred years ago, or even thirty. In the leading manufacturing countries, however, new products are constantly being evolved (the manufacture of jet aircraft engines and atomic power stations are examples), and for years, if not decades, they can expect to remain the only producers of these.

VI. CONSUMPTION AND LIVING STANDARDS

THE uneven nature of the world shareout of agricultural, mineral, and industrial production results, not surprisingly, in great differences in standards of living between one country and another and even from one region to another within countries (e.g. in Brazil, Turkey, Italy). Although, however, everyone knows that the U.S.A. is more prosperous than India, and Switzerland richer than Paraguay, it is no easy matter to compare them with accuracy. The standard of living in a country could be measured roughly by dividing total production (by all branches of the economy) plus imports, minus exports, by the total number of inhabitants. Looking at it in another way, it could be measured by assessing what an average family might expect to purchase and consume during a given period, although in reality the average family (or inhabitant) is a myth, created for the convenience of statisticians, and in poorer countries particularly there is usually a small number of families enjoying a relatively high standard of living and a large number that can only hope to possess somewhat less than the average family.

Since many world problems are closely related to differences in living conditions, and therefore to production per inhabitant, it is necessary to have some idea of the extent of the differences between extremes of prosperity and poverty, and to be able to rank the countries of the world approximately according to their living standards.[1] To illustrate the first point, conditions are compared in three sample countries: the U.S.A., Argentina, and India. To show the second point, as many countries as possible (this depends on availability of statistical material) have been arranged on scales indicating *per caput* consumption of energy (table 6) and *per caput* consumption of steel (table 7).

In most respects (but by no means all) the U.S.A. has a higher standard of living than any other country in the world. India, without any doubt, comes among the poorest countries. Somewhere between is Argentina, a country with good conditions for farming over an appreciable part of its total area and a certain amount of modern industrial development. These three countries are compared in table 5.

The fact that most of the figures in table 5 are only approximate should not deter us from making a comparison on these lines merely through lack of accurate data. In addition to the items included in the table, many others could be shown : opportunity to travel for pleasure, availability of entertainments, of books, of modern cooking and heating appliances, and so on. In every case the average U.S. family is better off than the average Argentinian or Indian family. Another item that is even more urgent than food, namely domestic water supply, should not be forgotten. In most poorer countries an abundant supply of good water is assured only to a small part of the community.

1. The reader who is interested in the economics of the uneven share-out of world production and consumption should consult *Economic Theory and Under-Developed Regions* (London, 1957) by G. Myrdal, a Swedish economist. He is concerned with the widening gap between the poorer and more prosperous countries of the world and searches for ways in which the latter can help the former and how the former should set about helping themselves. This may not be only by grants and credits but by agreeing to terms of trade that are fairer on the poorer countries. One of the many important points argued by Myrdal is that free trade does not work for equality among nations but that (p. 26): 'the play of forces in the market normally tends to increase, rather than to decrease, the inequalities between regions.'

TABLE 5

	U.S.A.	Argentina	India
Food: calories consumed per day per inhabitant	3200	2800	1800
Rooms per 10 inhabitants	10	4*	2*
Kilograms of cotton yarn per inhabitant per year	10	4	2
Doctors per 100,000 inhabitants	120	70	20
Dentists per 100,000 inhabitants	50	20	2
Percentage of population over 10 years of age literate	Almost 100	87	18
Students enrolled in higher educational establishments per 10,000 inhabitants	150	40	12
Copies of daily newspapers published per 1000 inhabitants	340	155	8
Radio receiving sets per 1000 inhabitants	750	140	2
Motor vehicles per 1000 inhabitants	390	33	1

* Very approximate figure.
NOTE: The figures can only be compared in a horizontal direction.

TABLE 6

	Anglo- and Latin America	Non-Communist Europe and all Africa	Communist Bloc	Rest of Asia and Australasia
10,000–				
	U.S.A. 8250			
	Canada 7570			
5000–		Norway 5340		
		U.K. 4870		
4000–		Sweden 4150		
		Belg.-Lux. 4100	Czecho. 3760	Australia 3660
3000–		W. Germ. 3350	E. Germ. 3530	
		Switz. 2870		N. Zealand
		France 2440	Poland 2650	2750
2000–	Venezuela 2030	Un. S. Afr. 2280	U.S.S.R. 2020	
		Finland 1850	Hungary 1670	
			Romania 1220	
	Chile 1020	Italy 1050		Israel 1050

Continued on p. 100

TABLE 6 (*continued*)

	Anglo- and Latin America	Non-Communist Europe and all Africa	Communist Bloc	Rest of Asia and Australasia
1000–				Japan 990
	Argentina 890			
	Puerto Rico 750	Spain 800		
	Mexico 710		Bulgaria 610	
	Cuba 640			
500–		Rhodesia 550		
400–	Colombia 470		Yugoslavia 470	Lebanon 490
	Brazil 360	Portugal 360		Malaya 390
300–	Peru 300	Greece 330		Turkey 310
		Morocco 240		Iraq 270
		Egypt 230		
200–		Algeria 200		Syria 190
	Bolivia 160	Kenya 160	China 160	Philipp. 150
	Guatemala 150	Ghana 130		S. Korea 150
	Ecuador 140	Belg. Cong. 110		India 120
100–				Indonesia 100
				Ceylon 100
		Mozambique 90		
50–		Sudan 50		Pakistan 50
40–	Haiti 40	Nigeria 40		Thailand 40
		Uganda 40		
30–	Paraguay 30	Fr. Eq. & W. Afr. 30		Burma 30
		Liberia 30		
20–				
		Ethiopia 10		

Consumption of energy (expressed in terms of coal equivalent) in kilograms per inhabitant in 1955 or nearest year.

NOTES 1. In order to fit all the names on one page a logarithmic scale has been chosen. The scale therefore decreases up the table.

2. Lack of space in the table has made it necessary to omit the following important countries: Denmark 2430, Netherlands 2220, Austria 2220, Uruguay 810, Formosa 460, Tunisia 180, Cambodia–Laos–Viet Nam 40.

SOURCE OF FIGURES: *United Nations Statistical Abstract, 1956*, Table 127: Estimated consumption of commercial sources of energy expressed in terms of coal.

	Anglo- and Latin America	Non-Communist Europe and all Africa	Communist Bloc	Rest of Asia and Australasia
500–	U.S.A. 620			
400–		W. Germ. 410		
		Sweden 402		Australia 333
300–	Canada 322	U.K. 367	Czecho. 300	
		Belg.-Lux. 292		
		France 235		
200–			U.S.S.R. 200	
			E. Germ. 200	New Zealand
		Austria 182	Poland 150	208
		Un. S. Afr. 138	Hungary 150	Israel 149
	Venezuela 109	Italy 118		Lebanon 118
100–	Argentina 108			
				Japan 82
50–	Chile 54	Ireland 53	Yugoslavia 51	
		Spain 50		
40–	Uruguay 36			Malaya 36
	Cuba 35	Portugal 32		Iraq 33
30–	Mexico 31	Greece 27		
	Colombia 27	Algeria 26		Syria 24
20–	Brazil 25			
		Egypt 14		Turkey 19
	Peru 14	Belg. Cong. 13		Iran 15
				Philippines 13
10–				
				Thailand 9
		Fr. W. Afr. 7		India 7
			China 6	Ceylon 6
5–		Br. W. Afr. 5		
4–				Pakistan 4
3–				Indonesia 3

Consumption of steel (expressed in terms of crude steel) in kilograms per inhabitant in 1955 or nearest year.

NOTES 1. In order to fit all the names on one page a logarithmic scale has been chosen. The scale therefore decreases up the table.

2. Figures for the countries of the communist bloc are only very approximate.

SOURCES OF FIGURES: *United Nations Statistical Abstract, 1956*, Table 131: Apparent consumption expressed in terms of crude steel.

An important point is brought out in table 5. While the ratio of food consumption in the U.S.A. and India is about two to one, the ratio of the availability of radios and motor vehicles, which in India are luxuries, is several hundred to one. Air, domestic water, and food are essential anywhere, and a certain amount of shelter and clothing is desirable almost everywhere. There is clearly a downward limit below which the consumption of calories could not descend without the consumer dying. There is also an upward limit beyond which the consumer would become ill or fail to digest all the food consumed.[1] In contrast, people can go on living without any of the numerous products of our modern machine age, and just as happily, probably, without them as with them.

Any classification of different parts of the world according to living standards is bound to be to some extent subjective. Even if figures were available to measure production and consumption in all branches of the economy of every country in the world it would be impossible to reach agreement as to how much importance should be attached to each particular branch.

Food consumption per inhabitant is no doubt a useful measure of living standards, especially when the actual content of the food (e.g. the proportion of protein) is taken into account. Unfortunately, figures are not available for many parts of the world, while, as already shown in the case of the U.S.A. and India, the range is relatively small between the countries with the highest and lowest *per caput* consumption (see *Statistical Yearbook of the United Nations, 1956*, Table 126). In Anglo-

1. The lower limit must be somewhere in the vicinity of 2000 (otherwise half of the population of the world would die) although about 2750 calories has been suggested as the desirable minimum. The upward limit might be about 4000–5000, but there are so many variables to be considered that rigid limits cannot be set. The amount required by each individual varies. A baby needs fewer calories than an adult, a large man more than a small one, an Eskimo more than an inhabitant of the tropics (but not many more, perhaps), and a person doing physical work more than one lying down all day. The average American is larger than the average Indian and lives (mostly) in a cooler environment. On the other hand the Indian is probably obliged to perform more physical work.

America, Northwest Europe, and Australasia it generally exceeds 3000 calories per inhabitant daily. In Latin America it ranges from 3000 to 2000 and in Asia it is mainly between about 2200 and 1800.

Per caput national income is also interesting, but again many countries, including those of the communist bloc, do not publish figures that would be of any use for purposes of comparison. If the national income (see *Statistical Yearbook of the United Nations, 1956*, Table 161) of countries is divided by the total number of inhabitants and then converted into U.S. dollars at the most suitable rate of exchange quoted, figures can be obtained for the annual *per caput* national income in many parts of the world. Unfortunately, the real value of the dollar equivalent of national currencies varies widely from country to country owing to the artificial nature of exchange rates. Even so, the figures are not without interest for comparative purposes. In the U.S.A. the annual *per caput* national income is about $U.S. 2000. In Northwest Europe it ranges from about $U.S. 1000 (Sweden and Switzerland) to about $U.S. 600 (Netherlands). Australia and New Zealand are also around $U.S. 1000 but Canada is nearer $U.S. 1500. In Latin America the range is between about $U.S. 500 (Venezuela) and $U.S. 60 (Haiti and Paraguay). In Asia it is between about $U.S. 250 (Turkey and Japan) and $U.S 60 (India and Pakistan).

For the purposes of this book, figures of *per caput* consumption of energy (in terms of coal equivalent) and of steel have been chosen to illustrate differences in living standards throughout the world (see tables 6 and 7). One reason why these figures have been chosen is that they are available for almost every important country in the world, including the members of the communist bloc. Another is that there is such a great range between the highest and lowest consumers that a useful grading is possible. In the U.S.A., for example, the annual *per caput* consumption of commercial energy in terms of coal equivalent is about 8 tons, whereas in Ethiopia it is about one-hundredth of a ton (it is not, of course, implied that living standards are therefore 800 times as high in the U.S.A. as in Ethiopia). A third reason why figures for energy and steel consumption are useful is that they are a measure, though a very approximate one, of the economic and military strength of a country. When considering tables 6 and 7, the reader should bear in mind that the numbers on the scale refer to *per caput*, not *absolute*, consumption. Although, for example, 400 kilograms of steel are consumed annually *per inhabitant* in Sweden and only about 200 in the U.S.S.R., the *total* consumed in the U.S.S.R. is far greater because this country has about thirty times as many inhabitants as Sweden.

Table 8 is an attempt to summarize differences in living standards by classifying countries in five main groups. The most prosperous are at the top, the poorest at the bottom. The reader should appreciate that the choice of five groups (fewer or more might have been made) and the decision as to the rank of each country are subjective. Certain countries where there are great differences in living conditions between Europeans and non-Europeans (e.g. Algeria and the Un. of S. Africa) or between different parts of the country (e.g. Brazil and Italy) are difficult to classify. Furthermore, certain countries are so near a division between one group and another that they might be put in either.

What is significant about the table is that it is no easy matter for a country to move up from one group into another. The U.S.S.R. has done so during the last three decades. It is the ambition of its leaders to take it up two more places into the top group and then to replace the U.S.A. at the top. Most political leaders would be satisfied to move their countries up even one place. Another feature of the table is that the countries in the bottom group have more than half of the world's population. The population shareout is approximately as follows: Group 1, 7 per cent; 2, 8 per cent; 3, 20 per cent; 4, 10 per cent; 5, 55 per cent.

Bearing in mind the great difference in output and in consumption per inhabitant between the countries in the highest and lowest groups, might we not question whether in reality there is any possibility that the poorer countries will ever catch up the more prosperous ones? Surely living conditions in the U.S.A. and India were closer 150 years ago than they are now. The gap

TABLE 8

	Anglo- and Latin America	Non-Communist Europe and all Africa	Communist Bloc	Rest of Asia and Australasia
1	Canada U.S.A.			
2		Austria Benelux France Scandinavia Switzerland U.K. W. Germany	Czecho- slovakia E. Germany	Australia New Zealand
3	Argentina Chile Cuba Uruguay Venezuela	Italy Spain Un. S. Africa	Hungary Poland Romania U.S.S.R.	Israel Japan
4	Brazil Colombia Mexico Peru	Algeria Egypt Greece Morocco Portugal	Bulgaria Yugoslavia	Iraq Syria Turkey
5	Bolivia Ecuador Guatemala Haiti Paraguay	Colonial Africa Ethiopia Liberia Sudan	China	Afghanistan Burma Ceylon India Indonesia Iran Korea Pakistan Philippines Saudi Arabia Thailand Viet Nam

Classification of principal countries into five main groups according to production and consumption per inhabitant in all branches of the economy.

NOTES 1. The members of each group are arranged alphabetically, and not in order of rank.

2. A classification of this kind (and even the choice of the five categories themselves) is bound to be subjective.

has *widened* over that period, not *narrowed*. What justification is there for hoping that it will start to close, instead of continuing to widen?

We, as Europeans, or people of European origin, are obsessed with the idea of material progress, and have witnessed such remarkable examples of it both in peace and war in Europe, Anglo-America, and more recently the U.S.S.R. We therefore assume not only that progress is desirable everywhere in the world, but also inevitable. It is merely a matter of time before the underdeveloped countries of the world (and these contain between 60 per cent and 70 per cent of the world's population, depending where the line is drawn) achieve a standard of living for all their inhabitants comparable with the present standard in North America and Northwest Europe. But even if we are justified in assuming that this is desirable, have we any grounds for assuming that it is inevitable or even probable?

There are several reasons why the assumption should not be accepted without many reservations. One reason is related to population changes. In both the U.S.A. and Canada (7 per cent of the world's population) population is increasing rapidly, but in these countries the exploitation of resources is organized very efficiently (if wastefully at times), more and more raw materials are being imported from abroad and output has been increasing even more rapidly than population, though in a somewhat erratic manner. In most of the countries in group 2 (8 per cent of the world's population) the rate of increase of population is low; as a result, there is not the urgency here to increase output. But most of the countries in the remaining groups have high rates of increase of population, and for various reasons the rates are likely in some cases to become even higher in the near future. In most of the countries in the two lowest groups (more than 60 per cent of the world's population) output has been increasing only slowly, while in some it has even decreased. The point is this, and we must face it: at present, the richer countries are mostly becoming more prosperous and the poorer ones are remaining poor and are even tending to become poorer. In addition to over-population there are questions connected with soil erosion, loss of soil fertility, the working out of more accessible mineral deposits, the great growth of urban areas. These affect all countries, but less can be done in the poorer ones to deal with them.

On the other side are the benefits that financial aid, technical assistance, increased trade, and other means of increasing output can bring to poorer countries. What of financial aid? Most has been given by the U.S.A., during and since the Second World War. If we examine it in detail (see ch. 9) we realize that most of the aid has gone to help countries which before the war had a reasonably high standard of living – the U.K., W. Germany, France, Italy, Japan. In ten years since the war (1945–54) India has received less than $U.S. 300 m. from U.S. Government foreign grants and credits. The generosity of the U.S.A. is not questioned here. Why, after all, should anything be given at all? What we should appreciate is that as a result each Indian has received less than one U.S. dollar in a decade. In the U.S.A. a haircut costs more than a dollar. Considering the small size of Jordan's population, the U.K. grant to this country up to 1956 was substantial – something in the order of several £ per inhabitant each year, yet little was done even with this amount to improve living conditions. What about oil royalties in certain countries? Only after its oil output moved up to tens of millions of tons per year did Venezuela begin to receive enough from these to do something about the development of its economy. The story is the same in the oil countries of Southwest Asia. So far the financial and technical aid to poorer countries has, with a few exceptions, been merely a drop in the ocean. The exceptions include Soviet aid to China (but this must eventually be repaid) and United States aid to Western Europe, to its own dependencies, former dependencies, or 'strategic' allies, such as Puerto Rico, the Philippines, Japan, and Formosa.

There are signs that Western Europe and the U.S.A. are now beginning to appreciate the need for a re-appraisal of the whole situation of aid and underdeveloped countries. The matter was apparently discussed, for example, during Mr Macmillan's visit to the U.S.A. in June 1958 (*Observer*, 15 June 1958). That it will be difficult to do anything is suggested by Dr Hjalmar Schacht's opposition to Mr Macmillan's suggestion (*News Chronicle*, 14 June 1958) that Germany should put its surplus gold into a project to help underdeveloped countries. The general impression is that the idea is good as long as you can get someone else to provide the money.

VII. URBAN REVOLUTION

CLOSELY related to questions of population change, mining and manufacturing developments, and differential living standards is the question of modern urban expansion. A great deal has been written about modern revolutions in agriculture and industry. Less is known by most people about the parallel urban revolution.

Farm workers live principally in small rural communities. Mining, industrial, and most other workers live mainly in urban types of settlement. Not surprisingly, the great development of modern industry, mining, and associated activities has led to the rapid expansion of many existing towns and to the creation of new ones. Advances in agriculture released farm workers from the land and enabled them to take up other activities in towns.

Large-scale migration from rural areas to industrial centres was a feature of England in the later 18th and 19th centuries. At present it is taking place in almost every part of the world, but varies in intensity from one country to another. Although the whole process of urbanization is closely connected with the changing employment structure[1] of countries, various immediate reasons decide individuals or whole families to move into towns. Among these are the attraction of various amenities and services; the almost universally higher and more reliable wages in manufacturing and other urban activities than in farming; government policy (as in the U.S.S.R. and, more recently, China) forcing people into cities; and at the other end, overpopulation in rural areas, and the introduction there of agricultural machinery, reducing the number of farm workers needed in a given area. A rapid increase of urban population in a short period is caused by the inflow of people from rural areas rather than by the natural increase of population in the urban areas themselves, though this can contribute as well.

1. The percentage of the total employed population in each branch of the economy.

The urban population, then, is tending to take up a larger and larger proportion of the total population of the world. In the U.K. more than 80 per cent of the population is defined as urban. Two hundred years ago it was only about 20 per cent. In the U.S.S.R. urbanization is a more recent feature: in 1913 (within the present limits) the total population was 159 m. and the urban population only 28 m. or 17·6 per cent; in 1956 the total had increased to 200 m. and the urban population to 87 m., 43·4 per cent of the total.

Fig. 9 is intended to give a very generalized picture of the present world distribution of urban population. Each circle is proportional in area to the total population of the region (see ch. 3) it represents. Black sectors in the circles represent the percentage of the total that is urban. It will be appreciated that on this map urban population is being measured against total population and that it must be shown in relation to some symbol (in this case, the circle) representing population, and not against land area.

A point to bear in mind is the fact that although the ratio of urban to rural population in India and China is low the total number of inhabitants is so large that there are more urban dwellers in these countries than in the U.K. or Germany, which are highly urbanized. The percentage of urban dwellers in China is about 13 per cent, but this represents 80 m. people. The U.S.A. has the largest absolute number of urban dwellers (about 110 m.). The percentage of urban inhabitants in selected countries of the world is shown below.

1. *More than about* 60 *per cent:* U.K. (81%), Germany (70%), Australia (69%), U.S.A. (64%), Belgium (63%), Argentina and Canada (62%).

2. *About* 30–60 *per cent:* Venezuela (54%), France (53%), Sweden (50%), Czechoslovakia (49%), U.S.S.R. (44%), Mexico (42%), Spain (37%), Brazil (36%), Hungary (35%), Portugal (31%), Egypt (30%).

3. *Below* 30 *per cent:* Peru (25%), Romania (23%), Turkey (22%), South Korea (20%), Morocco (18%), India (17%), China (13%), Pakistan (11%), Thailand (10%), Kenya (5%).

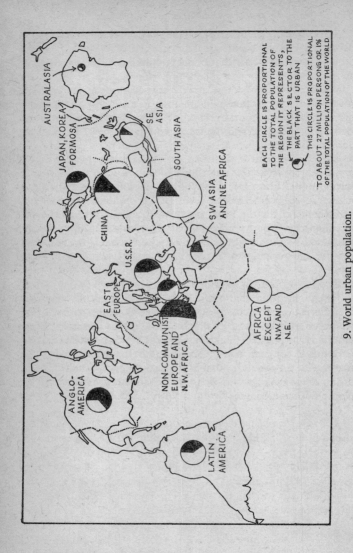

EACH CIRCLE IS PROPORTIONAL
TO THE TOTAL POPULATION OF
THE REGION IT REPRESENTS,
THE BLACK SECTOR TO THE
PART THAT IS URBAN

THIS CIRCLE IS PROPORTIONAL
TO ABOUT 27 MILLION PERSONS OR 1%
OF THE TOTAL POPULATION OF THE WORLD

AUSTRALASIA

SE ASIA

JAPAN, KOREA,
FORMOSA

SOUTH ASIA

CHINA

SW ASIA
AND N.E. AFRICA

U.S.S.R.

EAST EUROPE

NON-COMMUNIST
EUROPE AND
N.W. AFRICA

AFRICA
EXCEPT
N.W. AND
N.E.

ANGLO-
AMERICA

LATIN
AMERICA

9. World urban population.

Unfortunately these figures are only broadly comparable because they are for different years between 1945 and 1954 and because the definition of 'urban' varies from one country to another.

A great deal of work will have to be done by sociologists, psychologists, and geographers before all the implications of the urban revolution can be appreciated. One feature is becoming clear. In some respects urban centres all over the world resemble one another more closely than they resemble adjoining rural areas. Traffic jams and road accidents, bank robberies and organized prostitution, slums and overcrowding, neurosis and lonely people, spivs and teddy boys can be found in some form in any large urban centre, whether it is communist like Moscow or capitalist like New York, prosperous like Stockholm or poor like Bombay. On the other hand, one would hardly expect to find these, at least in their urban forms, in farming communities in China or Nigeria, Portugal or Mexico. Nor would these rural areas have libraries, theatres, higher educational establishments, well-run hospitals, or elegant department stores.

The great urban centre is detached from the land on which it depends, often precariously placed with regard to food and water supply, strategically a tempting target for a carefully placed guided missile and beset by innumerable other problems. But the urban revolution is in progress, and no more can be done to reverse the process of urbanization than to prevent advances in the technological revolution, which is constantly enlarging the possibilities and dangers before the human race.

PART TWO

This Part consists of a brief account of each of twelve regions into which the world has been divided for the purposes of this book. Although the particular features of each region are stressed, all regions are dealt with on more or less the same lines: location and outstanding characteristics, population, economic life, problems, and notes on some of the more important countries. Less importance has been given to naming mountains, rivers, and towns (which can be found in ordinary atlases) than to discussing the possibilities of the environment (with special reference to farming) and the minerals, industries, and communications. Nor has a distinction always been made as to the particular crops or livestock found in a given area. Only important mineral producing and industrial areas are shown on the regional maps.

The reader is asked to be careful in distinguishing throughout the book, and especially in the tables, between figures that are for absolute production (e.g. 560 m. tons of coal produced in the U.S.A. in 1950) and figures that are for output per inhabitant or *per caput* (e.g. in 1950 about $3\frac{3}{4}$ tons of coal were produced in the U.S.A. per inhabitant – i.e. the 560 m. tons measured against the 150 m. people) or output per worker (the 560 m. tons was produced by about 500,000 coal miners, which means that each worker produced rather more than 1,000 tons in one year). The twelve regional maps have a standard set of symbols, the key to which is shown opposite.

On the maps showing the hemisphere of seven of the twelve regions, circles centred on the central point of the projection (zenithal equidistant) are drawn at distances of a thousand miles apart. Distance is correct along any straight line from the central point towards the periphery, but exaggeration in other directions increases away from the centre, so that towards the edge area is exaggerated appreciably.

Symbols used in regional maps, figs. 14*a*, 16, 18, 20, 22, 23, 24, 25, 26, 28, 29, 31*a*.

LAND USE

Main areas of farming. Here most, if not all, of the land suitable for agriculture is now in use

Areas at present only partly utilized for agriculture. Here there seem to be opportunities for extending cultivation

Dry areas, at present used mainly for grazing but in which cultivation might be extended

AREAS OF VERY LITTLE OR NO USE AT PRESENT

〰〰〰 Ice cap

||||| High mountain areas

↑↑↑↑ Coniferous forest

≡≡≡ Desert areas

〜〜〜 Cold desert (tundra)

♀ ♀
♀ ♀ Dense tropical forest

MINING (*only significant producing areas are shown*)

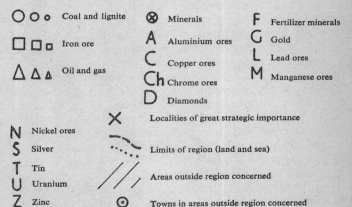

○ ○ ∘ Coal and lignite

⊗ Minerals

F Fertilizer minerals

□ ▢ ▫ Iron ore

A Aluminium ores

G Gold

△ ▵ ▵ Oil and gas

C Copper ores

L Lead ores

Ch Chrome ores

M Manganese ores

D Diamonds

N Nickel ores

S Silver

T Tin

U Uranium

Z Zinc

✕ Localities of great strategic importance

⋯⋯⋯ Limits of region (land and sea)

⁄⁄⁄ Areas outside region concerned

⊙ Towns in areas outside region concerned

–·–·– Political boundaries within region concerned

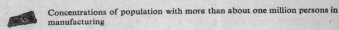

Concentrations of population with more than about one million persons in manufacturing

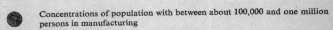

Concentrations of population with between about 100,000 and one million persons in manufacturing

Other important industrial areas

Large towns (mainly national capitals) with few industries

Chapter 5

THE REGIONS OF THE OUTER ZONE

I. ANGLO-AMERICA[1]

THE term Anglo-America is not infrequently used by U.S. geographers to describe America north of the Republic and Gulf of Mexico. In this book it also includes Greenland (a Danish possession) and the various U.S. islands in the North Pacific. Within the region there is great diversity both in relief and in climate. North America stretches almost from the tropics far into the Arctic. In spite of this physical diversity, considerable unity is given to the whole region by the fact that English is spoken almost everywhere (the French-Canadians form the largest non-English speaking minority). Similarly, most of the inhabitants are of European origin, but the Negroes of the U.S.A. (about 10 per cent of its total population) form a large non-European group. Another striking feature of the region as a whole is the form of its economic development during the last 150 years. The high degree of regional specialization in both the U.S.A. and Canada, and the close economic connexions between the two, mean that every part of the continent makes some particular contribution to the economy of the region as a whole. Finally, since the Second World War strategic considerations have contributed to reinforce the unity of Anglo-America. Alaska, North Canada, and Greenland are a forward line of defence for the U.S.A. against possible air attack across the Arctic or North Pacific, but the perfection of inter-continental rockets will no doubt reduce their strategic significance.

Anglo-America is separated by sea from all its neighbouring regions except Latin America (see fig. 10). To the north, across the Arctic Ocean, lies the U.S.S.R. To the west, many thousands of miles across the North Pacific, are Japan and China. Not so far across the North Atlantic is Europe.

1. See also ch. 9 for a study of the growth of the U.S.A. and its importance as a world power.

Anglo-America has about one-sixth of the world's land area but contains only about one-fifteenth of its population. The population is distributed thus: the U.S.A. 170 m. (1957), Canada 17 m., Hawaiian Islands (of which Hawaii itself is the largest)

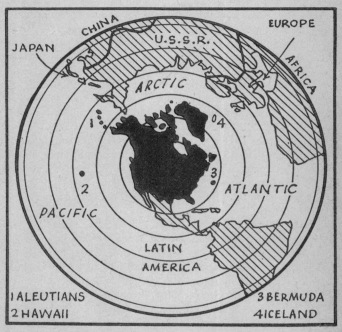

10. The hemisphere of Anglo-America. Projection: oblique zenithal equidistant. Centre of projection: Winnipeg, Canada. The circles are at thousand-mile intervals.

500,000, Alaska 200,000, Greenland 25,000. The U.S.A., with not much more than one-third of the total area of Anglo-America has almost 90 per cent of the total population. In the U.S.A. itself, about four-fifths of the population lives in the eastern half, while almost two-thirds of Canada's population is concentrated in a very small part of the national territory – southern Ontario and Quebec. Even in the most intensively used farming regions of Anglo-America, however, the density of population is low by European, Indian, or Chinese standards. On the other hand, the U.S.A. has some of the largest urban areas in the world (Greater New York has 13 m. inhabitants, Chicago and Los Angeles 5 m. each) and about 65 per cent of its population now lives in urban types of settlement, while even in Canada, which is less highly industrialized, more than 60 per cent is urban.

The population of Anglo-America is at present increasing rapidly. This is a result not only of the fairly high natural rate of increase but also of the arrival of hundreds of thousands of immigrants each year from Europe. The number of arrivals in the U.S.A. is much smaller than it was at the beginning of the century (e.g. about 200,000 in 1952 compared with almost 1 m. per annum during 1911–15), and there was very little immigration at all during 1930–45. In contrast, Canada, with only about one-tenth as many inhabitants as the U.S.A. received almost 200,000 immigrants in 1951. Canada's future policy appears to be to continue to encourage immigration, though not, perhaps, at the 1951 level.

Although agriculture is no longer the largest single employer of labour in Anglo-America, as it was in the last century, most of the U.S.A. is used for some kind of farming (see fig. 11). In Canada, on the other hand, only a small part of the total area is used for agriculture. The northern half of Anglo-America is too cold for farming. Almost all of Greenland is covered by an ice-cap. Northern Canada and much of Alaska are in the zone of tundra (or cold desert), while much of the remainder is occupied by the zone of coniferous forest, in which the soils are generally of little use for cultivation even where climatic conditions are favourable for the growth of certain crops. Much of the western two-fifths of the U.S.A. is too rugged for farming or too dry to be cultivated intensively without irrigation. Even the area of the Great Plains, to the east of the Rocky Mountains, often suffers from droughts and from strong winds that remove unprotected soil.

About three-fifths of the U.S.A. is in farms, but only about one-third of this farmland (or 20 per cent of the total country) is

11a. Anglo-America. For key see p. 115.

11b. Industrial Anglo-America. In the region shaded on the map industry overshadows other activities.

cropland. Twenty-eight per cent of the total area of the country is forest and woodland. In Canada no more than 2–3 per cent of the total area is cropland. About 34 per cent is forested. Most of the U.S. cropland is in the eastern half of the country, where only relatively small areas, such as the higher parts of the Appalachians, are not used for some kind of farming.

In the U.S.A. the number of persons engaged in agriculture is surprisingly small. In 1920 the farm population of the U.S.A. (workers and dependants) was 32 m., or 25 per cent of the total population. In 1954 it was only 22 m., and no more than $13\frac{1}{2}$ per cent of the total population (which had itself increased over that period). In 1950 there were only 8 m. full-time agricultural workers and some 3 m. seasonal workers, and the number has continued to diminish since then. Even so, total farm output has tended to increase, which means that output per worker is far higher than some decades ago.

The very high output per worker in agriculture in the U.S.A. (only rivalled in a few countries, including Canada, Australia, and New Zealand) is the result of several developments. In the U.S.A. (with the exception of certain regions) farms tend to specialize in the production of one or a small number of crops or one type of livestock. Generally only a very small proportion of the produce is consumed on the farm itself. When a farm specializes in one particular branch of agriculture (such as grain cultivation or dairying), the farmer can become an expert in that branch and needs only a limited range of equipment. Two other features of U.S. farming are the high degree of mechanization and the large amount of manufactured fertilizer applied per unit of area. Tractors and other machines have been applied widely in the U.S.A. because much of the best farmland is level or gently undulating, and because in most areas fields are large. Obviously, the introduction of mechanization has been much more widespread in the U.S.A. and Canada than in countries such as China or those bordering the Mediterranean, not only because Anglo-America is highly industrialized and can therefore mass-produce farm equipment, but also because the farmland has not been divided into minute parcels by generation after generation of peasant farmers.

Yields per unit of area tend to be lower in the U.S.A. and Canada than in countries such as Denmark, the Netherlands, and the U.K., where the amount of land available for agriculture is so much more limited and is therefore used with great care. Nevertheless, Anglo-America supplies most of the agricultural commodities it needs and still has a surplus of wheat, meat, cotton, tobacco, and other products for export. Only tropical crops such as coffee and cocoa (which, of course, cannot be grown in Anglo-America), and wool, are imported in large quantities. There is, indeed, a superabundance of food in Anglo-America, and whereas in most other parts of the world there is a constant struggle to ensure sufficient calories for rapidly increasing populations, in the U.S.A. many citizens are disturbed because they eat too much. Typical of the situation is a sweetening substance with no calorific value, which can now be purchased by anyone wishing to reduce his (or her) intake of calories.

One aspect of U.S. farming is less encouraging. In a land where farmers and government officials are more concerned with surpluses than shortages it is ironical that much of the land at one time farmed in many of the drier areas between the Mississippi and the Rocky Mountains is now of little or no use because the soil has been, and still is being, blown away. A recent series of dry years has been making matters worse.

Anglo-America is fortunate in having extensive proved reserves of many of the more important economic minerals. Both the U.S.A. and Canada have large deposits of coal, oil, and iron ore.

Per caput coal production has always been higher in the U.S.A. than in Canada, but in both countries there has been a tendency during recent decades for total production to decline. In the U.S.A. about 400 m. tons were being produced annually in 1935–9. The total rose almost to 600 m. per year during the later years of the Second World War, but dropped below the pre-war level in 1954 (379 m. tons) only to pass it again in 1955 (448 m.). Other sources of energy, including oil, natural gas, and hydro-electricity, are tending to replace coal in many branches of the economy.

For several decades the U.S.A. (with 6–7 per cent of the world's population) has accounted for about half of the world's oil production. In Canada the oil industry was relatively insignificant until a few years ago, but output there is now increasing rapidly. Figures in the following table are in millions of metric tons.

TABLE 9

	1936	1945	1954	1955	1956
U.S.A.	149	232	313	336	383
Canada	*	1	13	17	24
World	245	351	691	779	869

* Negligible output.

There is some concern in the U.S.A. now about oil reserves. Although new sources are constantly being found, most fields only have a life of 10–20 years at present rates of production. More and more oil is now being imported because demand is increasing more rapidly than home production. In Colorado, however, shales have been discovered containing more than 130,000 m. tons of oil – 150 times the amount produced in the whole world in 1956. As a result of advances in cracking, it appears that the time is not far off when it will be possible to exploit this shale oil economically, an interesting example of how technical advances can suddenly change an economic situation. In Canada, too, the Athabaska tar sands of Northern Alberta contain very large reserves of oil in a form that can now be refined. Estimates put the reserves at between 15,000 and 45,000 m. tons.

Although the U.S.A. has many other minerals, it now imports part or all of its needs of almost every mineral. It is still the world's leading producer of iron ore, but now also the world's largest importer. It produces one-quarter of the world's copper, one-sixth of the lead and zinc, but still has to import additional supplies of these metals. It produces at home little or none of its requirements of bauxite, tin, manganese, chrome, tungsten, and nickel. On the other hand it has good deposits of fertilizer minerals – phosphates, potash, and sulphur (about one-half, one-quarter and nine-tenths respectively of world output).

Canada produces and exports many of the minerals deficient in the U.S.A. It is the world's leading producer of nickel, platinum, and asbestos, and a large producer of lead, copper, and zinc. Its deposits of uranium are four times as large as those of the U.S.A. In recent years it has become the main supplier of U.S. imported iron ore (from Labrador).

The U.S.A. leads the world both in absolute and in *per caput* production in almost every branch of industry. The rapid expansion of industry there during the last hundred years results from the combination of a number of favourable circumstances. It has had abundant supplies of coal, some of the most accessible deposits being in the Northeast, where the Industrial Revolution began in the U.S.A. During the present century oil and natural gas, of which it has large reserves, have come to play an important part in industrial development. The U.S.A. has also had many of the mineral and plant raw materials needed for modern industry. From Europe there has been a constant inflow of settlers, among them persons from industrial areas. The U.S.A. itself has formed from the start a large and expanding market. Then there have been few traditions and restrictions to impede the development of industry in such a young nation. Behind everything has been the idea of material progress.

In industry, as in agriculture, there has been a high degree of local specialization in production. This has been possible because a close network of railway lines already covered the more populous part of the U.S.A. by the end of the last century and has been supplemented during the present century by a remarkable system of roads, gas and oil pipelines, and electricity transmission cables. Cheap transport has been called the great key to American progress.

A feature of U.S. development in recent decades has been the concentration of much of the industrial capacity in a small number of large concerns. One of the consequences of this trend has been the standardization of products, facilitating mass-production and resulting in high output per worker. Less than one-third of the employed population of the U.S.A. is engaged in manufacturing – about 15 m. persons – yet almost every branch of modern industry is to be found there, and only Western Europe and the U.S.S.R. can be considered possible rivals with regard to capacity, though no single European country has such a wide range of products.

The earliest centres of modern industry in the U.S.A. were in New England. From there industry spread to the west, to the vicinity of the Great Lakes, and southwest along the Atlantic seaboard and into the Appalachians. Even today much of the industrial capacity of the country is concentrated in this north-eastern region, while many of Canada's principal industrial centres lie at no great distance across the boundary. In recent decades there has been a trend towards decentralization, and industry has expanded in the cotton-growing states of the south-east, in the oilfield areas of the south, and in the larger urban centres of the Pacific Coast states where, around Los Angeles, most of the U.S. aircraft factories are located. A project of great significance to many of the interior industrial centres of Northeast U.S.A. and southern Ontario is the St Lawrence seaway (to be completed in 1959), along which large ocean-going vessels will be able to pass from the Atlantic into the Great Lakes. One of the main functions of the seaway will be to enable ore-carrying ships to transport iron ore most of the distance between the Labrador fields and the ports on the Great Lakes.

Although foreign trade has always played an important part in the economic life of the U.S.A. and Canada since the earliest colonial days, they depend less on it than the U.K. does.

The pattern of U.S. trade has changed fundamentally during the last hundred years. The following figures represent the percentage of the total value of exports taken up by semi-finished and finished manufactures (as opposed to crude materials and crude and manufactured foodstuffs): 1850s, 16 per cent; 1890s, 26 per cent; 1915–20, 55 per cent; 1931–5, 57 per cent; 1941–5, 81 per cent; 1954, 77 per cent. During the same period, crude materials and foodstuffs have come to occupy a larger and larger part of the imports. The U.S.A. therefore now exports mainly manufactured goods; motor vehicles and other products of the engineering industry account for one-third of the value of all exports. Even so, U.S. farm products such as grain, cotton, and tobacco are still significant items in international trade. Imports, which are mainly raw materials and foodstuffs, fall into several main groups: tropical foodstuffs and beverages (cocoa, coffee, tea, sugar, and fruits); tropical plant raw materials (rubber); animal raw materials (wool and hides); forest products (wood and paper pulp); non-metallic minerals (oil); and non-ferrous metals (copper, lead, zinc), iron ore and ferro-alloys (manganese), and nuclear fuels (uranium). Although the U.S.A. has important trading connexions with many non-communist countries in different parts of the world, a large proportion of its foreign trade is with Canada and certain Latin American countries.

The *per caput* value of Canada's overseas trade is about twice as high as that of the U.S.A. In contrast to the U.S.A., most of Canada's exports are raw materials (often processed, but not manufactured). Canada is more fortunate than most Latin American countries, which depend on one particular raw material for export, because it has a wide range of products for sale abroad. Forest products (wood, pulp, newsprint, and paper) make up about one-third of the value of exports, minerals (aluminium, nickel, copper, and asbestos) another one-fifth, and wheat and flour about one-twentieth. Canada also exports various manufactures. In recent years, about three-quarters of Canada's imports have been coming from the U.S.A., and about one-tenth from the U.K. The U.S.A. takes about 60 per cent of Canada's exports. Clearly, then, the two countries have close trading connexions. These connexions are strengthened by the fact that some 30 per cent of all U.S. foreign investments are in Canada.

Little need be said about living conditions in Anglo-America. Undoubtedly the standard of living here is the highest in the world, though there are appreciable differences between different regions. In the U.S.A., in particular, it is not difficult to see from the *Statistical Abstract of the United States* that the average income of Negro and American Indian families is far below that of the whites.

Although there are no serious problems in Anglo-America connected with pressure of population on land or resources, the U.S.A. and Canada are not without other problems.

Two problems in the U.S.A. are worth noting, one connected with the inequality of opportunity between the people of European descent and the various groups of non-Europeans (in this

125

group are included the Mexicans, mainly American Indians, who are employed in the U.S.A.), the other connected with the inequality of *per caput* production between the U.S.A. and most other parts of the world.

While the original inhabitants of North America, the Indians, have by now either been exterminated or accommodated on reserves, the Negroes live and work in the same areas as the whites both in the cotton-producing states and in the urban centres of industrial U.S.A. It is ironical that in the stronghold of freedom, equal opportunity, and progress, the Negroes should still remain underprivileged almost 100 years after the Civil War, during which they were freed from slavery. On the other hand, it would be surprising, in view of current prejudices regarding questions of race, if they had been assimilated into the American community in the way that each group of European settlers has.

A second great problem now facing the U.S.A. is the widening gap between living standards and production there and in other parts of the world. The U.S.A. can now hardly trade on equal terms with any part of the world except Canada and Australia. Other countries need its surplus foodstuffs and raw materials such as cotton and wheat just as much as they need its machinery and other manufactures. They simply cannot afford to buy them – they have little to offer that the U.S.A. needs. In recent years U.S. imports have been about $U.S. 10,000 m. and exports $U.S. 15,000 m. per year. The gap has been closed largely by the granting of various forms of aid and credit. As living standards continue to improve and production costs to rise in the U.S.A., it has to give away or sell cheaply what it is unable to sell at current world market prices. For example, it is becoming more and more difficult for the U.S.A. to sell cotton in foreign markets because this commodity can be produced more cheaply in other cotton-growing countries of the world where living standards are lower. In recent years the U.S.A. has had a surplus of cotton in spite of the restriction by the national government on the acreage under this crop. Even the giving away or selling at reduced prices of surplus commodities such as flour and cotton can cause complications by interfering with the foreign trade of other producers. The expansion of U.S. foreign investments in poorer countries in a way tends to aggravate the situation. The production of raw or processed materials is organized by U.S. companies in many different parts of the world, but the materials produced are frequently exported to the U.S.A. and other manufacturing nations, and therefore do not contribute directly, except by providing royalties, to raise living standards in poorer countries.

The reader who has played the game Monopoly might agree that the U.S.A. is like the player in the game who has acquired much of the best property and is embarrassed when other people land on it because they would go out of the game if they had to pay all that the rules required. In this game the U.S.S.R. is clever. It has made its own set of rules and moves round on its own circuit, without landing on other people's property.

Canada, like Australia, is one of the few countries in the world that suffers, or professes to suffer, from under-population. Although Canada has very great forest, fishing, and mineral resources, however, only a very small part of the country – perhaps 5 per cent – has good or reasonable conditions for farming. With present farming techniques Canada could never feed more than a few tens of millions of people. The Canadian environment in many ways resembles that of Siberia (see ch. 7). In time, of course, some means may be found of utilizing the soils of the coniferous forest zone for agriculture. Not surprisingly, however, most of Canada's capital investment is at present in the development of mineral, forest, and water-power resources. Examples are the rapidly expanding oil industry, the projects to increase aluminium output, and the work on large power stations in British Columbia.

Canada's social problems are largely connected with the difficulties of integrating the two main European communities – those of British and French origin. Problems arise from differences in language and religion. About one-half of the total population is of British, and one-third of French, descent.

In the economic and strategic spheres, Canada is closely connected with the U.S.A. In many respects Canada's economy is dominated by its more powerful neighbour, although it also has important ties with the U.K. and other parts of the British Commonwealth. In geographical terms it has the doubtful privilege of being located between the U.S.A. and the U.S.S.R., a fact that has not prevented (and may even have encouraged) it from acting independently of the U.S.A. in many post-war political crises.

Although both Alaska and Greenland are thinly populated and relatively unimportant economically they have become vital areas in the defence of the U.S.A. since the Second World War. Alaska's population has increased three times since the 1930s, largely as a result of the establishment there of important U.S. bases, facing the remote northeast extremity of the U.S.S.R., the Chukhotka Peninsula. Many U.S. and West European expeditions have visited Greenland since the war, while the U.S.A. and U.S.S.R. have both given great attention to the exploration of the Arctic Ocean in recent years.

II. LATIN AMERICA

LATIN AMERICA consists of twenty independent republics and a number of small colonial territories. After almost 150 years of freedom from European colonial rule, national consciousness has grown strong in most of the republics. The enormous extent over which Latin America stretches (almost 7000 miles from Northwest Mexico to Southern Chile), and the great diversity of physical conditions, contributed to the breaking up of the former Spanish American Empire into eighteen modern nations, but in contrast the Portuguese colonies in South America remain united in modern Brazil. Although most of Latin America has therefore been independent from Europe for about 150 years, Iberian influence was so powerful there during the three centuries (16th–18th) of European domination that today a Mexican or a Cuban feels closer in many respects to a distant Brazilian or Argentinian than to a North American living only a few hundred miles away in the U.S.A. A considerable degree of cultural unity is therefore to be found in Latin America in spite of its physical diversity. Spanish is the official language in all the independent nations except Brazil (Portuguese) and Haiti (dialects of French), although in many areas the languages of the original inhabitants, the American Indians, are still used.

Roman Catholicism is almost universally professed if not actively practised, even if pre-Christian characteristics have been incorporated in it in some regions. Throughout Latin America many social and economic features of the Iberian colonial period are still preserved. Much of the land remains in the hands of a relatively small number of landowners of European origin. Most of the republics still specialize in the production of raw materials for Europe (and now Anglo-America as well) as they did when colonies, though one by one during recent decades they have been breaking away from this economic tradition.

Latin America has about one-fifteenth of the world's population and almost one-sixth of its land area. About three-quarters lie within the tropics. Fig. 12 shows the hemisphere of Latin America. The only land frontier is with the U.S.A. Africa, with which there is very little contact, and Europe, with which there are significant cultural and commercial ties, are several thousand miles away even from the nearest parts. The other eight regions of the world are located outside the hemisphere of Latin America. It is therefore not surprising that Latin America has generally been little concerned with events in other parts of the world, and was probably less affected by the Second World War than any other extensive land area.

Table 10 contains some basic economic statistics concerning the eleven most populous independent nations. In cols I and II it can be seen that the countries vary greatly both in size and population. The most extensive, Brazil, is larger than the U.S.A, or Australia, while even Uruguay, the smallest in South America. exceeds England in area. Col. III shows, again, that density of population varies considerably from one country to another. Many of the smaller islands, not shown in the table, have even higher densities than Cuba – some have several hundred inhabitants per square mile. Unfortunately the figures fail to bring out the fact that in every country there are also great differences in density between urban and closely settled farming regions on the one hand and almost uninhabited regions such as the interior of the Amazon basin on the other. In South America, a considerable part of the population lives within about one hundred miles of the coast, partly a result of colonization from overseas,

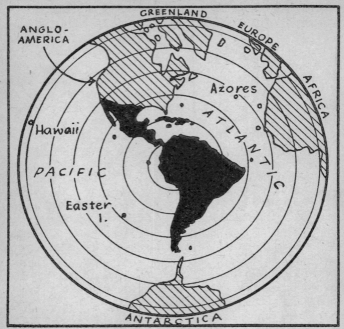

12. The hemisphere of Latin America. Projection: oblique zenithal equidistant. Centre of projection: Iquitos, Peru. The circles are at thousand-mile intervals.

partly because much of the best farmland is located in coastal areas.

The population of Latin America is characterized by the great diversity of its origin. The indigenous inhabitants, the American Indians, were to be found almost everywhere before the arrival of European explorers, but were most numerous in two main areas: Central America (including Mexico) and the Northern Andes. They, not Columbus, nor even the Vikings, must have been the discoverers of America, for all archaeological and anthropological evidence available at present suggests that they entered America from Asia. In the 16th–18th centuries Spaniards

TABLE 10

	I	II	III	IV	V	VI	VII	VIII	IX	X
	Area	Pop'n	Dens.	Cropland	Oil	Steel	Rlys	Motor vehs	Trade	Main export
Mexico	760	30	39	9	13	700	5	17	83	Cotton 25
Cuba	44	6½	148	25	*	*	5	23	75	Sugar 85
Venezuela	350	6	17	1	129	*	1	36	68	Oil 95
Colombia	440	13	30	2	6½	200	1	8	67	Coffee 80
Ecuador	105	3½	33	4	½	*	2	5	64	Bananas 30
Peru	480	10	21	1½	2½	*	2	10	55	Cotton 25
Bolivia	420	3½	8	½	½	*	5	4	32	Tin 60
Chile	290	7	24	4	½	300	8	14	52	Copper 60
Argentina	1080	20	19	10	4½	300	13	31	18	Pastoral 55
Uruguay	71	3	42	7	*	*	6	35	24	Pastoral 75
Brazil	3290	60	18	2	½	1200	3	12	42	Coffee 75
U.K. (for comparison)	94	51	540	20	*	20,000	4	135	—	—

* Negligible output or no production.

I. Area in thousands of sq. mls. III. Density of population in persons per sq. ml.
II. Population in millions. IV. Cropland as a percentage of total national territory.
V. Production of crude oil in 1956 (millions of metric tons).
VI. Steel output (thousands of metric tons).
VII. Miles of railway per 10,000 inhabitants.
VIII. Motor vehicles in circulation per 1,000 inhabitants.
IX. Percentage of value of all imports now supplied by the U.S.A.
X. Main item of export expressed as percentage of value of all exports.

and Portuguese colonized Latin America in relatively small numbers, while larger numbers of African Negroes were imported as slaves. In the 19th–20th centuries large numbers of Europeans – not only Iberians, but also Italians, Germans, and others – have migrated to South America, mainly to extra-tropical areas (South Brazil, Argentina, and Chile). Smaller numbers of Asians (mainly Japanese, Chinese, and Indians) have also been received in certain countries. There is therefore a great variety of races, with some degree of mixing in almost every part of Latin America. Often, however, one race predominates: African Negroes in Haiti; American Indians in Mexico and the Andes of Ecuador, Peru, and Bolivia; and Europeans in Argentina, Chile, Uruguay, and South Brazil.

In all Latin American countries farming is the occupation of a large proportion of the population. In some areas, including Haiti and parts of Central America and the Andes, it is almost the only activity, and each community or small group of communities is to a large extent self-supporting. In other areas, including most of Argentina and Uruguay, parts of Brazil and Chile, and many of the islands, agriculture is run largely on a commercial basis with specialization in one or more crops or pastoral products for sale to urban areas or for export to foreign markets. There is a tendency to exaggerate the importance of the special crops such as sugar, coffee, and cotton, and to forget that most of the cropland in Latin America is used for the cultivation of such food crops as maize, tubers, beans, and rice, which are the main items of diet for most of the inhabitants.

Fig. 13 shows the main areas of rural settlement in Latin America and the areas where conditions are not favourable for farming. The least favourable areas include: the high zone of the Andes, where only limited areas are suitable for cultivation or grazing in the north and the southern part is hardly used at all; the desert areas of Northwest Mexico, coastal Peru, Northern Chile, and the interior of Argentina; and the dense forests of the Amazon lowlands. Nowhere, except where altitude reduces temperature, are conditions so cold that they prevent some kind of farming.

Considering that these unfavourable regions only account

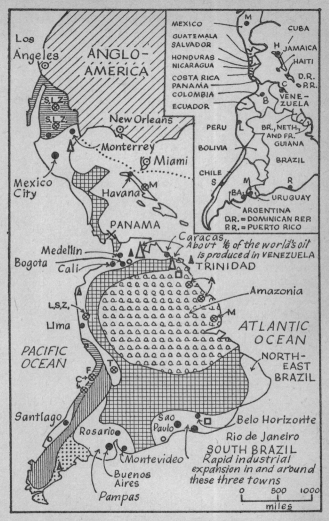

13. Latin America. For key see p. 115. The inset map shows the main political divisions.

133

for perhaps half of the total area of Latin America, the figures in col. IV in the table show that at least in the larger countries the area under cropland is remarkably small. Grazing land is not of course shown, and in most of the South American countries pastoral activities are no less important than cultivation. Even so, many large areas are at present little utilized and could be used for some kind of farming. The countries in which possibilities for extending cultivation and grazing appear most promising are those in tropical South America: Brazil, Venezuela, Colombia, Ecuador, Peru, and Bolivia, each of which has a portion of the vast Amazon–Orinoco lowland. In Chile, Argentina, and Uruguay, most of the better quality farmland is now utilized, although much of it could be used more intensively. The same is true in Central America and the islands, but in Haiti, Puerto Rico, and the smaller islands, the pressure of population is becoming a much more serious problem than it is in Cuba or on the mainland.

Perhaps the most significant feature of mineral production in Latin America is the fact that only one country, Colombia, has extensive proved reserves of coal. The total annual coal output of the continent is merely a few million tons – less than the U.S.A. mines in a week. Only in Chile, Colombia, Brazil (about 2 m. tons each), and Mexico is home-produced coal significant in the national economy, though even here output per inhabitant is very small by U.S. standards. The lack of good coal supplies has been one of the main reasons why modern industrial growth has been so restricted in Latin America.

The region as a whole is in a much better position with regard to oil deposits, though some countries have very small proved reserves and others none at all. In the interwar period Mexico for a time produced more than one-quarter of the world's oil. The industry was nationalized in 1938. Much of the most accessible oil had by then been extracted and Mexico now has little surplus for export. It was eclipsed by Venezuela in the 1930s, and this country now accounts for several times as much as all the other producers of Latin America together, though it consumes only a small part of its output, which is produced entirely by foreign companies. Colombia, Peru, Ecuador, and Bolivia are smaller producers consuming most of their output, but

Argentinian production only meets part of that country's needs, while at present Brazil produces only a very small proportion of its requirements.

Latin America is a leading world producer of several metallic ores and metals. The following countries produce a significant percentage of the world's total: Netherlands Guiana, Br. Guiana, and Jamaica together about 50 per cent of the world's bauxite; Venezuela, Brazil, Chile, and Peru, iron ore; Chile, copper; Mexico and Peru, lead and zinc; Bolivia, tin; Cuba and Brazil, manganese.

In many respects the mining industry of Latin America is typical of that in the poorer, little industrialized areas of the world. Most of the countries have been unable to explore, let alone exploit, their own mineral deposits in the period of modern world industrial expansion. Almost everywhere, therefore, mining establishments are owned, financed, and organized by European or U.S. companies. The labour supply is of course local. Most of the metallic ores and metals, and much of Venezuela's oil, are exported to industrial countries outside the region. There has so far been little industrial development based on local minerals, though Latin American countries do benefit from the royalties paid by foreign companies on concessions and production, while Latin Americans employed in foreign companies generally receive higher wages and enjoy better living conditions than their compatriots in agriculture. On the other hand, their standard of living is far below that of mining workers in the U.S.A. or Western Europe. What is more, even the great oil industry in Venezuela directly employs only about 60,000 workers, while the labour force in farming in Venezuela must be at least thirty times as large. Consequently only a very small proportion of the national labour force benefits directly. At all events, the attitude of most Latin American governments appears to be that it is a doubtful blessing to have one's minerals in the hands of large foreign companies. The more powerful countries, including Argentina and Brazil, have therefore attempted to control their mining activities. An eminent Colombian economist, Jorge Mejía Palacio, recently (*Américas*, vol. 9, no. 8, Aug. 1957) expressed the view about 'colonial' investments that they contribute little, apart from their royalties, to the general economy of Latin American nations.

For many reasons, industrial development on modern lines has been slow and slight in most Latin American countries. The absence of extensive reserves of good coal except in Colombia has almost completely prevented the earlier phases of the Industrial Revolution from spreading into the region. Oil has only begun to play an important part as a source of fuel and power in the last two or three decades, while hydro-electric power has so far been utilized on a large scale only in South Brazil. Another disadvantage is connected with organization and labour supply. With almost no tradition of manufacturing in the colonial period, the supply of labour accustomed to industrial activities has been small. Moreover, the lack of interest in machines and technical matters, which has been typical of the Spaniards and Portuguese, has left the European settlers in Latin America short of technicians. Even now little technical literature is available in Spanish or Portuguese on such subjects as geology and engineering, and a knowledge of English is essential for an expert. Thirdly, again partly a result of the Iberian tradition, the Europeans with capital have often preferred to keep it invested in agricultural establishments or to buy land and build in expanding urban centres rather than to risk investing in industry. The countries are poor, anyway, and lack the capital to build up large industrial enterprises. Finally, many of the republics have too few inhabitants (and the majority of them with little or no purchasing power) to provide big enough markets to make large and therefore economic industrial undertakings possible, while to ensure their survival many existing national industries have to be protected by heavy tariffs on imported manufactures from the U.S.A., Europe, and elsewhere.

Certain branches of light manufacturing, working entirely with imported machinery, and frequently financed and assisted technically by parent establishments in Europe or the U.S.A., do flourish in some of the more populous countries. Cotton spinning and weaving is carried on in almost every republic; most republics satisfy their basic needs in clothing and shoes, various processed foodstuffs and beverages. Some produce items like paper and rubber tyres, while bulky goods such as cement and bricks, which are costly to transport over great distances, are mostly produced locally. In other words, most simple products that can be made with foreign machinery and relatively unskilled labour are manufactured in Latin America. It is the machines themselves, the complicated pieces of equipment – locomotives, motor vehicles, generators – that have to be imported. The engineering industry hardly exists in Latin America, though imported parts of machines are frequently assembled and machines repaired and maintained. Only in Brazil are the beginnings of a large-scale engineering industry to be found.

Until relatively recently Latin America produced almost no steel, the basic raw material in the engineering industry. Even now it turns out little more steel in a year than the U.S.A. does in a week. At present only Brazil, Mexico, Chile, Colombia, and Argentina produce appreciable quantities of this metal, while only the first four have modern blast furnaces to produce the pig iron for steel making. Even today several hundred thousand tons of Brazilian iron ore are smelted with charcoal – an interesting indication of the state of industrial development in Latin America, for coking coal had almost completely replaced charcoal in Britain 150 years ago and even in Russia 40 years ago. In striking contrast are some of the industries introduced into the São Paulo area of Brazil in the last decade: the smelting of aluminium, the manufacture of railway and electrical equipment, and of sewing machines and pharmaceuticals.

Developments in all branches of the economy in Latin American countries have been hampered to a considerable extent by poor communications. The great era of railway building with European capital ended about 50 years ago, leaving large areas tens and even hundreds of miles from the nearest line. Moreover, for obvious reasons, many of the lines run from the interior to a coastal port. Only Cuba and parts of Mexico, South Brazil, Argentina, and Chile are adequately served by rail. Almost all existing lines are single track, and few new lines have been built in recent decades. Interest has turned to the construction of roads generally cheaper than railways to build and maintain and therefore more suitable where traffic is not expected to be heavy.

Air transport has now become the main form of passenger transport in many parts of Latin America, linking the principal towns of each country and the capitals and larger towns of different countries. The rivers Orinoco, Amazon, and Paraná and their tributaries remain the chief lines of movement in the interior of South America.

With regard to foreign trade, the nations of Latin America have a number of features in common. Col. x in table 10 shows how dependent most of the large countries are on one item of export (and the same is true of the smaller ones and the colonies). In some countries it is a farm product, in some a mineral. The whole economy of Colombia and Brazil, for example, has been greatly affected for several decades now by the fluctuations in the world coffee trade. Almost every country is thus dependent on one or a small number of raw materials for its foreign currency – with which it buys its machinery and vehicles as well as various other raw materials, and in some cases considerable quantities of food and fuel as well. The demand for Latin American meat, cereals, and sugar is generally more constant than the demand for semi-luxuries such as coffee or for minerals such as copper and tin, the prices of which often change. In this respect, therefore, Argentina, Uruguay, and Cuba are particularly fortunate, while Venezuela, of course, benefits from the continuing expansion of the world demand for oil.

Another feature of Latin American foreign trade is the growing share taken by the U.S.A. In the colonial period (except the later stages) trade was with Spain or Portugal. In the 19th century Britain and other industrial countries of Europe handled a large share. Largely as the result of two wars in Europe and of the industrial expansion of the U.S.A., this country now supplies about half of all the imports of Latin America and takes about two-fifths of the exports. Broadly speaking, the closer the country to the U.S.A., the larger is the proportion of its trade with it. In contrast, there is relatively little trade among Latin American countries themselves, largely because in so many respects their economies are similar. Most striking of all, perhaps, is the decline during the present century of Britain's trade with many Latin American countries, the result of growing competition from the

U.S.A., from other West European countries, and even from Japan.

Although living standards in Latin American countries are far below those in the U.S.A. and the more prosperous countries of Europe, there are considerable differences within the region itself between one country and another and between different regions within individual countries. The more prosperous countries of Latin America are those situated south of the tropics – Argentina, Uruguay, and Chile, and the southern part of Brazil. Paraguay, Bolivia, and Ecuador, the islands except Cuba, and the smaller Central American republics, are the poorest. The contrast within countries is generally between the capital city and some other large towns on the one hand and the rest of the country on the other. Most of the wealthier citizens reside either permanently or periodically in the larger towns and most of the industrial establishments are located there. Towns such as Havana, Caracas, Lima, and Rio de Janeiro are the showpieces of their countries. Their luxurious commercial and residential buildings and superficial air of prosperity hide from the brief visitor the general poverty to be found in the rest of the country and even in the poorest quarters of many of the towns themselves.

Although each country in Latin America has its own particular problems there are several groups whose members have many features and problems in common. There follows a note on each of six sub-regions of Latin America.

Mexico, with 30 m. people, barely feeds itself at present. Successful attempts have recently been made to increase yields in farming areas and new areas are being irrigated. Even so, the position is critical and the rate of increase of population high. There is an alarming movement of population to urban areas, and Mexico City alone now has more than 3 m. inhabitants. Mexico was the first country in Latin America to set up a blast furnace (at Monterrey in 1900) and the first to produce oil on a large scale. Economically it has close ties with its neighbour, the U.S.A., but even so, industrial development has been slow and farming remains by far the most important activity, employing about 60 per cent of the working population.

The six republics of mainland Central America – Costa Rica (population 1 m.), Salvador (2¼ m.), Guatemala (3¼ m.), Honduras (1½ m.), Nicaragua (1¼ m.), and Panama (1 m.) – suffer from the small size of their internal markets, which make the introduction of large modern industrial establishments uneconomical. Little has been done so far to realize a proposed union of a number of these small republics. The transcontinental Panama Canal provides a large source of revenue for the Republic of Panama and the importance of the canal to the U.S.A. gives this country a particular interest in the security of the whole of Central America.

The islands, consisting of three republics, Cuba (population 6½ m.), the Dominican Republic (2½ m.), and Haiti (3½ m.), and a large number of British, French, U.S., and Netherlands possessions, are all relatively small and densely populated. Sugar is almost everywhere the leading export crop. Cuba, which produces sugar and tobacco for the U.S. and European markets, is from an economic point of view virtually part of the U.S.A., though politically it remains independent. Puerto Rico, a U.S. possession, is now a commonwealth. It is much more overcrowded than Cuba but is also an exporter of sugar. Haiti, again, is overcrowded, as are most of the small British and French islands of the West Indies.

On the mainland of South America, the five republics of Venezuela, Colombia, Ecuador, Peru, and Bolivia have two important features in common: firstly, much of the population lives at considerable altitudes above sea-level; secondly, the high ranges of the Andes form great barriers between the coastal lowlands (except in Bolivia), the high inhabited plateaus and valleys, and the interior forested lowlands of the Orinoco and Amazon. Of these countries Colombia possesses the greatest industrial capacity, although Venezuela's oil industry is much more spectacular than any single enterprise in Colombia. The other three are poorer countries. Peru suffers from an excessive concentration of its wealth and industrial capacity in the capital, Lima. Bolivia is in a precarious economic position, resulting from the decline of tin output in recent years, partly a consequence of nationalization.

Argentina, Chile, and Uruguay are among the most prosperous and most highly developed Latin American countries, but Chile suffers from its dependence on one item of export, copper, while the Argentinian economy still appears to be suffering from the war, when the country supported (if somewhat half-heartedly) the Axis cause.

Of all the nations in Latin America, Brazil is the only one that can claim to rank as a major world power. It can almost feed 60 m. people when only 2 per cent of its area is cropland and 10 per cent used for grazing. Even if only 10 per cent is suitable for intensive cultivation, the possibilities for extending farm production are enormous. As it is, farm output has only risen by about 20 per cent since 1940, barely keeping pace with the increase of population. Industrial development has been much more rapid. Most of the manufacturing establishments are in South Brazil, in the triangle São Paulo–Rio de Janeiro–Belo Horizonte, where hydro-electricity is the main source of power. South Brazil is also responsible for almost all of the country's production of coffee, the principal export. The Northeast is much poorer and the interior, with more than 1 m. square miles of tropical forest, has hardly been developed at all. The planned development of the Brazilian economy started in 1956 with the inauguration of an impressive plan to co-ordinate all schemes now under way and to take the country towards its 'economic emancipation'.

In spite of spectacular material development in certain parts of Latin America, however, there are many serious obstacles to progress. Politically, the governments are, with a few exceptions, notoriously unstable. After a century and a half of independence, democracy on European or U.S. lines can hardly be said to have triumphed anywhere, except perhaps in Uruguay. One reason may be that the individual leader rather than the party is the motive force in political life. A single individual can more easily be replaced than a party and, with exceptions, is less likely to use his period in office to benefit the country as a whole than to concentrate on undoing what his predecessor has started and use his power to advance himself, his relatives, and his followers. As long as only a small proportion of the electorate is educated and the wealth and administrative organs are concentrated in the capital city, there seems little possibility that the situation can change.

Political instability does not favour harmonious economic development and it hinders the inflow of foreign capital. Foreign investors will only put their money in enterprises such as large mineral workings which, unless openly opposed or nationalized, can continue operating without suffering from changes of government.

Against this background of political instability, social unrest, and erratic economic development, the rapid increase of population throughout Latin America becomes a problem of great magnitude. In many areas the rate of increase exceeds 2 per cent per annum and in some it even exceeds 3 per cent. If present trends continue, Latin America's population of 170 m. will reach about 500 m. by the end of this century. What is unfortunate, and even alarming, is the fact that much of the increase is taking place in urban areas and not in pioneer areas, not in new areas of cultivation. Whatever else they do, Latin American countries will have to devote far more attention and capital than at present to building roads and railways into new areas and establishing colonies of settlers there. Most important of all, agriculture, the basis of Latin America's prosperity, needs modernizing almost everywhere. How ironical, then, that less than 2 per cent of Peru's 1957 budget was devoted to agriculture (and about 20 per cent to defence).

III. AFRICA EXCEPT NORTHWEST AND NORTHEAST

FOR the purposes of this book the continent of Africa has been divided into three parts. Northwest Africa, with most of its population close to the Mediterranean and separated from the rest of Africa by the Sahara Desert, more than 1000 miles in width, is in many respects closely connected with Europe. Indeed, the Mediterranean to the north is a far less formidable obstacle to the movement of people and goods than the waterless desert to the south. Northeast Africa is likewise partly cut off from the rest of Africa by the Sahara to the southwest, but in the south it merges into Central Africa along the mountain ranges of the eastern part of the continent. In Northeast Africa, Egypt is certainly more closely connected with Southwest Asia than with

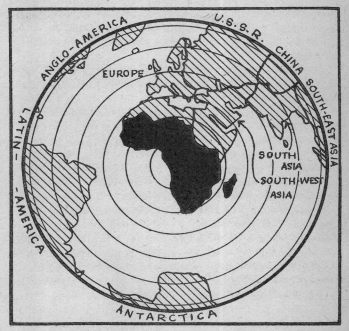

14. The hemisphere of Africa. Projection: oblique zenithal equidistant. Centre of projection: Leopoldville, Belgian Congo. The circles are at thousand-mile intervals.

Africa, and, indeed, the whole of the Nile basin has been influenced by long cultural connexions with Asia. The Red Sea is an insignificant obstacle to movement between Arabia and Northeast Africa. These northern parts of Africa differ greatly from the rest of the continent, Africa south of the Sahara, about which this section is concerned.

Until about one hundred years ago Africa was hardly penetrated by European colonial powers. There were many footholds along the coasts, points where European ships took on supplies and, in many localities, captured or purchased slaves. Only in the southern part of Africa did Europeans (Dutch settlers) colonize the continent in considerable numbers. The systematic exploration of Africa by Europeans only began during the second half of the last century, yet by 1914 almost all of the continent had been annexed.

Africa, excluding the northwestern and northeastern parts, has about one-eighth of the world's land area and about one-twentieth of its population. The region has a number of distinctive features. It has been colonized only relatively recently by European powers, and this is one main reason why so far European influence has been felt much less strongly in Africa than in Latin America, a continent not without certain features and problems resembling those of Africa. What is more, unlike Latin America and Australasia, the population is, with the exception of the Un. of S. Africa, almost entirely indigenous. Even in the Un. of S. Africa more than three-quarters of the inhabitants are Africans or mixed. The primitive subsistence economy of most of the population of Africa has only been modified superficially by European penetration. Railways have been built between interior farming and mining areas and coastal ports to carry raw materials, but large plantations specializing in particular crops are generally much less important in Africa than in parts of Latin America and Southeast Asia. Many export commodities, such as cocoa and palm kernels, are grown in small quantities by a large number of communities and collected at certain centres for shipment overseas. Outside the Un. of S. Africa there has so far been almost no development of manufacturing on modern lines and little urban development. Educational and medical facilities in Africa are poor or non-existent outside a small number of towns.

Although few statistics are available even for the most important aspects of life in many of the colonies of Africa, table 11 has been prepared to enable the reader to compare some features of the more important countries. For most countries, even

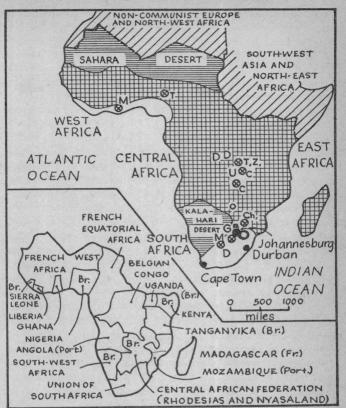

15. Africa except the Northwest and Northeast. For key see p. 115. The inset map shows the main political divisions.

the population figures are only very approximate. The table shows clearly the great difference between the Un. of S. Africa and the rest. This, of course, is largely a result of the relatively high (for Africa) proportion there of people of European origin.

Almost everywhere in Africa except in a few urban centres the non-indigenous population forms only a very small minority.

TABLE 11

	I	II	III	IV	V	VI	VII
				Percentage of			
	Area	*Pop'n*	*Dens.*	*Europeans*	*Energy*	*Newsp.*	*Doctors*
Liberia	43	1	23	*	30	1	30,000
Ghana	80	4	50	*	130	18	18,000
Nigeria	340	30	88	*	40	5	57,000
Fr. W. Africa	1830	18	10	*	30	1	28,000
Fr. Eq. Africa	970	8	8	*	30	1	28,000
Belgian Congo	910	13	14	1	140	?	20,000
Angola	480	4	8	*	40	4	28,000
C. Afr. Fed.	490	7	14	4	550	46[1]	4100[2]
Un. S. Africa	470	14	30	20	2280	57	2000
Madagascar	240	5	21	1	40	2	9000
Mozambique	300	6	20	*	90	2	34,000
Tanganyika	360	8	22	*	40	1	20,000
Uganda	94	6	64	*	40	1	21,000
Kenya	230	6	26	1	160	5	10,000
U.K. (for comparison)	94	51	540	—	4870	570	1100

1. S. Rhodesia only. 2. S. Rhodesia only, N. Rhodesia 11,000
Nyasaland 32,000

I. Area in thousands of sq. mls.
II. Population in millions.
III. Density of population in persons per sq. ml.
IV. Europeans as percentage of total population (* – less than 1 per cent of total).
V. Estimated consumption of commercial sources of energy expressed in terms of coal equivalent, kilograms per inhabitant in 1955.
VI. Number of copies of daily newspapers in circulation per thousand inhabitants.
VII. Number of inhabitants per doctor.

The proportion of Europeans varies from one area to another, but in most colonies is less than 1 per cent of the total population. In the Un. of S. Africa, however, there are some 2¾ m. Europeans (whites) and 400,000 Asians, in addition to the Africans (Bantus) and mixed inhabitants (Coloureds), of which there are about 10 m. In certain other regions of Africa, including the Rhodesias and Kenya, there is a significant percentage of Europeans who have settled permanently and are landowners. Elsewhere, as in Fr. W. Africa, Nigeria, and the Belgian Congo, the Europeans are almost entirely administrators, doctors, teachers, technicians, and other persons serving there generally only for limited periods. In some areas, including Liberia, there are almost no Europeans at all. It is in the areas where Europeans have settled permanently and own land that the more serious racial problems exist or may be expected to occur in the future.

There are few figures to show whether population is increasing as rapidly in Africa as it is in such regions as Latin America and South Asia. It is worth noting, however, that in the Un. of S. Africa the rate of increase is higher among the non-Europeans than among the European settlers. Elsewhere in Africa it is improbable that the effects of modern medical science have yet been felt widely enough to affect appreciably the death rate and infant mortality rate. Little has yet been done to eliminate the diseases that have so far contributed to keep the density of population relatively low in most of Africa, even where there has been no shortage of land suitable for farming. The number of inhabitants per doctor (see table 11) gives a rough indication of the availability of medical services. The number will have to be much lower before the benefits of medical science can be expected to upset the balance between the birthrate and deathrate to the extent that it has in many other parts of the world.

In Africa there is no great concentration of population comparable with that in China or India. There is a zone of relatively high density in West Africa between the Sahara in the north and the Gulf of Guinea in the south. The largest urban centres, on the other hand, are in the Un. of S. Africa, though towns are now growing fast elsewhere.

Africa is essentially a farming continent. Most rural communities are concerned almost entirely with producing food for their own needs. The food crop may be millet or sorghum (mainly in the drier parts), maize (in many of the more humid parts), rice, bananas, or various tubers (manioc, sweet potatoes, and yams). Livestock is generally of poor quality, relatively unimportant as as a source of food, and often merely a symbol of wealth and prestige.

In addition to the many diseases that affect plants, animals, and human beings in Africa and make the development of

147

agriculture difficult, there are many areas where physical conditions are unsuitable for intensive farming. Northwards the climate becomes increasingly arid towards the centre of the Sahara as the rainy season grows progressively shorter. There is also a smaller area where conditions are too dry to support more than a poor cover of vegetation, the Kalahari desert of Southwest Africa. Parts of East Africa, on the other hand, are too rugged to be of much use for farming. Owing to its proximity to the equator, nowhere in Africa is too cold for agriculture, except the highest parts of the mountainous east and south. Within a limited area in west and central Africa, the rainfall is very heavy and a dry season almost non-existent, and as in the Amazon region of Latin America, clearance of the forest vegetation is difficult without suitable equipment. When all these unfavourable conditions have been taken into consideration, a large part of the continent remains suitable for farming. It is the primitive and frequently wasteful methods of cultivation that have kept the density of population low in these parts of Africa. With the elimination of plant and animal diseases, the introduction of new types of plant and livestock, and the wider use of fertilizers, the more favourable parts of Africa could undoubtedly be made to produce far more than they do at present. Production could be increased both by obtaining higher yields in existing areas of farmland and by the utilization of new lands.

For the industrial nations of Europe and Anglo-America, which lie outside the tropics, Africa is an important source of a number of tropical plant commodities. While far less important than Latin America for the production of coffee, Africa accounts for much of the world's cocoa. Ghana is the world's leading producer, while Nigeria rivals Brazil for second place and Fr. W. Africa also produces a large quantity. Palm kernels and groundnuts are important items of export from Nigeria and other parts of West Africa. On the other hand, little of the world's rubber comes from Africa, although there are large areas where climatic conditions are suitable for its cultivation. In the Un. of S. Africa, which lies outside the tropics, agriculture is generally more specialized than in the rest of Africa. The country is able to support a number of large urban centres and to export several farm products, including wool and sub-tropical fruits. Central Africa has extensive areas of forest, the Belgian Congo having the largest reserves. At present little timber is exported.

The large-scale modern mining industry of Africa is organized entirely by non-Africans. The equipment and technicians come from outside the continent and the production is almost all exported for consumption in the leading industrial countries of Europe and Anglo-America. The main mineral-producing zone in Africa extends north–south for a distance of about 1500 miles between Kabinda in the Belgian Congo and Kimberley in the Un. of S. Africa, the central part being in the Rhodesias. There are other mineral-producing areas of some importance in Angola, Nigeria, and Ghana.

Africa is poorly endowed with proved coal and oil deposits (not counting the oil recently discovered in Algeria, which is in Northwest Africa). The Un. of S. Africa has the largest proved reserves of coal and accounts for almost all of the coal produced in the continent (30 m. tons per annum) while S. Rhodesia mines most of the remainder (3 m. tons). There are extensive deposits of high grade iron ore in several parts of Africa, but only in the Un. of S. Africa is this used locally for the production of pig iron. Sierra Leone and Liberia have in recent years become exporters of iron ore. Africa is an important source of certain other metals: manganese from Ghana and the Un. of S. Africa; chrome from S. Rhodesia and the Un. of S. Africa; copper from N. Rhodesia (one-quarter of world's smelter production) and the Belgian Congo; zinc from the Belgian Congo; and tin from Nigeria and the Belgian Congo. An example will serve to show, however, that outside the Un. of S. Africa, mining gives direct employment to only a very small part of the total population: in the Belgian Congo, with 13 m. people, only 100,000 are employed in mining.

For the production of three other minerals, Africa is of particular importance. The Un. of S. Africa accounts for about one-third of the world's gold, while the Belgian Congo has in recent decades produced most of the world's diamonds. It is not without significance to world affairs that since the early 1930s the U.S.S.R. has been rivalling the Un. of S. Africa in gold production, while in 1956 enormous deposits of diamonds were discovered in Siberia (see *Times Review of Industry*, Aug. and Sept. 1957). The third mineral is uranium. Since the war, the Belgian Congo has been one of the world's leading producers of this.

There are several reasons why there has so far been very little industrial development on modern lines in Africa, outside the Un. of S. Africa. The most important reason, perhaps, is that European penetration began relatively late, and even when most of the continent was held by European powers it was regarded as a source of raw materials and a market for European manufactures. The absence of an industrial tradition, the lack of educational facilities, the primitive economic structure of the various colonies, and the colonial policy of the European powers have been more significant in preventing industrial expansion than the lack of good coal and oil deposits. Indeed, it should be remembered that there are many suitable sites for the construction of hydro-electric power stations. The Belgian Congo, with its many rapids on the Congo and its tributaries, is alone calculated to have 20 per cent of the world's hydro-electric potential.

The Un. of S. Africa is by far the most important industrial country in Africa. Industrial expansion has no doubt partly been a consequence of mining development and the concentration of an appreciable part of the population in urban areas. The output of iron and steel per inhabitant is higher in the Un. of S. Africa than in any Latin American country, though not so high as in the leading industrial countries of the world. *Per caput* production of cement and fertilizers (particularly superphosphates) is again high by Latin American and, of course, African standards. Heavy industry is relatively more important than light industry in the Un. of S. Africa, an unusual feature for a young industrial country outside Europe and Anglo-America. Usually such branches of industry as the manufacture of textiles are established before metallurgical and chemicals industries.

In the Rhodesias and the Belgian Congo there has also been some recent industrial expansion, and here again the influence of the older mining activities has been significant. Elsewhere only the beginnings of modern industrial expansion are to be found. Since the war, for example, some large modern cotton mills have been opened in Nigeria.

In general, Africa is very poorly provided with communications. Railways are few and modern motor roads almost non-existent outside the Un. of S. Africa. The number of inhabitants per motor vehicle in circulation is extremely high in most colonies. Again, the *per caput* value of overseas trade is very low, and most colonies export only one or a small number of agricultural or mining products.

From what has so far been said here about Africa the reader will appreciate that living standards are very low. Indeed, in most rural communities conditions hardly differ from those prevailing perhaps for several thousand years. The shortage of statistical data does not hide the fact that medical services are few and educational facilities non-existent in many areas. Almost everywhere, however, some form of European influence has already been felt, and the old economic and social structure has been modified, if only slightly.

Africa's problems are numerous. Two, in particular, are of great importance in the study of world affairs: the development of national consciousness in colonies and former colonies, and the presence of appreciable numbers of Europeans in certain areas.

Not only has europeanization modified many features of Africa's former economic and social life. It has even aroused feelings of national consciousness within colonial territories. The colonies were carved out by the various European nations with little regard to existing cultural features, and many administrative units, including, for example, the Belgian Congo and Nigeria, contain peoples with different dialects and even languages as well as different religions and social institutions. In a way, therefore, African nationalism is superficial and even artificial, and has only come about through the creation of colonies by European powers. Nations formed from these could easily disintegrate once there is no European control of the administration and no guidance on economic matters.

The second question concerns both Europeans and Africans. In some parts of Africa, Europeans have settled in appreciable numbers and, largely as a result of their military superiority, have acquired land. In Southern Rhodesia, for example

(*Observer*, 6 May 1956) more than 30 m. acres (seven times the size of Yorkshire) are in the possession of a few tens of thousands of Europeans. Less than 4 per cent of this land is actually under crops. A situation such as this is hard to justify.

It is unfair for an outsider to judge the racial policy of Europeans who have settled in Africa, but in time it will be the Africans who have the last word. As Mr Tom Mboya put the matter with particular reference to Kenya (*Observer*, 8 July 1957): 'Let us be frank about the alternatives that face Kenyans. In the long run the fate of the colony must be determined by the unalterable fact that there are about six million Africans compared with 50,000 Europeans, 250,000 Asians, and 30,000 Arabs. The only question to be decided, therefore, is whether the Africans will achieve their objectives with the co-operation of the immigrant races and the British Government or despite them.'

Africa is more fortunate than most of South and East Asia in that it is not overpopulated. There is no doubt that the continent could produce much more food than it does, though even approximately how much more, it is impossible to say. Non-African help in the form of experts, farm equipment, and fertilizers is essential if progress is to be made, yet the failure of a large, highly planned enterprise like the groundnut scheme suggests that improvements can more confidently be expected if gradual changes are brought about in existing methods of farming than if attempts are made to reorganize African agriculture completely. A large amount of financial aid must be given to Africa before substantial improvements can be expected. In recent years the U.S.A. has invested large sums in African mining enterprises, while direct financial aid has been granted to Liberia. Little, however, has so far been done either by the U.S.A. or by the European colonial powers to tackle this fundamental question of farming in Africa.

Africa is the only remaining extensive area of European colonialism. Already the Un. of S. Africa and Ghana are self-governing, though still within the British Commonwealth, while the Federation of Rhodesia and Nyasaland has been granted a considerable degree of self-government. Undoubtedly the British policy is to grant self-government to all the British territories eventually. Whether Belgium and France have the same intention is doubtful. Portugal, the other important colonial power in Africa, still lives in the Middle Ages and from its attitude over Goa (its possession in India) we may surmise that any change in the status of its colonies in Africa is not at present envisaged. At all events, the British example cannot fail in time to influence the policy of the other three powers. What is perhaps most unfortunate for the colonial territories of Africa is that their European mother countries (and particularly Portugal) are not themselves in a position to give to or invest large sums of money in tropical Africa, any more than the six Latin American nations with a share of the Amazon-Orinoco lowlands can afford to develop tropical South America. Germany and the U.S.A. are among the industrial countries of the world that could afford to help in the development of tropical Africa, yet they have only limited opportunities and incentives to do so as long as these lands are tied to one or other of the four European colonial powers.

IV. AUSTRALASIA

AUSTRALASIA consists of a large number of islands, the most extensive of which is Australia, which is so large that it has come to be thought of as a continent. New Guinea, and the two islands of New Zealand, are sizeable, but the remaining islands, mostly in groups, but some separated from the nearest neighbours by hundreds of miles of ocean, are small. Australia and New Zealand have mostly been colonized by settlers of British origin and many of the smaller islands are also in the British Commonwealth. This fact gives some unity to the region. The eastern part of New Guinea is also in the British Commonwealth, but west New Guinea is a colony of the Netherlands. The whole of New Guinea and the smaller neighbouring islands are generally considered as part of Australasia, though in their climate, vegetation, indigenous population, and economic life they resemble the neighbouring islands of Southeast Asia more closely than they do Australia or New Zealand.

Australasia has about one-fifteenth of the world's land area, but only about one-two-hundredth of its population. Fig. 16 shows the hemisphere of Australasia. The closest neighbour region is Southeast Asia (hence the importance attached by Australia to its relations with Indonesia, formerly the Netherlands East Indies) and, at no more than a few thousand miles are South Asia, China, Japan, and the U.S.S.R. The regions with which

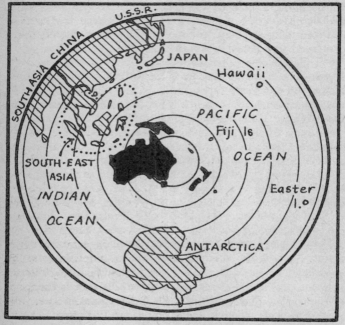

16. The hemisphere of Australasia. Projection: oblique zenithal equidistant. Centre of projection: Brisbane, Australia. The circles are at thousand-mile intervals.

Australasia has the closest cultural and commercial connections – Western Europe and Anglo-America – are in the other hemisphere, although the U.S. sphere of interest in the Pacific extends into the hemisphere of Australasia (Hawaiian Islands, etc.).

Australasia has only relatively recently attracted European settlers – Australia for little more than 150 years, New Zealand for not much more than 100. The European settlers, most of them of British origin, number about 10 m. in Australia and about 2 m. in New Zealand. In these countries the indigenous population has been exterminated (as in Tasmania), has had lands confiscated (as during the Maori Wars in the last century in North Island, New Zealand) or, in places, has been left almost undisturbed (as in Northern Australia). In contrast to Australia and New Zealand, there are very few Europeans in New Guinea and the other islands of the Southwest Pacific.

The density of population in Australia, not much more than 3 persons per square mile, is exceedingly low (cf. U.K. 540, U.S.A. 57) and in reality much of the country is uninhabited, while more than half of the total population is concentrated in the five most populous urban areas.

We tend to think of both Australia and New Zealand as essentially farming countries. Although each is more or less self-supporting in food and each has a large surplus of farm produce for export, only about 15 per cent of the employed population is engaged in agriculture in Australia and about 20 per cent in New Zealand. So great is the degree of mechanization in the various activities connected with farming that although agricultural output has increased enormously during the last decades, the number of persons employed in agriculture has hardly changed. In both countries only a surprisingly small proportion of the total area (not much more than 1 per cent in Australia and about 2 per cent in New Zealand) is cropland (excluding sown pastures), but much of the remainder is used for grazing. In Australia the greatest obstacle to agriculture in most areas is shortage of water. About one-third of the interior is desert, not used at all for farming, while another third is poor quality grazing land. The most humid part of Australia, the southeast, includes, ironically, the most rugged part of the country. New Zealand is nowhere too dry for some kind of farming, but there are extensive rugged, high mountain areas, especially in South Island. In both countries agricultural production has been increased in recent years less by extending farming into new lands than by improving pastures with the introduction of the most suitable fodder plants and fertilizers. The optimistic forecasts made in the interwar years about possibilities of settlement in Australia have been revised, and a recent booklet for prospective immigrants (*Australia in Brief*, 1956) suggests that the 600,000 square miles of 'temperate' country, including most of the best farmland, might eventually support a total of 25 m. people enjoying present living standards.

It was gold that attracted many settlers to Australia and New Zealand in the last century. Mineral production is no longer of great importance in the New Zealand economy, while in Australia gold is no more important now than several other minerals, of which lead and zinc are exported, coal and iron mainly used locally. Australia is fortunate in having good reserves of coal, including coking coal for the smelting of iron ore. Until recently, on the other hand, the search for oil has proved fruitless, but in 1953 oil was struck in Western Australia. In addition to coking coal, Australia has extensive reserves of iron ore. These are located at a considerable distance from its main coalfield. Finally, important deposits of uranium ore have been found in several localities and uranium oxide is mined.

It is somewhat surprising to learn that in Australia there are now approximately twice as many persons employed in various branches of industry as in farming. Most of Australia's industrial development has taken place in the last forty years, having been stimulated by the two world wars, during which the supply of manufactured goods from Europe was reduced. The emphasis has not only been on the production of consumer goods, as in Latin America, but also on the establishment of heavy industry, as in the Un. of S. Africa. In spite of the modest number of inhabitants of its home market (which for many purposes can be said to include New Zealand), Australia now has an engineering industry of considerable capacity. New Zealand is not so highly industrialized as Australia and produces mainly light manufactures. Even so, it now has more persons employed in industry than in farming, though here, as in Australia, much of the industry is not manufacturing but merely the processing of farm products.

Both countries are well served by railways, but road transport and, in Australia, coastal shipping services, have taken much of the former traffic of the railways. Air transport is important for the movement of passengers and mail and, in remoter parts of Australia, even for the transport of livestock.

In both countries there is a high degree of specialization in farm production and various commodities are exported in large quantities – wool, wheat, beef, and fruits from Australia, wool,

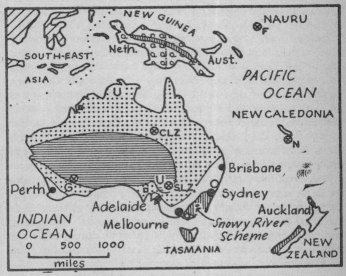

17. Australasia. For key see p. 115.

dairy produce, mutton, and lamb from New Zealand. In addition, minerals and, in recent years, manufactures, have figured among the exports of Australia. Neither country therefore depends on a single item of export to the extent that most Latin American countries do. New Zealand has now come up to second place (figures for the U.S.S.R. are not available) below Australia, among the world's producers of wool.

Australians and New Zealanders enjoy a high standard of living. The best idea of the high level of production is perhaps given by the following comparison between Latin America and

Australia: Latin America has seventeen times as many inhabitants as Australia, but produces less than half as much coal and about the same amount of steel; it has in circulation approximately the same number of motor vehicles. In total farm output Australia rivals Argentina, which has twice as many people. The average farm worker in Australia produces about ten times as much as the average farm worker in the U.S.S.R., a thought to bear in mind when discussing the advantages of communist organization in general and of collectivization in particular.

Australia and New Zealand play a more important part in world affairs than their small total population alone would merit. There are several reasons for this. Australia itself is large territorially, if not in population, and an even larger part of the earth's surface is occupied by Australasia (or Oceania) with its numerous British islands and island groups scattered over the southwest quarter of the Pacific Ocean. Then there is the fact that Australia and New Zealand could both hold at least two or three times as many inhabitants as they do at present – hence their potential importance in the future. In addition, there is the high level of productivity and in particular the great export trade in high-grade wool, which reaches all the important industrial countries in the world. Australia produces 30 per cent of the world's wool and 60 per cent of its merino wool. New Zealand accounts for 10 per cent of the world's total (thereby producing considerably more per inhabitant than its more populous neighbour).

Australia and New Zealand are not without their problems. They are as far away as they could be from the mother country, with which they have such important cultural and commercial links. They are underpopulated, yet are unwilling to receive immigrants that are not 'white'. The interior and northern parts of Australia are empty. It is doubtful, however, if even with the most elaborate and costly works of irrigation the empty northern part could support more than a few million people (most conservative estimates put the figure rather in the region of a few hundred thousand) – at present there are only a few tens of thousands of inhabitants, many engaged not in farming but in mining. In other words, Northern Australia, might, over a long period, absorb the surplus population *of a few months or a few weeks* from India or China – a drop in the ocean.

Another matter of some concern is the tendency for immigrants who arrive in Australia to settle in the larger urban areas rather than in smaller centres or rural areas. Greater Sydney and Greater Melbourne together have more than one-third of Australia's total population. In New Zealand, again, the same trend is evident, and the four largest urban areas now have about 40 per cent of the country's population.

When thinking of Australia as a world power, we should therefore remember how small is its population. We should not forget that both Australia and New Zealand have been developed almost entirely by British settlers and only since the beginning of the Industrial Revolution. They have been important sources of food and raw materials for the industrial population and industries of the mother country. Their economies are complementary to that of the U.K., though they rely much less on British manufactures and send a much smaller proportion of their exports there than they did a century, or even fifty years ago.

New Guinea and the other islands of the Southwest Pacific contrast in almost every way with New Zealand and Australia. They mostly lie within the tropics, and their natural vegetation is mostly dense forest. It is heartening to think that in New Guinea there may even still be communities that have had no direct contact with Europeans. The Japanese invasion of that island in 1942 and the search for oil there during the last few decades have at last begun to open it up. Apart from their obvious strategic significance, some of the other islands of the Southwest Pacific are important sources of minerals (Nauru, phosphate rock; New Caledonia, chrome ore and nickel) and of tropical crops for Australia and New Zealand.

Australia and New Zealand, then, are still capable of receiving many millions of settlers, and although the reader should hesitate to accept the excessively optimistic forecasts of the future made in the interwar years, the possibilities of development in these two underpopulated countries are without doubt great. In agriculture new methods are constantly being introduced to increase pastoral production, while the discovery of oil and uranium means the beginning of new lines of development in the Australian economy. Finally, the multi-purpose Snowy River project, a long-term scheme to utilize rivers in Southeast Australia to generate electricity and irrigate new lands for farming, is an impressive undertaking, of great importance to the country's economy.

Chapter 6

THE REGIONS OF THE INNER ZONE

I. NON-COMMUNIST EUROPE AND NORTHWEST AFRICA

FIFTY years ago it would have been difficult to make a simple division of Europe into two parts on the basis of different political systems. Now, in contrast, it is impossible to ignore the great barrier existing between the communist and non-communist parts of the continent. The barrier already began to appear as the Soviet Communist Party cut Russia off from the rest of Europe in the 1920s. It was pushed westwards during and after the war. The barrier may well disappear as suddenly as it was created.

The presence of communist-controlled governments in about three-fifths of the area of Europe imparts considerable unity to the remaining non-communist countries. As a result of the danger of further communist expansion the various nations of Western Europe, including the former maritime empire builders, rivals for several centuries, have finally appreciated the need for co-operation. So far it has mainly been in the military sphere.

Although Northwest Africa differs greatly from non-communist Europe in many ways, its close economic connexions with Europe and with France in particular, and the presence there of more than 1 m. European settlers in Algeria, and several hundred thousand in Morocco and Tunisia, make it more realistic from the point of view of world affairs that the region should at present be considered with Europe instead of with Africa or even Southwest Asia (see also ch. 5, section III).

Although non-communist Europe is small territorially (about 2 per cent of the world's land area without Northwest Africa) it has more than 10 per cent of the world's population and is characterized by its great diversity of environment. The whole area is broken into a number of islands and peninsulas by seas that penetrate far inland. No part is more than a few hundred miles from the coast. The great variety of land forms to be found in Western Europe is matched by the diversity of languages and customs and by the presence of a large number of nations and an even larger number of small language and dialect groups within nations. Yet racially there is a general resemblance between most Europeans, while culturally the whole area has long been influenced by Christianity. Moreover, the languages

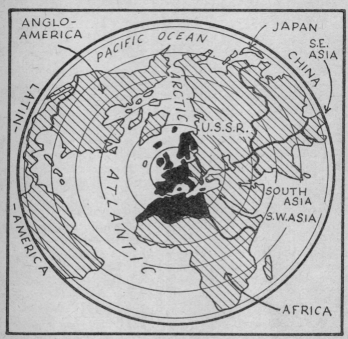

18. The hemisphere of Europe. Projection: oblique zenithal equidistant. Centre of projection: Brussels, Belgium. The circles are at thousand-mile intervals.

for the most part belong to the Romance or Teutonic groups of the Indo-European family and some, such as Spanish and. Portuguese or German and Dutch, do not differ greatly from each other.

Non-communist Europe lies near the centre of the hemisphere that includes the highest proportion of land. Fig. 18 shows how

TABLE 12

	I	II	III	IV	V	VI
			Energy	Steel	Steel	Pass.
	Pop'n	Coal	per cap.	prod'n	cons.	cars
1 Finland	4	*	1850	*	166	18
2 Sweden	7½	*	4150	2	402	71
3 Norway	3½	½	5340	*	249	31
4 Denmark	4½	*	2430	*	183	43
5 U.K.	51	225	4870	20	367	61
6 Eire	3	*	1380	*	53	41
7 W. Germany	52	162[1]	3350	21	410	29
8 Netherlands	11	12	2220	1	235	20
9 Belgium & Luxembourg	9	30	4100	9	292	45
10 France and Saar	44	73	2440[2]	16	235	57
11 Italy	48	1	1050	5½	118	16
12 Switzerland	5	*	2870	*	229	48
13 Austria	7	*	2200	2	182	13
14 Spain	29	12	800	1	50	4
15 Portugal	9	½	360	*	32	9
16 Greece	8	*	330	*	27	2
17 Algeria	10	½	200	*	26	9
18 Morocco	8½	½	240	*	19	11
19 Tunisia	4	*	180	*	17	8

* Negligible output or no production.
1. Including lignite.   2. Excluding Saar.

NOTE. The following are not included: Iceland (150,000 inhabs.), Libya (1 m.), Malta (320,000), Spanish Sahara.

 I. Population in millions, 1954.
 II. Coal production in millions of metric tons.
 III. Estimated consumption of commercial sources of energy expressed in terms of coal equivalent, kilograms per inhabitant in 1955.
 IV. Steel production in millions of metric tons.
 V. Apparent consumption of steel expressed in terms of crude steel, kilograms per inhabitant in 1955.
 VI. Passenger cars in circulation per thousand inhabitants in 1954.

all the main land areas of the world except Antarctica, Australia, and the southern part of Latin America lie within its hemisphere. Non-communist Europe has land frontiers with the U.S.S.R., East Europe, Southwest Asia, and Africa.

Table 12 includes figures (for 1954 or 1955) for all the countries of non-communist Europe and Northwest Africa, except a few of the smallest in population. Col. I shows that the member nations vary greatly in population. They vary appreciably also in size, but all except Algeria and Libya are small when compared with such areas as European U.S.S.R., the U.S.A., or Australia. Most, however, are densely populated, and England and the Netherlands are among the most densely populated countries in the world. The remaining columns of the table cover industrial capacity and living standards.

Parts of Europe have been inhabited by farming communities for several thousand years, and already towards the end of the Middle Ages most of the land suitable for agriculture was in use and limits to further expansion were becoming evident. In much of Scandinavia, in the north and west of the British Isles and in Iceland, conditions are generally too rugged and cold (and in places even too windy) for cultivation. The higher parts of the Alps and other mountain areas are unsuitable for similar reasons. Southwards, increasing aridity limits the amount of good farmland. Parts of Spain suffer from lack of rain, while only small areas in Northwest Africa can be used for cultivation and much of Algeria and Libya is desert. In spite of these unfavourable conditions a large percentage of the total area is used intensively for farming in France, Iberia, Germany, Italy, and England as well as in some of the smaller countries.

European farming is characterized by its high yields per unit of area. In general, however, yields per farm worker are much lower than in the U.S.A. and other areas outside Europe recently settled by Europeans, where the rural population density is lower and there is a higher degree of mechanization. Complicated systems of land tenure, small fields, and, particularly in the Mediterranean countries, steep, often terraced slopes, make the introduction of certain modern techniques difficult or impossible. Another feature of farming in non-communist Europe is the small opportunity for extending cultivation, while further appreciable improvements in yields can hardly be expected in such countries as Denmark, the Netherlands, and England, where great progress has already been made in achieving high output per unit of area.

Non-communist Europe is unable to feed itself. Some countries, including Switzerland and the U.K., import about half of

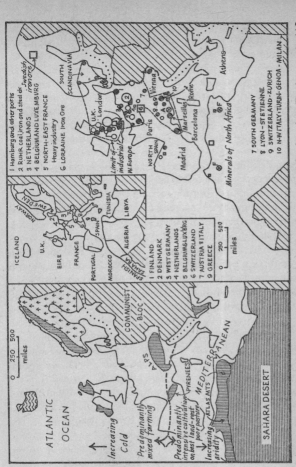

19 *left* Non-communist Europe and Northwest Africa. Areas used for farming. For key see p. 115.
Right Non-communist Europe and Northwest Africa. Minerals and industries. For key see p. 115.
The principal concentrations of mining and manufacturing outside the U.K. are named. The
inset map shows the main political divisions.

the bulk of their food. Most import an appreciable though smaller part of the food they require, in addition to most of the agricultural raw materials they consume in industry. The emphasis in European farming is on food production, and few industrial raw materials of plant and animal origin are produced. These, as well as tropical and sub-tropical crops such as cocoa and coffee, which cannot be cultivated owing to the climate, have to be imported. In addition, cereals, meat, and dairy produce are needed in varying quantities by the U.K. and other industrial countries.

Forestry and fishing are important activities in parts of non-communist Europe. Much of Scandinavia is forested and the higher parts and areas of poorer soil are often forest-covered in the rest of Europe. With increasing aridity southwards the conditions become unsuitable for forest growth and the Mediterranean woodland is generally of poor quality and little commercial use. Fish is a significant source of protein food in several European countries. The main fishing grounds are in the northern seas and the countries such as the U.K. and Norway with long coasts facing these are among the world's leading fishing nations.

Apart from its large deposits of coal and iron ore, non-communist Europe is on the whole poorly provided with mineral resources. Even the coal and iron ore deposits are limited to certain areas. The U.K., W. Germany, France, and Belgium together account for almost all of the coal output (U.K. about 40 per cent, Germany with the Saar about 30 per cent). The leading coal producers, however, are poorly supplied with high-grade iron ore (over about 50 per cent iron content) but Sweden, Spain and Algeria have large deposits. France, the U.K., Germany, and Benelux all make use of their own low-grade iron ore.

Relatively little oil and natural gas is produced in non-communist Europe – altogether about 10 m. tons of oil, not much more than 1 per cent of the world's total. About ten times as much is imported. It is hoped that in a matter of years Algeria and Libya will become important producers of oil.

Many other minerals are produced in non-communist Europe and Northwest Africa, but mostly in relatively small quantities. Algeria, Morocco, and Tunisia together account for one-quarter

166

of the world's phosphate rock and also supply Europe with iron ore and manganese ore. France and Germany produce potash, and France, Italy, and Greece bauxite. Most of the region's needs of oil, nuclear fuels, copper, lead, zinc, and tin, and several ferro-alloys have to be imported from other parts of the world.

In spite of the lack of many raw materials, manufacturing employs a considerable part of the labour force in most European countries – as much as half in the U.K. and Belgium, and not much less in W. Germany, Sweden, and Switzerland. In the Mediterranean countries, however, agriculture employs several times as many people as industry. The large proportion of urban dwellers in most European countries is partly a consequence of industrialization.

Coal, used for producing steam power, and coke for smelting iron ore, formed the basis of industrial expansion in the earlier period of the Industrial Revolution. The U.K., Belgium, France, and Germany, with good coalfields, were the earliest to apply the techniques of the Industrial Revolution on a large scale. Towards the end of the last century it became possible to utilize hydro-electric power, and certain parts of Europe, which produced little or no coal, were able to develop manufacturing with electricity. They include Sweden and Norway, Switzerland, North Italy, and Catalonia (Spain). Until very recently oil has been of little importance as a source of power in European industry, most of it being used for transportation. Nuclear fuels are not produced in large quantities in Europe and the utilization of this source of energy, like oil, will have to be based on imported materials.

From the earliest years of the Industrial Revolution, Europe has had to import cotton. Since then the list of imported materials has constantly been growing. Other fibres such as wool and jute, timber, and most of the metals needed are among the items imported for industry.

Europe has a long tradition of industry, and several hundred years ago a number of areas were already specializing in manufacturing. Among them were parts of Spain, Northern Italy, Germany, and Flanders. There was also an important trade between different parts of Europe. The Hanseatic towns in the north and Genoa and Venice in the Mediterranean handled much of the maritime traffic. In many respects England was less developed industrially and commercially than some parts of the Continent. It was in Britain in the 18th century, however, that many techniques were applied for the first time in industry and agriculture and large modern factories run by steam-driven machinery were first built. Iron ore was smelted with coke instead of charcoal, complicated machinery was used in textile and later in other establishments, and railways and steamships revolutionized transportation. These new techniques subsequently spread to other parts of Europe where coal was available, and to other parts of the world, such as the U.S.A.

In non-communist Europe almost every branch of modern manufacturing is now somewhere represented. Metallurgical and heavy engineering industries tend to be concentrated on or near the main coalfields or in port areas. Textile industries and particularly light engineering are generally more widely distributed.

In total industrial capacity non-communist Europe exceeds the U.S.S.R., and in many branches of production rivals or exceeds the U.S.A. Some of the countries, particularly those having to import much of their food, fuels, or raw materials, export an appreciable proportion of their industrial output. Certainly the basis of fuels and raw materials for further expansion is not so favourable in non-communist Europe as it is in the U.S.A. and the U.S.S.R., and European industry is bound to be more affected by fluctuations in world trade than either U.S. or Soviet industry. Indeed, the search for raw materials and markets was one of the stimuli to colonial expansion by European powers in the 19th century and even the present century (Italy in Abyssinia in 1935–6). The U.K. and France still benefit to some extent from their colonies, while the postwar prosperity of Belgium is closely connected with its possession of the Congo. Portugal also has extensive colonial territories, but, being predominantly agricultural itself, has little trade with them and little money to invest in them.

The trade between non-communist Europe and the rest of the world consists mainly of the exportation of manufactured goods and the importation of oil, raw materials, and foodstuffs. A disturbing trend is the growing dependence of non-communist Europe on U.S. and Polish coal. Also of growing importance is the importation of factory equipment from the U.S.A. Just as the U.K. supplied many parts of the world with textile machinery in the last century (and still does, of course), so now the U.S.A. supplies many of the machines for the engineering industry of Europe. In particular, many war-damaged industrial establishments have been re-equipped with U.S. machinery. Within non-communist Europe itself there is also a considerable movement of goods – coal from the coalfield areas, timber from Scandinavia, and minerals from Northwest Africa, finding their way to many countries.

Living standards vary greatly from one part of Europe to another. In general, standards vary according to the degree of intensity of industrialization. One important reason why Portugal and Greece, for example, are relatively poor, is that they possess few important industries and much of the population is engaged in farming. In contrast, Switzerland and Sweden, which are highly industrialized (and have kept out of two world wars), are among the most prosperous. The last two columns in table 12, showing the *per caput* consumption of steel and the number of passenger cars per 1000 inhabitants, help to pick out the haves and have-nots in non-communist Europe.

Non-communist Europe has many problems. One of the most serious is the question of food supply. Fortunately, the population is increasing only slowly in the industrial countries. In Iberia, South Italy, Greece, and Northwest Africa, on the other hand, the rate of increase is still high, yet these areas have few manufactured goods and raw materials to export in exchange for foodstuffs. Another set of problems results from the presence of such a large number of nations in such a small area. Each nation aims at some degree of self-sufficiency, protecting its economy by tariff barriers and subsidies, which hinder the exchange of commodities and reduce the possibilities of regional specialization. One of the main arguments for economic union is that, as in the U.S.A., each region would be in a better position to specialize in what it most economically produces. There is already a core in the European Coal and Steel Community, which includes France, West Germany, Italy, and the Benelux countries. Yet another set of problems in non-communist Europe is connected with the spread of communism and the dominant military position of the U.S.S.R. in Europe. Indeed, it might be said that the non-communist countries of Europe have been forced to accept U.S. economic domination to save them from Soviet political domination.

The reader will find a further section on European union, with special reference to the U.K., in ch. 10. This section is concluded with a brief note on the different parts of non-communist Europe.

Northern Europe (20 m. inhabitants) is one of the most prosperous parts of the continent. In Finland, Sweden, and Norway the principal source of power for industry is hydro-electricity, and timber is an important raw material. Sweden has large deposits of high-grade iron ore, while the fishing industry is an important part of Norway's economic life. Only in Denmark is agriculture the predominant activity. In all these countries, population is increasing only slowly, and although most of the total area is unsuitable for farming there is no serious pressure on resources.

The British Isles (54 m.) differs considerably from the rest of Europe in many respects. Its insular location has enabled it to be less involved in European affairs than most of the other countries of the Continent. For almost four centuries it has traded with and sent settlers to other parts of the world, and it has important economic connexions with the Commonwealth it has created. The British Isles is poorly provided with most resources. It barely produces enough food to feed half its population, though it has been suggested that if no livestock were kept and only plant foods for human consumption were produced, most of the population might be kept alive on an unpalatable diet. Apart from its reserves of coal and low-grade iron ore the U.K. lacks the minerals as well as the plant and animal raw materials for its industries.

West Germany (52 m.), with approximately the same number of inhabitants as the U.K., is not much better off with regard to the supply of fuel and raw materials, its large coal-mining industry being the basis of its economic prosperity. A much larger area is suitable for intensive farming in W. Germany than in the U.K., however, and consequently the dependence on imported foodstuffs is not nearly so great. Much of the industrial capacity is concentrated on and in the vicinity of the Ruhr coalfield. Switzerland and Austria are not unlike South Germany in some respects and in all three areas the availability of hydro-electric power has formed the basis of industrial development in the present century.

The Benelux countries (20 m.) resemble the U.K. in some ways. They are densely populated, and although the land is farmed intensively, imported food is required. Belgium and Luxembourg, with their important coal and iron ore deposits, are together the seventh largest producer of steel in the world. The Belgian Congo, with its many minerals and other raw materials, is an important source of wealth for the mother country and leaves Belgium in a better economic position than the Netherlands, which since the Second World War has lost its most important colonial territory, the East Indies (now Indonesia). Moreover, the rate of increase of population in the Netherlands is higher than in Belgium, and new areas can be made available for agriculture only by the slow and costly reclamation of land from the sea.

France (44 m.) has a larger area of farmland per inhabitant than the U.K. or W. Germany, but its coal deposits are not so extensive and are for the most part more difficult to work. Being able to provide almost all its own food requirements at home, France depends less on the exportation of industrial products than does the U.K., and it is not so highly industrialized. In spite of a sudden increase in population in the postwar period, the number of inhabitants in France has changed little during the present century and there has been relatively little emigration from France for a long time.

Italy (48 m.) which is only slightly more than half the size of France, also produces at home almost all the food it needs. It has few industrial raw materials, and, what is more significant still, has no coal deposits of importance. Some industrialization has taken place in North Italy on imported coal, hydro-electricity, and (in recent years) natural gas. This is also the most fertile part of the country. The remainder, peninsular Italy and the islands, is predominantly agricultural, and as population is still increasing fairly rapidly and opportunities to emigrate have been few during the last four decades, serious unemployment has now resulted from overpopulation.

Iberia (Spain 29 m., Portugal 9 m.) is about the same size as France, but generally conditions are less favourable for agriculture, many areas suffering from low rainfall. There has been little industrialization except in Catalonia (Barcelona area) in the east, where hydro-electricity is available from the Pyrenees, and in certain areas along the north coast where there are deposits of coal and iron ore.

In Greece (8 m.), where the population is increasing rapidly, farming is the principal activity, yet only a small proportion of the total area is good agricultural land.

Northwest Africa (23 m.), which for many centuries has been connected culturally and politically with Southwest Asia, was part of the Ottoman Empire until the last century. Its annexation by France began not much more than 100 years ago. As well as having about $1\frac{1}{2}$ m. European settlers (mostly French and mostly in Algeria) it is an important source of minerals and wine for France. Only limited areas near the coast and small oases in the interior are suitable for intensive farming. The remainder is poor grazing land merging southwards into useless desert country. Culturally the countries of Northwest Africa belong more to the Arab world and to Southwest Asia than to non-communist Europe. Economically, and, in the case of Algeria, also politically, they are, if only temporarily, part of Europe.

II. SOUTHWEST ASIA AND NORTHEAST AFRICA

No part of the world has for so long been the home of civilization and the scene of conflicts as the region between and including the Nile in Northeast Africa and the Indus in South Asia. Archaeological evidence suggests that here were the earliest cultivators, the first irrigation works, the first cities, and the oldest empires. Here also the Christian and Muslim religions had their origins.

Today, Southwest Asia might be called the centre of world affairs, even though the individual countries belonging to it are among the poorest and weakest in the world. It lies between Europe and the rest of Asia, between the U.S.S.R. and Africa. It has land frontiers with the U.S.S.R. in the north, with South Asia and even China in the east, with East Europe and non-communist Europe in the west, and with Africa in the south.

The region of Southwest Asia and Northeast Africa is given considerable unity by a number of features. Firstly, from the centre of the region, Arabia, the Muslim religion spread almost everywhere over it and, indeed, was carried far beyond its limits, into parts of Africa and Europe to the west and into Asia to the east. Today most of the inhabitants of the region are still Muslim. Secondly, several hundred years ago almost all of the region came under the control of the Ottoman Empire, centred on Turkey. During the period of Turkish control, little material progress was made, and, indeed, irrigation works were even neglected. Since the disintegration of the Ottoman Empire, Turkey has remained somewhat aloof and apart from the rest of Southwest Asia. Thirdly, the language of much of the region is Arabic, though the Turkish (Turco-Tatar family) and Persian (Indo-European family) languages belong to completely different families, which is why Turkey and Iran (Persia) are outside the Arab group of countries. Finally, the whole region is poor, good farmland is restricted by dry conditions to very limited areas, and irrigation is vital to the agriculture of several of the countries.

In only two respects does the region resemble non-communist Europe. It is broken into a number of peninsulas by seas that penetrate far inland, and it is divided into a large number of political units. Here the comparison with Europe ends.

As Turkish control of the region weakened in the 19th century and collapsed as a result of the First World War, other powers were able to extend their influence in the region. Britain, with its interest in a reasonably direct route to India, was one of the first, and France, with its expanding empire in Northwest Africa, was also interested. Before this, Russia had started to penetrate into the region and it annexed the Caucasus and Transcaucasia early in the 19th century. Germany was particularly interested in

1 AFGHANISTAN   2 IRAQ
3 SYRIA   4 CYPRUS
5 LEBANON   6 ISRAEL
7 JORDAN   8 YEMEN
9 ERITREA   10,11 FR. AND BR.
SOMALILANDS   12 ADEN PROTECTORATE (BR)
NOTE Several small political units
          are not shown

20. Southwest Asia and Northeast Africa. For key see p. 115. The
inset map shows the main political divisions.

174

establishing a sphere of influence between Central Europe and the Persian Gulf, but defeat in the First World War put an end to this project. Italy also established colonies in Libya before 1914 and attempted to build up a sphere of influence in Northeast Africa, the annexation of Abyssinia being a further step in this direction. By the beginning of the Second World War, therefore, much of the region had been annexed or influenced in some other way by European powers, and even the distant U.S.A. had economic interests there. Since the war the tide has turned against the Europeans and, in particular, Britain, France, and Italy have lost influence in the region. A number of independent states have begun to exploit the growing national consciousness of their inhabitants and to enter the already complicated game of power politics now being played in the region. Two important recent examples were the formation early in 1958 of the United Arab Republic (Egypt, Syria, and the Yemen) and the Arab Federation (Iraq and Jordan). Finally, the appearance of Israel on the scene shortly after the Second World War has further added to the confusion. Its inhabitants may claim that they are not Europeans, but certainly many have been educated in Europe or Anglo-America and in technical and organizational matters are far superior to their Arab neighbours.

When considering Southwest Asia and Northeast Africa the reader should always bear in mind the great differences in size and population between the various countries (see table 13). Israel and the Lebanon, for example, are each roughly comparable in size with Yorkshire, while together they have fewer inhabitants than this county. Turkey, on the other hand, is six times as large as England, and Iran and Saudi Arabia are each twelve times as large. Some of the small territories of the Persian Gulf have only a few tens of thousands of inhabitants, while Egypt, Turkey, and Iran each have more than 20 m. The whole region has about 130 m. inhabitants, 80 m. in Southwest Asia and 50 m. in Northeast Africa. For most of the countries, population figures are only estimates.

Population is distributed very unevenly over the region. In Egypt, for example, almost all of the inhabitants are concentrated in the lands irrigated by the Nile – about one-thirtieth of the

TABLE 13

	Area	II Pop'n	III Dens.	IV Oil	V Per cent of World	VI Steel	VII Energy	VIII Newsp.	IX Doctors
Turkey	300	23	77	*		16	340	32	3100
Syria	70	4	57	*		21	} 240	44	5000
Lebanon	4	1½	375	*		79		77	1300
Israel	8	1½	210	*		185	900	202	380
Jordan	38	1½	39	*		?	?	9	7400
Afghanistan	250	12	48			?	?	1	75,000
Iran	630	21	33	26½	3	5	?	6	8500
Iraq	172	5	29	31	3½	18	270	21	6400
Saudi Arabia	620	7	11	49	5½	6	?	2	?
Kuwait	8	¼	31	55	6½	?	?	?	?
Yemen	76	4½	59	*		?	?	?	?
Egypt	390	23	59	2		11	240	25	3600
Sudan	970	9	9	*		?	40	2	86,000
Ethiopia and Eritrea	420	16	38	*		?	10	1	100,000
U.K. (for comparison)	94	51	543	*		367	4870	570	1100

NOTE. The following are not included: Cyprus (½ m. inhabitants), Oman (¾ m.), Aden (¼ m.), Somalilands (2 m.), and smaller political units such as Bahrain. Oil output in millions of tons: Qatar 6, Neutral Zone Kuwait–Saudi Arabia 1½, Bahrain 1½.

I. Area in thousands of sq. mls.   III. Density of population in persons per sq. ml.

II. Population in millions.   IV. Production of crude oil (millions of metric tons).

V. Percentage of world total oil output.

VI. Apparent consumption of steel expressed in terms of crude steel, kilograms per inhabitant in 1955.

VII. Estimated consumption of commercial sources of energy expressed in terms of coal equivalent, kilograms per inhabitant in 1955.

VIII. Number of copies of daily newspapers in circulation per thousand inhabitants.

IX. Number of inhabitants per doctor.

total national territory. Indeed, most of the population of Southwest Asia and Northeast Africa is to be found either in irrigated lands or in the few areas of reasonably heavy rainfall. The more humid areas include the Mediterranean coastlands and some of the mountain areas, of which Ethiopia is the most densely populated. Although the average density is comparatively low, the density in the intensively cultivated parts is in reality very high.

There has been little urban development in the region so far. Turkey, with about 20 per cent of its population in towns, is probably the most highly urbanized of the larger countries, though, among the smaller ones, Israel has most of its population in non-agricultural settlements. Mining and industrial developments have recently been causing migration from rural areas to towns, and centres such as Baghdad in Iraq and Cairo in Egypt are growing rapidly.

Few figures are available to allow the rate of increase of population to be assessed with accuracy, but what data there are suggest that the increase is rapid. In Syria, the Lebanon, Jordan, and Egypt, for example, the population is increasing each year by 2–3 per cent.

In spite of the great expansion of the oil industry in certain countries in recent decades, agriculture is still by far the most important activity in all but a few districts. Only in Israel and some of the smaller oil-producing territories of the Persian Gulf do other activities overshadow farming. Agriculture is very much restricted by low rainfall over most of the region. In parts of Turkey, Iran, and Afghanistan it is also restricted by extensive rugged mountain areas. Only Ethiopia can be said to have an abundant rainfall for agriculture over an appreciable part of the national territory.

Most of the countries are more or less self-supporting with regard to food production and there is relatively little specialization in farming. There is a great contrast between the relatively small, intensively cultivated areas, producing crops such as rice, fruits, vegetables, and dates, and the extensive areas of generally scanty natural pasture supporting sheep, goats, or camels. Much of the region is of no use at all for farming. Only in a few areas

177

are specialized crops grown for export in appreciable quantities – cotton in Egypt and fruits in the Mediterranean coastlands.

Undoubtedly there are possibilities of increasing agricultural production in some areas. Higher yields could be obtained by the use of fertilizers and fuller use is now being made of some parts of Turkey with the introduction of mechanization. Except in Ethiopia and the Sudan, however, there are few areas into which cultivation could be extended greatly, and the only real hope of increasing the cultivated area is to provide large works of irrigation in the valleys of rivers such as the Nile, Tigris, and Euphrates, which still carry much of their water into the sea.

Forestry and fishing are of little or no importance in most of the region. There are few extensive stands of good timber, while the many seas in the region are of little use for fishing.

In view of the great fame of the oil industry of Southwest Asia the reader should be reminded that, apart from its oil reserves, the region appears to be very poorly provided with mineral deposits (though it has not yet been fully explored). What is more, the principal proved oil reserves are themselves restricted to a very small part of Southwest Asia. With regard to other minerals, Turkey is the only country with an appreciable production of coal, and it also accounts for about one-quarter of the world's chrome ore, while Egypt mines some phosphates. The oil industry is the only mining activity employing a large number of persons. Very little of the oil produced is actually consumed in Southwest Asia itself.

Of the world's proved oil reserves in 1956, Southwest Asia had almost two-thirds: world 26,000 m. tons; Southwest Asia nearly 17,000 m.; U.S.A. 4500 m.; Venezuela 1685 m.; U.S.S.R. 1330 m. New reserves are of course constantly being discovered and new techniques are making it a commercial proposition to utilize oil in shales. Even so, the present importance of Southwest Asia as a source of oil can easily be appreciated.

From col. IV in table 13, it will be seen that no more than four countries account for almost all of the oil production of the region and, together, Kuwait, Saudi Arabia, Iraq, Iran, and Qatar produced about 97 per cent (and more than 18 per cent of the world total). Egypt was the only important producer outside the Persian Gulf area. So far no large reserves of oil have been found away from the main producing fields around the Persian Gulf itself.

The oil production is almost entirely in the hands of a few European and U.S. oil companies, most of the oil is exported to Europe and other parts of the world, and the main benefit the producing countries derive from the industry is their 50 per cent share of the profits of production. Admittedly, these countries, like Venezuela in Latin America, themselves lack the capital and the technicians to develop oil production. Even so, the financial position is not altogether a happy one, and dissatisfaction with it was expressed in the nationalization of Anglo-Iranian Oil Co. property in Iran in 1951. Oil production dropped almost to nothing in the following years and the Iranian oil industry has only been put on its feet again by the assistance of a consortium of foreign companies. A recent agreement between Italy and Iran, whereby Italy is to receive only 25 per cent of the profits of oil production, may eventually lead to a revision of the financial situation in the region. Japan, too, has ignored the traditional 50–50 basis of profit sharing by recently agreeing to pay 57 per cent in royalties on production in its concessions.

It is often pointed out that the companies build towns and roads, which will remain even when oil production has ceased. Obviously these are built largely to serve the oilfields, and whether or not they will have any other future use can hardly be expected to concern the oil companies. As in all branches of mining, there invariably remains the question of finding employment for the workers if and when reserves are exhausted. At present this does not preoccupy the oil countries, for the industry is still expanding. A further question which is also of little concern to the oil companies, is the use made of the oil royalties. These may find their way into the pockets of a limited number of individuals or they may be spent on grandiose public buildings. They could more usefully be spent on works of construction to create alternative employment and a source of income for the government once the oil royalties begin to diminish.

The countries of Southwest Asia and Northeast Africa have almost no coal, and even very little timber for fuel. Educational standards are low and there is almost no tradition of manufacturing. Not surprisingly, then, there has so far been almost no development of industry on modern lines. Any future development of industry might be expected to be based on oil, for the region is one of the least suitable parts of the world for the construction of hydro-electric power stations, unless costly storage reservoirs are provided. As in the oil industry, foreign equipment and technicians are needed if industries are to be established. At present Turkey is the only country producing steel, while Turkey and Egypt produce small quantities of cement and fertilizers, and some light manufactures. Israel also has some modern industries. Elsewhere there has been little modern industrial development so far.

The region as a whole is very poorly provided with communications, but the economy does not require the exchange of goods between one region or one country and another. Only oil is moved in large quantities – either by pipeline or tanker.

Living standards are low throughout the region except in Israel. Here large amounts of foreign aid have enabled the inhabitants, with their superior technical experience, to provide living conditions closer to those of Western Europe than to those prevailing in Southwest Asia. Cols vi to ix in table 13 help to give an idea of differences in material and cultural levels between the various countries. Undoubtedly Ethiopia and Afghanistan are among the poorest. Almost no figures are available for Arabia. The oil countries must all have benefited from oil royalties, but it is impossible to assess precisely to what extent conditions have so far been improved. Turkey, Syria, the Lebanon, and Egypt, the countries closest to and longest influenced by Europe, are the most advanced economically, but hardly compare even with the poorest in Europe.

The problems of the region are many. In the end, aridity appears to be the greatest. If any significant improvements are to be made in agriculture, then here, more perhaps than anywhere else in the world, large sums of money will have to be invested in costly irrigation works. It has not yet been decided who will provide the necessary capital nor when it will be forthcoming, but whoever wishes to bring better living conditions to the region should not forget that agriculture is the principal activity almost everywhere.

With regard to oil production, Persian Gulf oil is at present essential to the economy of non-communist Europe, or at least to certain branches of its economy. Other sources of oil – in Algeria, Canada, or Latin America, for example – could be exploited rapidly within a matter of a decade, and Europe might by then begin to reduce its dependence on oil from Southwest Asia. European politicians, with their habitual inability to understand the impact of what they say on non-Europeans, openly boast that their aim is to become independent of oil from this precarious part of the world. They rarely express their indebtedness to Southwest Asia for the cheap oil received and they seem not to care if they suddenly cut off the one substantial source of revenue to these poorer countries by finding oil elsewhere.

In the field of world power politics Southwest Asia is a vacuum area, for although there are several great powers close to it there is no major power within it. Turkey, connected with NATO, is undoubtedly the strongest military power in the region. The Baghdad Pact countries, Turkey, Iraq, Iran (and Pakistan in South Asia), without the military backing of the U.S.A., have few resources to defend themselves, and the U.K., with so many financial and military commitments in other parts of the world, has in reality little to offer them.

The two outside powers now able to exert most pressure on the region are the U.S.S.R. and the U.S.A. Although the U.S.S.R. is so much closer to Southwest Asia than its rival, the U.S.A. benefits from its remoteness in one respect. Most countries would prefer to ally themselves to or receive aid from a distant power than one across their frontier or only a few hundred miles away. Turkey and Iran, the closest to the U.S.S.R., have certainly shown that this is true, and even Afghanistan has connexions with the U.S.A., though much of its foreign trade has for the last hundred years been with Russia.

III. SOUTH ASIA

SOUTH ASIA is not infrequently referred to in geography textbooks as the Indian sub-continent, and there is certainly some justification for this, because the region has more inhabitants than the whole of North and South America together, let alone Australia, which is regarded as a continent. Some unity is given to the region by the fact that almost all of it became part of the British Empire in the 18th or 19th century and during the period of British control enjoyed the benefits of the Pax Britannica. But British rule was imposed on a region with a great variety of languages, religions, and traditions, and it is perhaps surprising, therefore, that apart from Nepal and Bhutan, there emerged in South Asia in 1947–8 only four states, India, Pakistan, Ceylon, and Burma. All but Burma remain in the British Commonwealth, while Pakistan has challenged the decision to make Kashmir part of India. The whole region is characterized by its predominantly agricultural economy, dense population, and generally very low living standards.

South Asia occupies only about one-twentieth of the world's land area but it has more than one-sixth of the world's population. It has land frontiers with Southwest Asia, China, and Southeast Asia, but is almost completely cut off from these neighbouring regions by high mountain ranges, plateaux, and deserts, and to this day has no rail connexions with them and only long and difficult roads which, for the most part, can only be used by pack animals. Indeed, the region is more easily reached by sea than by land, and between about 1500 and the middle of the 18th century Portugal, Holland, England, and France all at various times established trading stations and forts in coastal areas.

Table 14 provides a few figures concerning the four independent states that emerged from the British Empire in South Asia (for Nepal and Bhutan almost no figures are available) as well as for Southeast and East Asia, which are dealt with in the next two sections of this chapter. In South Asia, India is the largest country both in area and in population, while Burma has the lowest density of population. Within each country the density varies greatly from one part to another. The Thar Desert and the

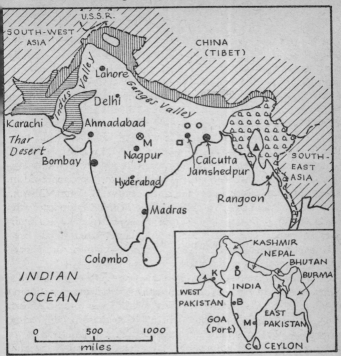

21. South Asia. For key see p. 115. The inset map shows the main political divisions.

high mountain areas are almost uninhabited, while the Ganges valley has a very high density of rural population over a large area. Although there are several large urban areas in India (Calcutta and Bombay each have more than 3 m. inhabitants, and Madras, Delhi, and Hyderabad 1–2 m.), only 17 per cent of the total population is classified as urban. The remaining 83 per cent is distributed over the surface of India in more than 550,000 villages (about 40 times as many as there are in Britain). The other countries of South Asia also have only a small proportion of urban dwellers.

TABLE 14

	I Area	II Pop'n	III Dens.	IV Energy	V Steel	VI Newsp.	VII Doctors
India	1265	382	302	120	7	7	7100
Pakistan	365	82	219	50	4	9	13,000
Ceylon	25	9	320	100	6	36	5300
Burma	262	19	72	30	?	8	8400
Indonesia	575	82	143	100	3	7	71,000
Philippines	115	22	191	150	13	19	8500
Viet Nam	127	26	204	40	3	?	61,000
Thailand	198	20	101	40	9	4	6800
Malaya	50	6	120	390	36	15	8000
Formosa	14	9	640	460	15	33	2400
Korea	85	28	300	150	?	?	4200*
Japan	143	89	602	990	82	397	1000
U.K. (for comparison)	94	51	543	4870	367	570	1100

* South Korea only.

I. Area in thousands of sq. mls.

II. Population in millions in 1955.

III. Density of population in persons per sq. ml.

IV. Estimated consumption of commercial sources of energy expressed in terms of coal, kilograms per inhabitant in 1955.

V. Apparent consumption of steel, expressed in terms of crude steel, kilograms per inhabitant in 1955.

VI. Number of copies of daily newspapers in circulation per thousand inhabitants.

VII. Number of inhabitants per doctor.

Agriculture is by far the most important economic activity in South Asia. Most rural communities are more or less self-sufficient with regard to food supply, although there is specialization in some areas in such crops as cotton, tea, rubber, and jute, and a small surplus of food is available from many districts to support the 60 m. or so urban dwellers.

Much of South Asia is too rugged for agriculture. Little use is made of the Himalayas or of the high ranges between India and Burma. Towards the west and northwest increasing aridity makes intensive cultivation impossible without irrigation. Most of West Pakistan and Northwest India comes within this arid or semi-arid zone, and the Indus and its tributaries, in particular, are vital as a source of water to an extensive farming region. Elsewhere in India, both in the Ganges Valley and the peninsula, the rainfall is frequently supplemented by water from rivers or wells, though in localities exposed to the full force of the monsoon rains, precipitation is abundant and even excessive. Only in the highest parts of the Himalayas are conditions too cold for agriculture. About half of South Asia lies within the tropics and the high ranges to the north help to prevent the cold conditions of the interior of Asia from being felt even in the more northerly lowland areas.

Much of the farmland of South Asia has been cultivated for centuries and even millennia, though, of course, by simple means. It is therefore to be expected that much of the best land is now settled and little remains to be brought under cultivation. In the arid parts of the region, as also in neighbouring Southwest Asia, there are still opportunities for irrigating new lands, while in the more humid areas, particularly in Burma, forested areas could still be cleared for farming. The possibilities of increasing farm production by obtaining higher yields in existing areas of cultivation are undoubtedly very promising, but there are various reasons why it is difficult to make more efficient use of the land. There is the problem of obtaining mineral fertilizers. The *per caput* production and consumption of these is at present insignificant in most parts of the region. The religious attitude to livestock in many areas makes it difficult to develop an efficient kind of mixed farming making the maximum use of available land and animals. Then there are questions of organization and land tenure. Finally, it is difficult for different regions to specialize in the crops (or livestock) they are best suited to produce (as happens in the U.S.A.) because the transport system would be unable to provide adequate facilities for the necessary inter-regional movement of goods.

The government of India obviously considers that a gradual all-round improvement of agricultural methods and yields is preferable to spectacular progress in a limited number of regions, and the inauguration of the India Community Projects Programme in 1952 was a significant development for the country.

The aim of the programme is to achieve 'the gradual transformation of the social and economic life of the villages by enlisting the co-operation of the people themselves in their own betterment through the practice of more scientific agriculture, better sanitation, the development of communications and cottage industries' (*Community Development Project, India* 1956, from Information Service of India, London). By 1956 the programme had affected about one-quarter of the population of India and by the early 1960s should reach every part of the country. The programme is applied in development blocks of about 100 villages (with 60–70,000 people per block) and teams of experts are present to advise on various matters. There is, of course, a great shortage of trained personnel. Without them, little can be done to improve educational standards, and an illiterate rural population can hardly be expected to instruct itself on technical matters. If successful, this scheme for improving agricultural methods and rural living conditions in India may serve as a model for application in comparable agricultural communities in Africa and other parts of the world.

With regard to mineral production, South Asia is fortunate in having both coal and iron ore deposits (in India). Burma is the only country with extensive proved oil reserves, although oil exploration is now being intensified in India as well. The region is poorly provided with most other minerals, but India accounts for about one-sixth of the world's production of manganese ore, most of which it exports. Coal production in India is about 40 m. tons per annum. This comes to about one-tenth of a ton per inhabitant, compared with more than 4 tons per inhabitant in the U.K.

Coal has formed the basis for heavy industry only in one main area of India, a district some 150 miles to the west of Calcutta. Elsewhere in South Asia the amount of power consumed in manufacturing is very small and modern industrial development is largely confined to a few large towns, including Calcutta, Bombay, and Hyderabad. Further industrial expansion based on hydro-electric power may be expected in parts of South Asia, but the importance of the traditional domestic industries in rural communities should not be underestimated and at least some of the future industrial expansion in the region may be expected here.

Today the industries of India are not unlike those in Russia fifty years ago (see ch. 8). A large market with a very low *per caput* consumption of industrial products is supplied by generally low quality home-produced goods such as cotton manufactures from centres like Bombay, Ahmadabad, and Hyderabad, while some of the basic needs of steel products are supplied by the iron and steel industry which, however, only turns out about 1½ m. tons of steel per annum, or one-sixth as much as Belgium and Luxembourg in absolute terms and less than one-two hundredth in terms of output per inhabitant. Since the war some progress has also been made in establishing engineering and chemicals industries, and particular importance is given to the production of fertilizers and cement. Without the employment of the drastic methods used in the U.S.S.R. and China to sacrifice the consumer and ensure that a large proportion of the national production is invested in expansion for the future, it is difficult to imagine rapid expansion of modern industries in India, and the targets set in the Second 5-Year Plan (1956–60) for heavy industry seem very ambitious. These figures are worth comparing with figures for China in ch. 7, section III. The difference in total population between India and China should be borne in mind.

TABLE 15

	1950–1	1955–6	1960–1
Irrigated areas (m. acres)	51	67	88
Electricity (capacity in m. kw.)	2·3	3·4	6·9
Iron ore (m. tons)	3	4·3	12·5
Coal (m. tons)	32·3	38	60
Steel (m. tons)	1·1	1·3	4·3
Cement (m. tons)	2·7	4·3	13

During the 1950s India also proposes to double the output of cotton textiles, satisfy all the country's needs of railway locomotives by 1960, increase the production of nitrogenous fertilizers 30 times and phosphatic fertilizers 15 times. It is hoped that eventually India will become self-sufficient industrially.

In the other countries of South Asia modern industrial development has been slight. In West Pakistan natural gas may make some future expansion possible.

Although the countries of South Asia inherited a railway system from the British period, the region is comparatively poorly provided with a network of communications, considering its size and population. The main defect of the system is the almost complete absence of motor roads to supplement the railway network. Emphasis is still on improving the railways rather than on providing roads, for the high price of imported motor vehicles and motor fuel make it impossible to develop road transport at a time when so many other projects require large capital outlays. Some idea of the insignificant role of road transport in South Asia is given by the fact that the whole region has fewer motor vehicles in circulation than a single metropolitan area in the U.S.A. the size of Baltimore or St Louis.

Per caput foreign trade is low in South Asia, but overseas trade is nevertheless vital to the economic progress of the region. Exports consist mainly of agricultural raw materials, but no less than one-quarter of the value of India's exports is now made up of jute and cotton manufactures. The largest group of imports is metals and machinery, and this includes the machinery needed to equip the industrial establishments of the region. About one-quarter of India's trade is still with the U.K. and about one-eighth with the U.S.A.

In many respects the problems of South Asia and China are similar. Both are poor agricultural regions with large, increasing populations, yet both lack the extensive tracts of little developed country still available for settlement in parts of Latin America, Africa, and Southeast Asia. So great is their dependence on agriculture that any improvements in living conditions can only be achieved by an increase in farm output. The main problem of India (and it is true of Pakistan as well) is neatly summarized by Mr Geoffrey Tyson in the following lines (*The Geographical Magazine*, Aug. 1957, p. 199) describing the view of certain Indians: 'Others were inclined to think that in spite of her efforts India was rather like a man travelling the wrong way on an escalator – just about able to hold his own against the moving staircase. In India's case the moving staircase is the remorseless increase in population and the unremitting struggle to match insufficient resources with ever-mounting responsibilities.' One recent figure puts the annual increase of population in India at 10 m.

To add to the many difficulties confronting economic progress in South Asia are the problems arising from political instability. India is a large country with a great variety of peoples and traditions – something only artificially welded into a whole by British rule. It is not surprising, therefore, that there has been dissatisfaction with the central government, for example, in the election of a regional communist government in Kerala. The question of introducing a national language may also lead to friction.

The main preoccupation of Pakistan is the fact that its two parts are about 1000 miles apart and separated by Indian territory. In addition, Pakistan has been disturbed by its heavy dependence on rivers rising in Indian territory, including Kashmir, for present and possible future supplies of irrigation water. On this question agreement seems near. Modern Burma, like India, is to a large extent a creation of British rule in South Asia. Now that China is growing more powerful it is challenging Burma's right to certain territories that formerly belonged, if loosely, to the Chinese Empire.

A problem that is likely to become more serious in the future than at present in South Asia is the question of raw materials for industry. While the region has certain plant and animal raw materials for industry, it lacks oil, most metallic minerals, and softwood. As long as the countries have to purchase machinery and equipment abroad to build up their industries they can hardly afford to import raw materials as well.

IV. SOUTHEAST ASIA

SOUTHEAST ASIA is a region of peninsulas, islands, and seas. Like Western Europe and Southwest Asia, no part of it is more than a few hundred miles from the nearest coast. The whole region lies within the tropics and nowhere is rainfall too low for some kind of cultivation. Much of the uncultivated area is covered with dense tropical forest. Movement across islands and from one mainland river basin to another is made difficult by the presence of high mountain ranges. The region is located at one corner of the great land mass of Eurasia and its chain of islands reaches out from the mainland like stepping stones in the direction of Australia.

Southeast Asia is on the sea route between South and East Asia and has been influenced by these regions for thousands of years, and by European powers for several hundred.

Buddhism spread into parts of the region by land from the north, while the Muslim religion reached it by sea from Southwest Asia. The first European navigators and traders arrived early in the 16th century, attracted by the region's tropical products, which could not be cultivated in temperate Europe.

In the 16th century Spain annexed the Philippines, and Portugal established footholds in various other islands, but during the following century the Dutch largely replaced the Portuguese in the East Indies and built up an important colony which subsequently became known as the Dutch East Indies and is now Indonesia. Only during the 19th century did European powers begin to annex large territories on the mainland of Southeast Asia. The British took the Malay Peninsula as well as the northern part of Borneo, where Dutch control had not been established. Towards the end of the century France moved into Indo-China, while in 1898 the U.S.A. acquired the Philippines, which had by then been a Spanish colony for some four centuries. In the whole of Southeast Asia, therefore, only Siam (now Thailand) remained free from European domination, a neutral zone between British and French possessions. The Japanese invasion of Southeast Asia in 1941–2 took the whole region out of European or U.S. control, and postwar attempts by France and the Netherlands to re-establish themselves have met with little success. The U.S.A., on the other hand, granted independence to the Philippines without attempting to reannex it. In 1957 Malaya was given its independence, and the British territories in Borneo and Singapore are therefore the only remaining European colonies in the region.

Japan has important economic connexions with the region, but China, rather than Japan, is now beginning to influence Southeast Asia, and the presence of a significant minority of

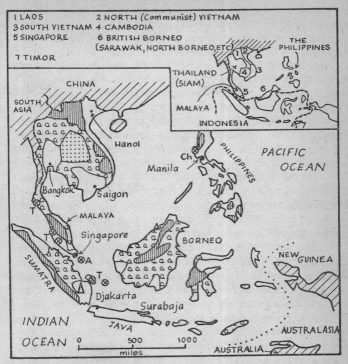

22. Southeast Asia. For key see p. 115. The inset map shows the main political divisions.

Chinese settlers in many areas of the region greatly strengthens China's position.

Table 14 on p. 184 provides some basic figures regarding the more important countries of Southeast Asia. Indonesia has about half of the total population of the region, but its inhabitants are very unevenly distributed among its many islands, Java alone having almost two-thirds of the Indonesian total. Throughout Southeast Asia the high density of population in the lowlands and on terraced hill slopes suitable for cultivation contrasts with the very low density in the rugged areas and in some lowland forest areas that have so far hardly been settled.

Agriculture is the principal activity of Southeast Asia, and everywhere the population is predominantly rural. Specialized commercial farming has acquired great importance in certain areas, especially in parts of Malaya and Java. Over most of the region, however, subsistence agriculture is practised, and each community provides most of its own food and other requirements. Rice is the principal food crop of the region, but manioc is an important food in Indonesia and bananas are widely cultivated. Of the specialized crops produced mainly for export to industrial countries outside Southeast Asia, natural rubber (Indonesia, Malaya, and Thailand account for about 90 per cent of the world's total) and copra (about 90 per cent of the world's total comes from the Philippines and Indonesia) are the most important, although it was the spices of the region that first attracted European traders.

Unlike South and East Asia, Southeast Asia still has large areas into which cultivation could be extended. The relatively small island of Java (about the size of England) has almost two-thirds of the population of Indonesia, yet accounts for less than one-tenth of its total area. Conditions on the larger neighbouring islands of Sumatra and Borneo do not differ greatly from those in Java, yet while Java has about 50 m. inhabitants they each have about 10 m. In the other countries of Southeast Asia there also appear to be opportunities for extending the farming area. In addition, of course, yields could be greatly increased throughout the region, as in many other predominantly rural parts of the world.

Although a large part of Southeast Asia is forested, timber is not widely exploited for export or consumption in industry. Fishing is not run on efficient lines, but even so, in some districts this activity provides one of the main sources of protein food.

Southeast Asia has a number of important mineral deposits, the exploitation of which has only been undertaken by European colonial powers. All but a small part of the output is exported. The region has no important coalfields. Oil, on the other hand, is produced in two main areas, Sumatra (Indonesia) and British

Borneo, which together account for about 2 per cent of the world's output. There may be oil deposits in other parts of the region, but in the dense forest and the rugged mountain areas the search for oil is more difficult and costly than in Southwest Asia and other parts of the world where there is little or no cover of vegetation. Of the metallic minerals, tin is by far the most important in the region, and Malaya (one-third) and Indonesia (one-sixth) together account for about half of the world's output. Other minerals produced in Southeast Asia include iron ore in the Philippines and Malaya, chrome in the Philippines, and bauxite in Indonesia. Japan is a large importer of these items.

Apart from essential processing industries connected with the production of commercial crops such as rubber and of minerals such as tin, there are almost no modern industries at all in Southeast Asia. Lack of coal has no doubt contributed to retard the development of manufacturing in the region. Equally serious obstacles have been the almost complete lack of facilities for advanced education, the absence of a tradition of manufacturing (except of village crafts), and the reluctance of former colonial powers to introduce industries into areas regarded by them as markets for their own home industries. Today, therefore, Southeast Asia, with some 160 m. inhabitants, produces no pig iron and steel, almost no fertilizers and cement, and even very few consumer goods. The large urban areas owe their growth to the expansion of administrative and commercial functions rather than industries.

The whole region, with the exception of Java and a few other small areas, is very poorly provided with railways and is almost without good motor roads. The movement of goods and passengers between the various islands and peninsulas and between Southeast Asia and other parts of the world is handled almost entirely by shipping services.

Foreign trade is largely limited to the export of a few agricultural and mineral raw materials (rubber, tin, and copra being the main items) and of rice (in quantities which vary greatly from year to year, depending on the surplus available). Most of the imports are manufactured goods. Except in Malaya, the *per caput* value of foreign trade is everywhere very low.

Living standards in Southeast Asia are among the lowest in the world. The main areas of agricultural settlement are already densely populated and many organizational problems confront governments wishing to resettle people in new areas. With almost no industries, even the few large and rapidly growing urban centres are something of a burden, depending as they do on a surplus of food from already overpopulated rural areas. Greater Djakarta (Indonesia) is estimated to have more than 3 m. inhabitants, and Manila, Saigon, Bangkok, and Singapore each more than 1 m. The value of exports is relatively small, and the amount of equipment that can be imported for agricultural and industrial projects is consequently not large. U.S. foreign aid has been of great importance to the economy of the Philippines, while large British investments in Malaya have, over several decades, transformed the former subsistence agricultural economy of parts of this country. Elsewhere the amount of foreign aid and investments received since the war has been very small in *per caput* terms. Indonesia's policy towards foreign, especially Netherlands, help, has not been aimed at inspiring the goodwill or confidence of foreign governments and investors. The attitude of the Indonesian government towards the Netherlands is particularly bitter, as the following lines from an Indonesian publication suggest (*Indonesia*, vol. 1, 1954, Ministry of Information, Djakarta): 'For centuries we lived the life of a subjugated nation, according to the will of others, for the interest of others. We had to follow the course of life which others imposed on us in the world society of nations. We were a mere object. We were deprived of our own individuality and personality as a free nation among free nations. However, at last this past fate of ours came to an end, but not without a struggle. ... The most important weapon to win this gigantic war of 80 m people in Indonesia against ignorance and poverty is ... peace.' The writer of these lines omits to mention that the former colonists brought many benefits to the East Indies and he makes the mistake of suggesting that it was a nation in the past and not merely a large number of rural communities with nothing to hold them together – which, perhaps, it still is now.

Indonesia is the only country in Southeast Asia that qualifies to be a major world power on the grounds of large area and population, and its recent threat to claim all the seas within its vast archipelago as territorial waters (see *The Times, 16 Dec. 1957)* is a reminder of its extent and strategic position, and of the influence it could exert on world affairs in the future. With no heavy industries, however, it remains of little significance militarily. One of the great problems of the country is the fact that it consists of some 2000 inhabited islands. This makes it difficult to exchange commodities between the various parts and, what is equally serious, makes the task of administering the whole country by a central government particularly difficult.

Although the Philippines are much smaller than Indonesia in population (20 m.) and area, they also consist of a large number of islands and consequently have many similar features and problems.

The former French Indo-China (which, since its independence, has been split up into the independent states of Cambodia, Laos, and Viet Nam – see fig. 22, inset map) and Thailand, consist of fertile, densely populated lowlands separated by high, rugged mountain ranges.

In many respects, the economic problems of Southeast Asia resemble those of South Asia. Indonesia is attempting to improve conditions in rural communities in very much the same way as India. The links with Europe are weaker, however, and the proximity of China and Japan cannot fail to bring this region more and more into the economic sphere of these two powers of East Asia. SEATO, to which the Philippines and Thailand belong, has been formed by the U.S.A., Australia, France, and the U.K. in an attempt to reduce the danger of Chinese communist penetration into the region. To the industrial countries of Europe and to the U.S.A. the tin and rubber supplies are at present vital, but there are important sources of tin in other parts of the world, while synthetic rubber is now being produced in several countries and rubber trees can be planted elsewhere.

In terms of geopolitics, Southeast Asia is a series of stepping stones between Asia and Australia (the Japanese reached the last important island in the series, New Guinea) and if controlled by a communist power, would constitute a threat to the empty northern lands of Australia and form a barrier between the Indian and Pacific Oceans. Now that communist China has unquestionably established itself as a leading world power, and is expanding its industries on modern lines, the countries of Southeast Asia have to decide what benefits they can derive from increased trade with their powerful neighbour without coming under its political domination. In the same way that many of the countries of Southwest Asia fear the nearest world power to them, the U.S.S.R., so the Southeast Asian countries may well be reluctant to establish too close ties with China and they may seek to establish or re-establish connexions with more distant powers in Europe and North America. It is worth noting in this connexion that there are several million Chinese settlers scattered about Southeast Asia, many of them in Malaya.

V. JAPAN, KOREA, FORMOSA

APART from the British and Portuguese footholds of Hong Kong and Macau on the Asian mainland (communist China), Japan, South Korea, and Formosa are the only parts of East Asia remaining free from communist control. These three countries (the whole of Korea, including the communist-controlled northern part, is considered in this section) differ in many respects from Southeast Asia, even if they might be considered a continuation of the zone of peninsulas, islands, and seas lying between the main land mass of Asia and the Indian and Pacific Oceans.

Although Japan, Korea, and Formosa differ from one another in many respects, they have certain features in common (see table 14 on p. 184). Formosa and Korea were the first overseas possessions of Japan. At present they form, together with Japan, a barrier between communist China and the Pacific Ocean. They have therefore acquired an important role since the war as outer bases of the U.S.A. and have all (except communist North Korea) received large quantities of U.S. military aid as well as considerable financial assistance for economic development.

Japan is now suffering from the consequences of the failure of its over-ambitious plan to conquer China and Southeast

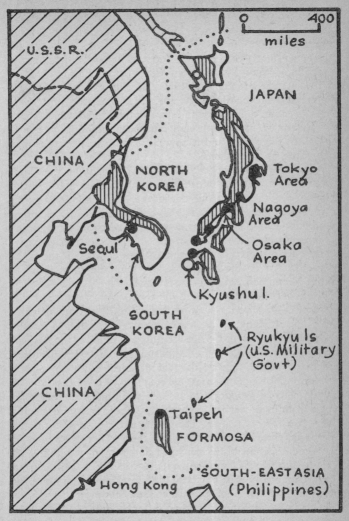

23. Japan, Korea, Formosa. For key see p. 115.

Asia. In the early 1930s its overseas territories had as many inhabitants as Japan itself and were several times as large. Manchuria was an important source of coal, iron, and steel, and, like Korea and Formosa, also supplied Japan with food. As a result of the Second World War, Japan lost not only its conquests in China, made in the late 1930s, and its vast new empire in Southeast Asia won during the war, but also its older possessions. Postwar Japan differs little in area from the Japan which started to industrialize itself on modern European and U.S. lines in the 1870s. On the other hand it now has about three times as many inhabitants as it had then.

Japan now has about 90 m. people, living in an area about two-thirds of the size of France. What makes matters more difficult is the fact that only about one-sixth of Japan's surface is cultivated and, indeed, cultivable, for most of the country is mountainous and the land too steep to cultivate or without a soil cover anyway. In other words, the home-produced part of Japan's food supply comes from an area about half the size of England. The arable land in Japan, scattered throughout the country in numerous small coastal lowlands and interior valleys, is intensively cultivated. Rice, the cereal with the highest yield per unit of area, occupies more than half of the area. To achieve the highest possible yields, large quantities of chemical fertilizer are used. As a result of the need to utilize so much of the farmland for rice, there is little room for pastures or for crops producing raw materials for industry. The fact that much of the non-agricultural surface of Japan is forest-covered is some compensation. The impossibility of producing more than small quantities of protein foods from livestock has forced the Japanese to obtain much of their protein from the sea. The fishing industry is efficiently run and its activities extend not only into the seas between Japan and mainland Asia, one of the best fishing areas in the world, but also far out into the Pacific. Japan catches about one-quarter of the world's tonnage of fish (in the late 1930s it accounted for more than one-half). As the population increases, however, the country depends more and more on imported foodstuffs.

Japan has important, though not large, deposits of several minerals. It produces some 50 m. tons of coal per annum (about half a ton *per caput* compared with more than 4 *per caput* in the U.K.). On the other hand, its oil deposits and production are insignificant. In addition to coal, Japan produces iron ore, manganese, copper, zinc, and sulphur.

Since the 1870s Japan has grown into an industrial nation of considerable importance. Coal and hydro-electric power form the basis of fuel and energy supplies, but the country has few home-produced raw materials apart from its timber and the above-mentioned minerals. *Per caput* consumption of energy is much lower in Japan than in the leading industrial countries of the world and the percentage of the total employed population engaged in manufacturing is much smaller than in the U.K. or Germany. Agriculture still employs about three times as many people as industry – an interesting contrast with Australia, where industry employs twice as many as agriculture.

Many branches of industry are represented in Japan and there is a basis of heavy industry, Japan ranking sixth (after the U.S.A., U.S.S.R., Germany, the U.K., and France) among the world's steel producers in 1955. The heavy engineering and chemicals industries are fairly well developed, but for its exports Japan relies largely on the products of its light engineering and textile industries. Like the U.K. and certain other countries of Western Europe, it must export manufactures in order to import food, the main items being basic foods such as rice, wheat, sugar, and soya beans, rather than luxury foods. In order to run its industries it must also import raw materials, including cotton and wool, which together make up more than one-fifth of the total value of imports.

The main problem of Japan, then, is to maintain its present living standards while its population continues to increase by between 1 and 2 m. per year. Already a large proportion of the population is committed to non-agricultural activities and lives in urban areas (Greater Tokyo has about 8 m. inhabitants and Greater Osaka about 4 m., while several other towns have about 1 m. each). U.S. aid has enabled Japan to expand its industries since the war, but the result has been an artificial trade balance with the U.S.A., with the value of imports 2–3 times as high as exports. Japan's problems of overpopulation might be solved in at least three different ways. Emigration could ease population pressure, but no part of the world is at present prepared to receive more than small numbers of Japanese settlers. The rate of increase of the population could be slowed down. There is a trend in this direction already, but its benefits will not be felt for some decades. Finally, there is the possibility of greatly increasing trade. This seems to be the greatest hope at present, and Japan is patiently waiting for the time when it can expand its trade with Southeast Asia and China and even with the Soviet Far East, India, and Southwest Asia.

Korea, like Germany and Viet Nam, is one of the countries unfortunate enough to remain divided as a result of the Second World War and subsequent conflicts. The communist-controlled northern half, with about 10 m. inhabitants, or one-third of the total population, has most of Korea's mineral and forest reserves and some hydro-electric power stations. South Korea, with about 20 m. inhabitants, depends almost entirely on agriculture, although here, as in North Korea, much of the land is too rugged for cultivation. Living standards are low in Korea and the war in 1950–3 created many new problems.

Formosa's current importance in world affairs is far greater than its size, population, or production merit. The island is only about twice the size of Wales, though it has nearly 10 m. inhabitants. About half of the population is rural, but some industries have been established with U.S. aid. The island has been settled by Chinese during the last three centuries, the original inhabitants having been relegated by these to the mountainous parts. It was occupied by Japan in 1895. It is claimed by communist China but held by Chinese nationalist forces backed by the U.S.A., and remains one of the major problem areas in world affairs today.

Chapter 7

THE COMMUNIST STATES

I. THE U.S.S.R. AND THE MONGOLIAN PEOPLE'S REPUBLIC[1]

THE U.S.S.R. is the oldest, most extensive and, at present, economically the most powerful member of the communist bloc or, as it is called in Soviet publications, the *socialist camp* – the member states of which are run by Communist Parties. The territorially extensive but thinly populated Mongolian People's Republic is at present very much a Soviet sphere of influence. The whole region covers about one-sixth of the world's land area and has about one-thirteenth of its population. It occupies the eastern half of Europe and the northern two-fifths of Asia. What

1. The important question of the reliability of Soviet statistical material should be mentioned here. Figures made available in Soviet publications during the last few years (particularly since 1956) have frequently been quoted in this chapter and the following one. For various reasons the author considers that recent figures have been little falsified. Two reasons are suggested here: firstly, they are published primarily for reference in the U.S.S.R. and the propaganda value they might have outside would not be worth the confusion that could arise at home if they were falsified; secondly, many sets of figures (e.g. for production of non-ferrous metals, most engineering manufactures) are omitted, obviously for security reasons, and those that are published are therefore presumably considered to be no longer worth hiding. For those who are inclined to indulge in wishful thinking and hesitate to accept Soviet production figures, the following lines by one of the members of the 1956 British Steel Missions to the Soviet Union are worth consideration: 'Seeing is believing and, in the days when Russia was completely cut off from the Western World, our mental attitude to the Five Year Plans was somewhat sceptical. Nobody who took part in the visits to Russia will any longer, however, cherish any false impressions that the figures were mere propaganda, that the targets were unobtainable or that the Industry was inefficient' (*Steel Review*, the British Iron and Steel Federation Quarterly, No. 6, Apr. 1957, p. 27).

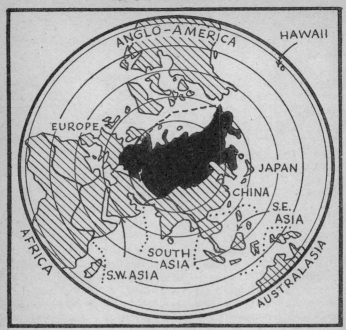

24. The hemisphere of the U.S.S.R. Projection: oblique zenithal equidistant. Centre of projection: Novosibirsk, Western Siberia. The circles are at thousand-mile intervals.

follows refers only to the U.S.S.R., not to the Mongolian People's Republic.

Although there is considerable diversity in relief, climate, and vegetation from one part of the U.S.S.R. to another, a high degree of political and economic unity is imparted to this giant state by the presence of the communist regime, which in 1957 celebrated the 40th anniversary of its acquisition of power. During the interwar years, when the U.S.S.R. was the only socialist state in the world, the aim of the regime was to make it as self-contained as possible.

The U.S.S.R. has land frontiers not only with the 'friendly' regions of communist China and East Europe but also with non-communist Europe and Southwest Asia. Japan and Anglo-America (Alaska) are separated from it only by narrow stretches of sea.

In 1956 the U.S.S.R. had about 200 m. inhabitants. About four-fifths of the population of the U.S.S.R. consist of Europeans and of peoples of European descent now living in the Asiatic part. Some two-thirds of the Europeans (or not much more than one-half of the total population of the U.S.S.R.) are actually Russians; the rest are Ukrainians and Belorussians (speaking languages that do not differ greatly from Russian) and smaller groups, such as Latvians and Moldavians. The Asian citizens of the U.S.S.R. belong to many different linguistic groups and range from peoples with a long tradition of culture, such as the Georgians and Armenians in Transcaucasia and the Uzbeks in Central Asia, to primitive tribes of pastoral nomads such as the Nentsy and Chukchi in Siberia. Strictly speaking, therefore, it is as inaccurate to refer to the U.S.S.R. and to Soviet citizens as Russia and Russians, as it is to call the British Commonwealth England and all its members English.

The U.S.S.R. is divided into fifteen Soviet Socialist Republics. The largest and most populous, the Russian Soviet Federal Socialist Republic (R.S.F.S.R.), is inhabited mainly by Russians, while the other republics, such as the Ukrainian S.S.R. and the Uzbek S.S.R., are formed round the more important of the various national groups after which they are named. In all the republics, however, there appears to be an appreciable percentage of Russians, while many Ukrainians have also settled outside the Ukraine itself, particularly in Asiatic parts of the U.S.S.R.

The population of the U.S.S.R. is very unevenly distributed over the national territory. About three quarters of the total lives in the European part, which occupies less than one quarter of the total area. In the Asiatic part there are two main concentrations of population: a long but relatively narrow zone between the coniferous forest and semi-desert zones, served by the Trans-Siberian Railway, stretching between the Urals and Lake Baykal, and settled mainly by Russians and Ukrainians; and a discontinuous zone of irrigated land in Central Asia, between the desert and the high mountain ranges, stretching between the Caspian Sea and the boundary of China, and settled mainly by Asians.

The population of the U.S.S.R. is now increasing by more than 3 m. per annum. Owing to the great losses in the war, however, the total has only recently passed the 1940 figure (subsequent boundary changes having been allowed for). At the same time, the percentage of town dwellers is growing, and at present about 45 per cent of the total population lives in urban types of settlement. Moscow itself has about 5 m. inhabitants and Greater Moscow is even larger, while Leningrad has 3 m. and several other urban areas have about 1 m. inhabitants each.

Before the 1917 Revolution, farming was by far the most important activity in Russia. It is still the largest single employer of labour, for not much less than half of the employed population of the Soviet Union is still in agriculture – a much larger proportion of the labour force than in Anglo-America, Australia, or industrial Western Europe.

In spite of its great size, the U.S.S.R. has not been producing enough from its farms to satisfy its growing needs. After more than three decades of Soviet planning and two decades of collectivization, farm production was not much higher in 1953 than before 1917. The reasons are partly organizational, partly environmental. On the organizational side the new Soviet leaders have made many changes since Stalin's death in 1953. Collective farms have been given greater freedom of choice as to what they can grow, an attempt has been made to increase the amount of animal fodder available by replacing other cereals by maize wherever possible, while new and long fallow lands have been ploughed for grain cultivation since 1953.

On the other hand, limits are set by environmental conditions to the expansion of the cultivated area and to the types of crop that can be grown. About 17 per cent of the U.S.S.R. is tundra (cold desert) and nearly 50 per cent is coniferous forest (with soils generally unsuitable for cultivation and the growing season too short for most farm crops to mature). In both these zones there are many areas where the subsoil is permanently frozen (permafrost). Another 10 per cent of the U.S.S.R. is desert or semi-desert. A small part consists of rugged high mountain areas. Even in the remaining 20 per cent, which is mostly steppe or cleared broadleaf forest, rainfall is not everywhere reliable, and dry seasons not infrequently reduce harvests. At present, then, about 10 per cent of the total area of the U.S.S.R. is cropland and another 10 per cent grazing land, though not much of the latter is of high quality.

Farming can only be extended into the colder two-thirds of the U.S.S.R. (as into the coniferous forest zone of Canada) when

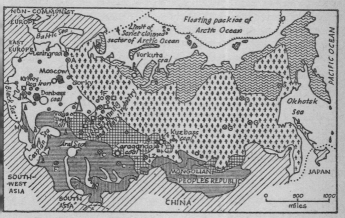

25. The U.S.S.R. and Mongolian People's Republic. For key see p. 115.

some means has been found to make the forest soils suitable for cultivation. Small areas are already utilized, but their economic significance is slight, though magnified by Soviet propaganda. To make use of the arid 10 per cent of the country, costly works of irrigation must be constructed. Here, however, the area that can ultimately be irrigated is limited to the amount of water entering the deserts by river from better watered mountain regions. At present, therefore, it seems that farm output can be increased more by obtaining higher yields in existing farming areas than by further extending agriculture into marginal lands.

Considerable importance has been attached by Soviet planners to the production of industrial raw materials, and the U.S.S.R. is more or less self-sufficient in the production of cotton and flax. Since no part of the country lies in or even close to the tropics, the range of crops that can be cultivated is limited, and the rubber tree (*Hevea brasiliensis*) is among the important tropical plants that cannot be grown. Sugar cane cannot be cultivated commercially, and most of the country's sugar requirements are produced from beet.

The timber reserves of the U.S.S.R. are more extensive than those of any other country in the world. So far, only the forests of European U.S.S.R. have been widely exploited. With coastlines on several different seas and oceans the country also has access to a number of important fishing areas. At present the Okhotsk and Caspian Seas are the most productive.

The U.S.S.R. is probably better provided with minerals than any other single country in the world. Its proved reserves of coal are only exceeded in size by those of the U.S.A. It also has abundant high grade iron ore deposits and, apparently, large oil reserves. In an article in *Pravda*, 4 Dec. 1957, it was claimed that the exploration of resources has now shown that no mineral that is vital to the country's economic expansion is lacking. There are deposits of uranium in various localities, and in 1956 diamonds were discovered in Eastern Siberia. Although gold is supposed to have no place in the Soviet economic system it is also produced in Siberia and is used in foreign trade.

The main producing coalfields are those of the Donbass, Kuzbass, Karaganda, and Vorkuta, which produce high grade coal, including coking coal for the smelting of iron ore, and those of Tula and the Urals where lignite or low grade coals are mined. The main sources of high and medium grade iron ore are at present Krivoy Rog and Kerch, about 200 miles from the Donbass, and in the Ural region, some 1200 miles from the coking coal of the Kuzbass and 600 miles from that of Karaganda. The Caspian–Caucasus area was the main source of oil until the 1950s, but for some time output has been increasing rapidly in the Volga–Ural region, and this now accounts for at least three-quarters of the total Soviet production. Important producing areas of other minerals include the Ural range and Kazakhstan.

The Communist States

Although the Soviet Communist Party claims the credit for the great progress that has been made in certain branches of industry during the last thirty years, nothing comparable could have been achieved without the many plant and mineral resources available in various parts of the country. The U.S.S.R. has abundant sources of fuel and power and many sites suitable for the construction of large hydro-electric power stations. Unfortunately for Soviet planners, some of the best deposits of coal (e.g. Vorkuta, the Kuzbass) are many hundreds of miles from large high grade iron ore deposits and far from the main concentrations of population and industry. Among the home-produced raw materials for industry are cotton, flax, and timber; non-ferrous metals such as copper, lead, zinc, aluminium ores; ferro-alloys such as manganese; and raw materials for the manufacture of chemicals, including fertilizers – apatite (for phosphate fertilizers), potash, and sulphur.

On the organizational side, heavy industry has benefited (even if Soviet citizens have suffered great hardships) from the drastic measures taken to develop mineral production and heavy manufacturing by investing a large part of the national income in these. But the reader should not overlook the fact that important industries were inherited from pre-Revolutionary times, so that in the early days of the communist period the U.S.S.R. was not without industrial plant and skilled workers (see ch. 8, section II).

During the Soviet period new branches of manufacturing have been developed. The most important, perhaps, are the engineering and chemicals industries, built up almost from nothing. Notwithstanding these great achievements, many branches of industry have been neglected. In particular, the U.S.S.R. is still far behind the U.S.A. and Western Europe in the production of consumer goods both in quality and in output per inhabitant.

In spite of attempts by Soviet planners to decentralize industry, much of the capacity is still concentrated in three main areas: the central part of European U.S.S.R. (around Moscow); the Donbass coalfield and associated centres on the Lower Dnieper and neighbouring areas; and the Ural region. Most of the Soviet pig iron and steel is produced in the Donbass area (one-half of the pig iron and one-third of the steel) and Urals (one-third of each), while the Moscow area is of outstanding importance for textiles and for engineering products requiring skilled labour. Outside these three main regions there are, of course, other important concentrations of manufacturing – mostly individual centres, such as the Baltic and Black Sea ports, with shipbuilding yards, and the Volga towns, with various branches of engineering. The Kuzbass coalfield area is something of an exception, for it has the best coal reserves in the U.S.S.R., a large iron and steel works, and a concentration of several large mining and manufacturing towns. Industries of regional rather than national importance have also been established in the parts of the U.S.S.R. that are most distant from the main areas of manufacturing – for example, in Soviet Central Asia and the Soviet Far East, but Soviet propaganda has tended to exaggerate their significance.

The U.S.S.R. is undoubtedly one of the leading industrial countries of the world. In certain branches of the engineering industry, the production of power station equipment, of excavators, and of aircraft, for example, it rivals the U.S.A. and Western Europe. On the other hand, Soviet industry has been built up over such a short period (the really impressive developments began less than thirty years ago, during the period of the First 5-Year Plan) that many branches – for example, the motor vehicles industry – have had to be neglected.

In a country the size of the U.S.S.R., with great distances between the various concentrations of population and the various areas of production, economic expansion has depended very largely on the provision of an efficient system of transport. In some respects progress has been held up through the inadequacy of the system. The railways carry about 85 per cent of the tonnage of all goods moved in the U.S.S.R., while the Volga (with associated rivers, canals, lakes, and seas) is at present the only important system of inland waterways, accounting for two-thirds of the traffic handled by these. Roads are largely feeders to the railways. To handle the constantly increasing volume of goods traffic the railway system of pre-1917 Russia (with about 40,000 miles of route in use after the First World War) has been used more and more heavily, its efficiency being improved by such means as double-tracking and electrification. New lines have also been built, and bring the present total route mileage to about 75,000 (cf. U.S.A. 230,000). Although the route mileage is less than double what it was four decades ago, the railway system is being used much more heavily now, for the volume of goods traffic (measured in ton kilometres) was about 16 times as great in 1956 as in 1913. It appears, however, that many key railways are working to full capacity and economic progress will therefore be held up unless new lines are constructed or the inter-regional movement of goods is cut down by the more rational use of local raw materials. At all events, even if the Soviet propagandists point out that their rail system is the most heavily used in the world, it should be remembered that it is cheaper to avoid carrying goods over long distances altogether, if possible. That is perhaps one reason why in 1957 about 100 planning regions were created to help in reducing the excessive power of Ministries located in Moscow. It was emphasized that each should make the fullest possible use of its local resources. Even now, in spite of the great inter-regional movement of goods, there does not appear to be the degree of regional specialization that is to be found in Anglo-America. In particular, the U.S.S.R. lacks the extensive highway system of the U.S.A., and so far has few long-distance gas and oil pipelines. A start has now been made on the provision of a national electricity grid.

Foreign trade is much less important to the economic life of the U.S.S.R. than to most countries of Western Europe, to Anglo-America, and to Japan. Much of the Soviet foreign trade is now with other members of the communist bloc. East Europe receives mainly raw materials and China mostly manufactured goods. Since the war the U.S.S.R. has imported large quantities of agricultural produce from non-communist countries, including wool from Australia, butter from New Zealand, meat from Argentina, and grain from Canada. This situation is regarded by Soviet leaders as temporary, but certainly it is evidence that all has not been well with Soviet agriculture during the communist period. One trend in Soviet trade is of particular significance in world affairs. In 1913, metals, machinery, and equipment only accounted for 1 per cent of the total value of Russian exports; in 1938, less than 7 per cent; but in 1955, more than 37 per cent.

The changing structure of Soviet foreign trade is worth study, for many items (e.g. raw cotton, machinery) that were being imported before the Revolution are now being exported. Although the U.S.S.R., like Anglo-America, is large, and well supplied with many raw materials, it seems probable that it must in time become a great trading nation, whether or not the Soviet leaders wish this to happen.

Some features and problems of the U.S.S.R. that are of particular importance in world affairs are discussed in ch. 8. Here, therefore, it is sufficient to point out that many problems of the U.S.S.R. result from the rapid but unharmonious development of the Soviet economy during the last four decades. Agriculture, road transport, light industry, and housing have been neglected because an excessive amount of capital has been invested in heavy industry in order to make the U.S.S.R. a powerful country militarily and to establish the foundations necessary for future general industrial development. That this policy saved the U.S.S.R. from defeat by Germany in 1941–2 surely justifies it, for the Germans quickly occupied the Donbass and would subsequently have overcome the Russians if they had not been provided with other heavy industrial areas built up in the 1930s beyond the reach of the enemy in the Urals and Kuzbass.

The following table shows how uneven has been the increase

TABLE 16

	1913	1926	1940	1956	U.S.A. 1955
Population (millions)	159	147	192	200	165
Rural	131	121	131	113	55
Urban	28	26	61	87	110
		1928		1955	
Coal (m. metric tons)	28	32	140	276	448
Lignite „ „	1	3	26	115	3
Oil „ „	10	12	31	71	336
Pig iron „ „	4	3	15	33	72
Steel „ „	4	4	18	45	106
Cement „ „	2	2	6	22	50
Fertilizers „ „	0·1	0·1	3	10	20
Cotton fabric (m. metr.)	2672	2678	3954	5904	9235
Motor vehicles (thous.)	—	7	145	445	9169
Cattle (millions)	52	60	48	61	97

of production in various branches of the Soviet economy. The last two columns include Soviet and U.S. figures for 1955.

1956 and 1957 Soviet figures show substantial increases in output on preceding years in many branches of the economy. The Sixth 5-Year Plan (1956–60) has, however, been modified, and Soviet leaders are now looking fifteen years ahead to a time when they hope to approach or overtake the U.S.A. in *per caput* production in important branches of the economy (*Pravda*, 9 Nov. 1957). Some approximate targets for fifteen years hence are given and they are worth comparing with figures in table 16: pig iron 75–85 m. tons; steel 100–120 m. tons; coal and lignite (proportion of lignite not specified) 650–750 m. tons; oil 350–400 m. tons.

II. COMMUNIST EAST EUROPE

THE only reason for making communist East Europe into a major world region is that since the Second World War all eight countries have been cut off from Western Europe by the establishment of a communist regime of one kind or another. The present political set-up can only be regarded as temporary, for nowhere else in the world have political boundaries altered and nations disappeared and re-emerged with such frequency as they have in this part of Europe during the last few hundred years. Even in the short postwar period there have been significant changes. Hardly had Czechoslovakia been brought into the communist herd when the Yugoslav Communist Party turned rogue and was expelled from the Cominform. In 1956 Poland acquired some degree of independence from the U.S.S.R., but Hungary's attempt to do the same was less successful. The countries in this region have frequently been influenced by more powerful neighbours – by the Ottoman Empire from the south, by Russia from the east, by Prussia and later Germany, and even by France (during the Napoleonic Wars), from the west. At present, then, Russian influence extends over the whole region except Yugoslavia. Situated between the inland Baltic, Adriatic, and Black Seas, the region has non-communist neighbours to the north (Scandinavia), to the west (Germany, Austria, and Italy) and to the south (Greece and Turkey).

26. Communist East Europe. For key see p. 115.

The Communist States

The following table gives some basic figures concerning all the countries except Albania (pop. 1¼ m.). They are arranged according to the degree of intensity of industrialization. Since the countries do not vary greatly in area or density of population, figures for these are not shown.

In all the countries of communist East Europe except Albania an appreciable proportion of the total area is cropland and all

TABLE 17

	I	II	III	IV	V	VI
		Crop-				Per cap. Cons.
	Pop'n	land	Coal	Steel	Urban	of Energy
E. Germany	18	48	70	2	65	3530
Czechoslovakia	13	44	36	4½	50	3760
Poland	27	55	96	4½	40	2650
Hungary	10	63	10	1½	35	1670
Romania	17	40	2	¾	25	1220
Yugoslavia	17	31	6	¾	20	470
Bulgaria	8	40	3	—	25	610

I. Population in millions.
II. Approximate percentage of total area cultivated.
III. Coal (including lignite in terms of hard coal equivalent) output in millions of metric tons, 1955.
IV. Steel output in millions of metric tons, 1955.
V. Urban population expressed as a percentage of total population.
VI. Estimated consumption of commercial sources of energy expressed in terms of coal equivalent, kilograms per inhabitant in 1955.

but a small part of the remainder grazing land or forest. Conditions, therefore, are good for farming over large areas and generally the tracts of poorer soil in both lowland and mountain areas are forested. All the countries are more or less self-supporting in basic foodstuffs and, unlike the more highly industrialized nations of non-communist Europe (such as Belgium and the U.K.), do not import much food. On the other hand, of course, both luxury foods from tropical and sub-tropical areas, and many animal and vegetable raw materials must be imported. Cotton, for example, is one of the principal imports of Czechoslovakia.

East Europe is well endowed with certain minerals, but many important ones are not produced in more than small quantities.

Only Poland and Czechoslovakia produce an appreciable amount of hard coal. Poland, producing about 100 m. tons per annum, is not far behind the U.K. in *per caput* production. All the countries produce lignite – East Germany by far the most (about 200 m. tons). Compared with ordinary coal, lignite is low in heating value, while its uses are more restricted and, in particular, it is not used for making pig iron. Oil is only produced in large quantities in Romania (but the 11 m. tons in 1956 was not much more than 1 per cent of the world's total). There are several deposits of iron ore in East Europe, though none is large, and East Germany, Poland, Czechoslovakia, and Hungary, therefore, have to import part of their requirements of this mineral. Several other minerals are produced in large quantities: potash in East Germany (about 25 per cent of world total); manganese ore in Romania and Hungary; bauxite in Yugoslavia and Hungary; and zinc in Yugoslavia and Poland.

The degree of industrialization varies greatly between the countries of East Europe. Albania has almost no industries, while Bulgaria, Romania, and Yugoslavia are still predominantly agricultural, although attempts have been made in the postwar period to set up large modern industrial establishments. Hungary is intermediate. The most highly industrialized areas are to be found in West Czechoslovakia, Southwest Poland, and the southern part of East Germany. Postwar communist policy has been to build up heavy industries in East Europe, and pig iron and steel output is now considerably higher in all the producing countries than it was before the war. Even so, *per caput* production is still several times higher in West Germany and the U.K. than in East Europe as a whole. The leading industrial countries of East Europe also have important engineering industries, while Czechoslovakia in particular has a surplus of consumer goods for export, mostly to its less highly industrialized communist neighbours and to the U.S.S.R. At all events, the total industrial capacity of East Europe is by no means small, though it can hardly be compared with that of the U.S.S.R. or non-communist Europe.

Much of the trade of the countries of East Europe is with fellow members of the communist bloc. The U.S.S.R. provides oil and industrial raw materials such as cotton, while it absorbs a considerable part of the manufactured exports of East Europe.

Lack of appropriate figures makes it difficult to compare living standards in East European countries with those in non-communist Europe and in the U.S.S.R. Certainly the level of production was considerably lower than in Western Europe in the interwar period everywhere except in East Germany and the western part of Czechoslovakia. It appears that both in agriculture and in industry production has nowhere been increased since the war as much as was hoped, partly, no doubt, because collectivization and emphasis on heavy industrial development, the cornerstones of Soviet economic planning, have not succeeded or have not been needed in East Europe.

Any future political and economic changes in East Europe depend largely on the attitude and policy of the U.S.S.R. At least until very recently, Soviet leaders appear to have considered East Europe vital to the U.S.S.R. as a protective zone several hundred miles wide between Soviet territory and the U.S. and allied bases in Western Europe. It has also made significant contributions to the Soviet economy.

From the point of view of the countries themselves, Soviet domination can hardly be enjoyed now any more than Russian, German, Prussian, or Turkish domination have been welcomed in the past. Under the 'dictatorship' of their national Communist Parties the countries have been forced to follow certain lines of economic development and they have been prevented or discouraged from trading with countries outside the communist bloc. The particular problems and interests of each country have largely been ignored. East Germany is bound to suffer as long as it remains separated from the rest of Germany. Poland, squeezed between its two more powerful neighbours, Germany and the U.S.S.R., at the moment looks to the latter to guarantee its western boundary, which includes a large part of prewar Germany. Czechoslovakia, perhaps, suffers less than its neighbours from its inclusion within the communist bloc, for as a result it has little outside competition for markets for its light manufactures. Hungary, which occupies a strategic position in the centre of the region (see fig. 26) is no less important than East

Germany as a Soviet base close to Western Europe and the Mediterranean. The remaining members of communist East Europe are less important as industrial powers, but the significance of Yugoslavia has been magnified by its resistance to Soviet influence. Its loss deprived the U.S.S.R. of a direct outlet on the Adriatic, for although the coast of Albania is on this sea, Albania is separated from Bulgaria and the U.S.S.R. by Greek and Yugoslav territory.

In conclusion, it might be suggested that alone none of the countries in East Europe can be considered a major world power (hence the inability of these countries individually to resist Soviet penetration). Nor are they countries with extensive areas of undeveloped land or large unexploited mineral deposits. They are all small territorially and, if and when their population increases appreciably, they will come to rely more and more on the export of manufactures to pay for food, fuels, and raw materials.

III. CHINA

THE emergence during the last decade of modern communist-controlled China as a major world power is perhaps one of the most significant events in world affairs in the present century. China has remained the most extensive and most populous region of the world never to be annexed by European empire-building nations during the last five centuries. As the Russians strengthened their hold on Siberia and Central Asia they did challenge the Chinese claim to certain thinly populated outer provinces, while Portuguese Macau and British Hong Kong are the last relics of attempts by the maritime powers of Europe to establish trading stations in the coastal provinces. Japan, the first Asian power to adopt modern European industrial techniques, was the only country to go far towards overcoming China when it annexed Manchuria in the early 1930s and later in that decade embarked on the conquest of the rest of China.

During the last decade, communist China has gone a long way towards establishing control over what in the 19th century was loosely called the Chinese Empire. The former Outer Mongolia remains outside, however, and part of it is now in the U.S.S.R., while part has become the Mongolian People's Republic, economically a Soviet sphere of influence. Formosa is held by Chinese nationalist forces but, like small areas in Burma and elsewhere, is considered by the Chinese communists to be part

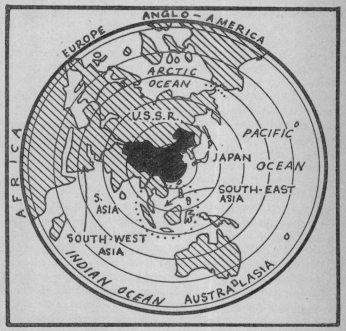

27. The hemisphere of China. Projection: oblique zenithal equidistant. Centre of projection: Wuchang, China. The circles are at thousand-mile intervals.

of the Chinese People's Republic. The control of the communist regime over the thinly populated western half of China, inhabited mainly by non-Chinese, has been greatly strengthened by the construction of railways and roads during the last few years (see fig. 28b). Modern China, then, is unified by the control of the Communist Party, with its capital in Peking, and, under the

217

5-Year Plans (the first from 1953–7), the economic development of the country is organized (as in the U.S.S.R. until 1957) by a single planning authority.

China covers about one-thirteenth of the world's land area (excluding Antarctica) but has, according to the most recent census, not much less than one-quarter of the world's population. Neighbouring regions with which it has long land frontiers are the U.S.S.R., South Asia, Southeast Asia, and Korea. It also has a short common frontier with Afghanistan (Southwest Asia) in the mountainous Pamir area. Japan and Formosa are at no great distance from China by sea. In addition, all the other regions of the world, except Latin America, fall wholly or partly within the hemisphere of China (see fig. 27).

Since the Chinese Communist Party has in many ways modelled itself on the Soviet Communist Party and has copied many features of Soviet economic development, the reader should constantly bear in mind the resemblances and differences between the two countries when studying the problems of modern China. If only temporarily, communist China has chosen to europeanize itself on Soviet lines. It has, for example, introduced collectiviza-tion in agriculture, and it stresses the importance of heavy in-dustrial development. In many respects contemporary China can be compared with the U.S.S.R. in the early 1930s, yet it would be a mistake to carry the comparison too far, because in area, population, and resources the two countries differ greatly.

According to a census held in June 1953 China had 602 m. inhabitants (including 8 m. in Formosa and 12 m. living abroad). More than 90 per cent are Chinese. The remainder, living mainly in the outer provinces, include Mongols and Tibetans. About 95 per cent of the total population of China lives in the south-eastern two-fifths of the national territory (see fig. 28b). Even here, great contrasts in density of population are to be found between the fertile lowlands of the main river valleys and the numerous steep-sided and, in places, high mountain ranges. In 1953, about 13 per cent of the population was urban, the remainder rural. There were nine cities with more than 1 million inhabitants. As a result of the recent expansion of industry, mining, and other urban activities, the proportion of town dwellers is increasing.

The population of China itself is increasing by about 12 million persons per annum. If this rate of increase continues the total population will double within a few decades to reach, perhaps, 1200 m. by the year 2000. There are already about twelve times as many people in China as in the U.K. In the year 2000 there could be 24 times as many.

Although urban centres have existed uninterruptedly in China for several millennia, farming is by far the most important

28a. China: use of land, minerals, and industries. For key see p. 115.

occupation, as it always has been, and most of the population still lives in rural communities. Moreover, each community is to a considerable extent self-supporting. In Russia before the 1917 Revolution, however, only 17 per cent of the total population was urban, yet now, after only 40 years, the proportion is 45 per cent.

Most of China is of little or no use for farming. About 20 per cent of the country's area, mainly the southwestern part, is too high, cold, and rugged to support more than very poor pastures except in a few small areas. Another 40 per cent, mainly the northwest and north, is too arid to be of much use for cultivation except where irrigated, and, like the high mountain areas, supports only poor-quality pasture. Even in the remaining 40 per cent, where almost all the population lives, much of the land is too rugged to be of use for cultivation. Not more than about 10 per cent of the total surface of China is intensively utilized for farming. Most of this better-quality farmland is occupied by the food crops that ensure the highest yields per unit area – rice in the south, soya beans, wheat, and koaliang in the north. Livestock is a luxury, and meat and dairy produce hardly enter the diet of most Chinese families, while even fish, such an important source of protein in Japan, is at present caught in relatively small quantities in China. Moreover, little land is available for the cultivation of industrial crops. Cotton, the principal textile raw material, occupies much of the land devoted to crops of this kind. Yet another disadvantage of China is the poverty of its forest reserves. Only about 5 per cent is forest covered (cf. almost 50 per cent in the U.S.S.R.).

Not surprisingly, great importance has been attached by the present regime to increasing farm production. Collectivization was introduced almost everywhere in the early 1950s. This form of farm organization does not itself automatically ensure higher output, and Chinese leaders must have learnt from the results of nearly three decades of collectivization in the U.S.S.R. not to expect great benefits from it. Also, following the Soviet example (in this case with a time-lag of only a few years) the Chinese have embarked on the ploughing of new lands for cereal cultivation (hitherto used for grazing) in poor steppe and semi-desert areas of Inner Mongolia, Sinkiang, and other interior and at present thinly populated regions. There is a danger here, as in the semi-arid areas now being used in the U.S.S.R., that strong winds will remove the soil from the land, as happened in the Great Plains of the U.S.A. in the interwar period. The Chinese new lands project is being held up as a result of a shortage of tractors needed for this extensive kind of cultivation.

It seems, therefore, that the most promising method of increasing farm output is to obtain higher yields in existing areas of cultivation. At present almost no chemical fertilizers are manufactured or consumed in China, and yields of such crops as rice are much lower than in Japan, where chemical fertilizers are widely used. In 1952 only about 250,000 tons of chemical fertilizer were produced – about one lb. per inhabitant. It is planned to produce 3 m. tons in 1962. Even this is a small amount

28b. China: towns with more than one million inhabitants and westward expansion. Only new roads and railways in the western part are shown.

in *per caput* terms. What is more, China appears to lack the minerals required for the manufacture of the more important types of fertilizers.

With regard to mineral deposits, China is not so well endowed as the U.S.S.R., though it is claimed that many new deposits have been discovered during the communist period. Most important of all, perhaps, is the fact that China has extensive deposits of high-grade coal. Among recently discovered minerals are large supplies of iron ore and oil. Iron ore is found in close proximity to coking coal in several localities. The oilfields, on the other hand, are in the interior of China, and the field at Yuming, where most of China's very limited output is at present produced, has only recently been linked by rail with the main centres of population to the east, while another oilfield at Tsaidam is not yet served by rail at all. China also has important deposits of certain other minerals, including tin, antimony, and tungsten. Other metals, including copper, lead, and zinc appear to be lacking.

In the U.S.S.R. the Soviets inherited important mines and industrial establishments (though damaged) from tsarist days. In the same way the Chinese communists have come into possession of the former Japanese-run iron and steel industry of Manchuria as well as the large textile factories of Shanghai and elsewhere, established by various foreign countries. Communist China, therefore, has not been without a base on which to build up its industries. Another advantage of China, not shared by the U.S.S.R. or India, is the presence of abundant reserves of coal in the vicinity of many of the existing large urban centres. In contrast, the oil deposits and many of the suitable sites for large hydro-electric power stations are located in inaccessible areas far from the principal concentrations of population and industry.

Home-produced raw materials for industry are not plentiful. Considering the large population of the country there is little timber, and there are few important minerals other than coal, iron ore, and oil. The amount of land available for the production of plant and animal raw materials is strictly limited owing to the need to use almost all of the better farmland for food production. The difficulty of transporting bulky goods between the different regions of the country is another obstacle to industrial expansion. China only has about 16,000 miles of railway – less than the U.K. or France. It has almost no modern motor roads, while the Yangtse is the only important inland waterway. In many respects, therefore, China is not in such a good position to embark on rapid industrial expansion as the U.S.S.R. was when it began thirty years ago. As in the U.S.S.R., the emphasis is on the expansion of various branches of heavy industry – iron and steel, engineering, chemicals (particularly fertilizers), and cement. The following table shows progress in certain basic industries.

TABLE 18

	Early 1940s Peak Year	1952	1957 Provisional	1962 Target
Coal (m. tons)	62	64	117	200
Oil (m. tons)	$\frac{1}{3}$	$\frac{1}{2}$	$1\frac{1}{2}$	$5\frac{1}{2}$
Electricity (thous. m. kwh.)	6	7	19	42
Steel (m. tons)	$\frac{9}{10}$	$1\frac{1}{3}$	5	$11\frac{1}{4}$
Chemical fertilizers (m. tons)	$\frac{1}{6}$	$\frac{1}{6}$	$\frac{3}{8}$	3
Cement (m. tons)	$2\frac{1}{4}$	3	7	13
Cotton yarn (m. bales)	$2\frac{1}{2}$	$3\frac{1}{2}$	5	$8\frac{1}{2}$

The first column shows the peak annual production before the communist period. 1957 figures are provisional and 1962 figures represent the targets set for the final year of the Second 5-Year Plan.

The production of consumer goods is not being neglected, and the output of such manufactures as cotton cloth, paper, bicycles, and rubber footwear has increased 2–3 times during the First 5-Year Plan (1953–7). Most impressive of all, perhaps, has been the creation during the last few years of China's engineering industry. The large iron and steel industry built up by the Japanese in Manchuria in the 1930s was regarded mainly as a source of pig iron and steel for Japan itself. Consequently, China has had to build up its engineering industry almost from nothing, and Soviet equipment and technical aid have therefore been vital. Soviet assistance has been given in more than 150 of the largest 700 industrial undertakings (not all, of course, engineering) of the First 5-Year Plan. The list of engineering products now turned out in China is impressive, and includes lorries, steam locomotives, rolling stock, various machine tools, scientific precision instruments and apparatus, and farm and textile machinery.

An important feature of communist planning in China has been the move to decentralize industry. Even now most of the steel is produced in South Manchuria, and many of the consumer goods are made in the Shanghai and Peking areas, while the Shansi-Shensi field accounts for most of the coal. Two large new iron and steel works are now being built in the interior of the country. This development is not unlike the establishment of iron and steel centres in the Ural region and Kuzbass in the U.S.S.R. during the 1930s. Likewise, new cotton manufacturing establishments are being opened in the cotton-growing regions of the middle Hwang-Ho and Yangtse valleys, as they were in the cotton-growing lands of the Soviet Union (Soviet Central Asia and Transcaucasia).

There are many obstacles to industrial expansion in China, and the reader should bear in mind that at present, and probably for some decades, the output is and will be very modest even in absolute terms, let alone *per caput* terms. At present, for example, China only produces one-quarter as much steel as the U.K., yet it has 12 times as many people. In 1962 it will still only be producing half as much, and then only if the targets of the Second 5-Year Plan are reached and if the output of the U.K. does not also increase. What is more, the population of China is so large and is growing so rapidly that *per caput* industrial production, which is extremely low at present, can hardly be expected to approach the *present* level in the U.S.S.R. until some decades have passed, and, indeed, may not do so at all.

The Chinese communists attach great importance to the expansion of foreign trade. At present, about 80 per cent is with other members of the communist bloc. Nevertheless, trade with Asian and African countries increased by 150 per cent during 1953–6. The only countries in America with which China had trade relations in 1956 were Canada, Brazil, Argentina, and Uruguay.

Traditional products such as silk and tea still figure among China's exports, but various new light manufactures are also being exported, even though they must be needed at home. China has to import many raw materials for industry and at the same time it requires industrial equipment and various machines.

In an interesting speech, quoted in *Pravda* (28 June 1957), Mr Chou En-lai made some points about prospects of future development in China. Some would surprise those people who accept the communist propaganda line that under a communist regime there are no limits to what can be achieved. In the speech he stressed that China is a backward agricultural country with limited resources, and that its future prosperity depends largely on the increase of farm output. He criticized people who expect immediate results from the introduction of socialism, and forecast only gradual improvements and these only from hard work and sound construction. You can't make a silk purse out of a sow's ear, even with the drastic methods employed by communist regimes.

If living standards are to be raised in China many obstacles have to be overcome. Two questions which lie behind all matters of economic progress not only in China but also in all the poorer countries of the world, have to be solved. Farm output must be raised and the rate of increase of population slowed down. Nowhere in the world is the problem more acute than in China. Only when measures are taken to solve these problems can the benefits of industrialization be felt by the whole community and improvements in education and living conditions be universally introduced. The Chinese communist government is concerned with both the problems mentioned, but in a country in which most of the inhabitants are poor, illiterate peasants, the task of introducing birth control is not an easy one. Even so, the recent moves to spread birth control and to legalize sterilization and abortion are significant.

With almost one-quarter of the world's population, China qualifies to rank as a major world power on the strength of its manpower alone. It does not yet challenge the leading world powers in industrial capacity. Indeed, it is hard to think of China challenging the present supremacy of the U.S.A. and U.S.S.R. during the next decade or two. It is equally hard to think of it not doing so before 50 years have passed. By then Southeast Asia and even Japan might well have fallen within its sphere of economic influence, and the status of former Chinese lands beyond the frontier (some of them now Soviet territory) challenged.

IV. THE COMMUNIST BLOC

THE communist bloc or *socialist camp* occupies about 25 per cent of the total land area of the world, has about 35 per cent of the world's population, and accounts for approximately 25 per cent the world's output of steel. The member countries vary greatly in extent, population, natural conditions, and industrial capacity. The contrast is enormous, for example, between Czechoslovakia and the Moscow area on the one hand and the arid pastures of Mongolia or the tropical rice-lands of South China on the other. The following table (mainly with 1955 figures) includes all the members of the communist bloc.

TABLE 19

	Area (m. sq. mls)	Pop'n (millions)	Energy[4]	Steel[5]
U.S.S.R.	8580	197	2020	45½
Poland	120	27	2650	4½
East Germany	42	18	3530	2
Czechoslovakia	49	13	3760	4½
Hungary	36	10	1670	1½
Romania	92	17	1220	¾
Bulgaria	43	8	610	*
Yugoslavia	98	18	470	¾
Albania	11	1	?	*
China	4120	600	160	3
Mongolian P.R.[1]	684	1	?	*
North Korea[2]	49	8	?	*
North Viet Nam[3]	63	10(?)	40(?)	*

* Negligible output or no production.

1. Mongolian People's Republic.
2. Democratic People's Republic of Korea.
3. Democratic Republic of Viet Nam.
4. Estimated consumption of commercial sources of energy expressed in terms of coal equivalent, kilograms per inhabitant in 1955.
5. Steel output in millions of metric tons, 1955.

Although apparently held together by the common interests of the Communist Parties that control the member states, the communist bloc has not been the solid unit its leaders have made it out to be. Since Stalin's death, in particular, it has become evident that there are many possible versions of communism. Even so, there is a high degree of economic self-sufficiency within the bloc, and the need for this has undoubtedly been dictated partly by the ban imposed by the U.S.A. and its allies on the export of many commodities to communist countries. The interdependence of the members of the communist bloc has been further reinforced by China's need for financial aid, equipment, and technicians, which have been provided by the U.S.S.R. and East Europe.

In several ways the communist bloc is artificial and improvised. Both China and the communist countries of East Europe surely appreciate, even if they say little about it, that the Soviet Communist Party has not only inherited the old Russian Empire but also the expansionist policies of its leaders. Present Soviet influence in East Europe is one of the most recent of many examples of a strong European nation interfering with the independence of smaller European nations – in this case influencing their political and economic life. On the other side of the communist bloc, Soviet relations with China are bound to be affected by the problems arising from contact by a former European empire builder and a non-European power, particularly since there are now within Soviet territory many lands that once belonged to the outer Chinese Empire. The idea of Soviet dominance is reinforced by the seniority (in terms of length of time in power) of the Soviet Communist Party, and by the great industrial capacity and unquestionable military superiority of the Soviet Union.

At all events, the postwar trend has been for trade to expand between the member countries of the communist bloc, but this itself has been difficult on account of the inadequacy of rail and sea links between the main industrial centres of East Europe and European U.S.S.R. on the one hand and eastern China on the other.[1] These two main concentrations of population in the communist bloc are separated by several thousand miles of thinly populated or uninhabited desert, forest, and mountain country, across which there is at present for a considerable distance (between Novosibirsk and Ulan-Ude) only one double-track railway (see fig. 29) and no motor roads. As well as being the only railway between Europe and China, the Trans-Siberian Railway is also the only land route between the Soviet Far East

1. See *Times Review of Industry*, Dec. 1957, p. 79, for a very useful article on this topic.

29. The communist bloc, showing routes across and round it. Projection: oblique zenithal equidistant. Centre of projection: Alma-Ata, Kazakh Republic, U.S.S.R.

region and the rest of the U.S.S.R., and the amount of traffic that it can carry between China and European U.S.S.R. must therefore be very limited (in Anglo-America there are about 10 trans-continental railways). Goods are also carried by sea, by the Northern Sea Route, when this is ice-free for 2–3 months in the summer, and via the Suez Canal for the whole year (but when this was blocked in 1956–7 Soviet vessels used the Panama Canal). Table 20 shows how great distances are between the two main concentrations of population in the communist bloc.

228

The Communist States

Furthermore, it should be remembered that the merchant fleet at the disposal of the 900 m. inhabitants of the communist countries is very small indeed. Although it is now possible to cover the 3500 miles from Moscow to Peking by air in eight hours, it will be a long time before the journey for all but the lightest and most valuable goods takes less than several weeks, whether by rail (even over the line to be opened in 1960 between Alma-Ata and Lanchow) or by sea.

The following table shows some distances (in statute miles) between Europe and the Far East.

TABLE 20

By	From	Via	To	Miles
Rail	Moscow	Soviet territory	Vladivostok	5,400
Rail	Moscow	Across Manchuria	Vladivostok	4,800
Rail	Moscow	Across Mongolia	Peking	4,400
Sea	Archangel	Northern Sea Route	Vladivostok	7,100
Sea	Odessa	Suez Canal	Vladivostok	10,800
Sea	Leningrad	Panama Canal	Vladivostok	15,600
Sea	Western Europe		New York	about 3,000
Rail	New York		San Francisco	about 3,000

The table appears in a short article on the subject of communist bloc sea routes in the *Manchester Guardian*, 21 Feb. 1957.

PART THREE

During the Second World War the U.S.A. and the U.S.S.R. emerged as the two major influences on world affairs. Some of the more important features of each are outlined in chs 8 and 9, with more space devoted to the Soviet Union than to the United States because less is easily available on it in English. Ch. 9 also contains a comparison of the two giant states, since Soviet leaders have committed themselves to overtake their rival in industrial production during the next fifteen years. Some aspects of the U.K. as a world power are discussed in ch. 10.

Chapter 8

THE SOVIET UNION[1]

I. TERRITORIAL EXPANSION OF RUSSIA[2]

THE state of Kiev, known as Rus, was in existence more than a thousand years ago. It was located in the lands between the Baltic and Black Seas, inhabited by East Slav peoples. By 1223, when the first Tatar invasion of European Russia took place, Rus had broken up into a number of principalities. Most of these were overrun and subjugated by Mongol and Tatar invaders in the 13th century. Only in the northwest, in the lands of Novgorod, did the Russians remain largely independent of their Asian conquerors. By about 1450, however, Asian influence was weakening and the principality of Moscow had already gained control over a considerable part of central European Russia. Between that date and 1533, when Ivan IV became Tsar, the Russian state in Europe expanded rapidly, absorbing the lands of Novgorod to the northwest, north, and northeast and recovering territory to the south from the Asian invaders. At this period Russia was emerging as a nation and becoming powerful enough to begin large-scale empire building in lands not inhabited by Europeans (see ch. 2).

Soon after the accession of Ivan IV in 1533, the Russians penetrated east and southeast to establish footholds on the Volga, capturing Kazan and Astrakhan on the middle and lower Volga in the 1550s. Eastward penetration into the coniferous forests of Siberia followed, and by the 1640s Russian explorers had reached the shores of the Pacific Ocean at points several thousand miles to the east of Moscow. By 1689, when the Treaty of Nerchinsk was signed between Russia and China, limiting further southward expansion by the Russians into Asia, several

1. In order that the reader may follow up various points and refer to the sources of the statistical data and controversial statements in this chapter a large number of references are given at the end of the chapter. Numbers in brackets in the chapter will be found here.

2. The reader is advised to refer to fig. 30 while reading this section.

million square miles of territory had already been annexed by Russia.

Siberia, which was several times as large as the Russia of 1533, was inhabited only by small scattered tribes, the members of which lived (and still do) by hunting, fishing, and reindeer herding. Climatic conditions in Siberia were even more harsh than those in European Russia, with long severe winters and spring flooding.

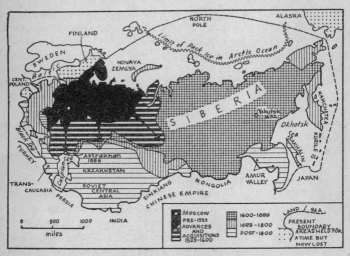

30. The growth of the Russian Empire, 1533 to the present. For a more detailed map of boundary changes in European Russia see fig. 31.

The Russian invaders moved mainly along the rivers. There was almost no cultivable land in the areas acquired in the 17th century. Few Russian colonists followed the soldiers, administrators, men of religion, and traders, largely because there were more favourable lands to settle nearer home and because movement was so slow and difficult anyway. There was abundant timber, but this commodity was not lacking in European Russia itself. There were also gold and furs, and these attracted some settlers, although the Russians did not colonize Siberia in large numbers until the present century, after the construction of the Trans-Siberian Railway.

After 1689 the eastward thrust of the Russians continued across the Bering Strait into North America. Alaska was annexed and a line of forts was established along the Pacific coast. The most southerly, Fort Ross, established by the Russians in 1812, was only sixty miles northwest of San Francisco, in what was then a Spanish colony and is now the state of California, U.S.A. Fort Ross was more than 9000 miles from Moscow by overland route across Siberia and then by sea along the Pacific coast. In this way the Russians and Spaniards, who had set out from opposite ends of Europe, and in different directions, met, after almost three centuries, on the other side of the world.

After the accession of Peter in 1682, interest in territorial expansion shifted to European Russia, and in spite of the drive into North America in the 18th century, efforts were largely concentrated on regaining lands inhabited by Russians and Ukrainians from foreign domination and on establishing footholds on the Baltic[1] and Black Seas, partly at the expense of the Ottoman Empire (Odessa and the Crimea were taken towards the end of the century). In Europe, the Russians were fighting the Swedes, Turks, and other peoples who were better equipped to resist Russian penetration than the tribes of Siberia had been in the previous century. Territorial gains were relatively small, though important. During and after the Napoleonic Wars, Finland and Poland were added to the Russian Empire, but at this time Russian interest in Asia was reviving, and three great advances were made there during the 19th century. Transcaucasia was overrun early in the century, Central Asia was gradually annexed between about 1840 and 1900, and the Amur valley and Sakhalin Island in East Asia were also taken during this period.

The Russian Empire in Europe and Asia reached its greatest extent by about 1900, though in 1867 Alaska had been sold to the U.S.A. for $U.S. 7,200,000, and Russia had thus lost its foothold in North America. Territory was lost in the war with Japan

1. Work began on the construction of the settlement of St Petersburg (now Leningrad) in 1703. The city was the capital of Russia between 1714 and 1918.

(1904–5) and during the First World War and the subsequent period of foreign intervention in Russia. The U.S.S.R. regained some of these lands, together with some other relatively small areas, only after the Second World War. The present territory of the U.S.S.R. is still slightly smaller than the Russian Empire was in 1900 (see fig. 31 for frontier changes in Europe), and it is obviously inaccurate, therefore, to talk of Soviet territorial expansion during the present century, though Soviet influence has, of course, been extended, without the actual annexation of territory, into East Europe and, to a lesser extent, into China. During the interwar period the U.S.S.R. claimed as Soviet territorial waters all of the Arctic Ocean lying between its northern coast and the North Pole, while possession of the Kurile Islands since 1945 has given it virtual control over the Okhotsk Sea.

During the last four hundred years, therefore, Russia has developed from a European state of modest dimensions into the largest state in the world, covering not much less than one-sixth of the total land area of the earth's surface excluding Antarctica. The strength of the U.S.S.R. lies in the fact that it is continuous and compact (and in this respect it may be compared with the U.S.A.) whereas the sea empires built up by other European powers during the same period have been scattered over the world and held together only by long, vulnerable sea routes.

II. INDUSTRIAL DEVELOPMENT IN RUSSIA

ALTHOUGH the expansion of certain branches of industry has been spectacular in the U.S.S.R. during the Soviet period, it is a mistake to assume that there were no industries in Russia before this. Before 1700 there were numerous ironworks in the area between Moscow and Tula and many small industrial establishments elsewhere in European Russia. During and after the reign of Peter the Great (1682–1725) Russians were sent to Western Europe for technical education, and foreign technicians were brought into the country. Shipbuilding industries were established in St Petersburg and Archangel, and what in the 18th century became one of the largest iron industries in Europe was developed

KEY (within map):
1914 BOUNDARY OF RUSSIA
INTER-WAR BOUNDARY
BOUNDARY ESTABLISHED IN 1945
AREAS HELD BEFORE 1914 BUT NOT NOW
AREAS HELD NOW BUT NOT BEFORE 1914
WESTERN AND SOUTHERN LIMITS OF COMMUNIST BLOC IN EUROPE EXCEPT YUGOSLAVIA

White Sea

SWEDEN

FINLAND

Helsinki

Leningrad

Stockholm

Baltic Sea

Moscow

Riga

Minsk

Hamburg

Berlin

Warsaw

Kiev

Prague

Vienna

Odessa

Budapest

Belgrade

Bucharest

Adriatic Sea

Sofia

Black Sea

Rome

Istanbul

TURKEY

0   250
miles

31. Changes in the European boundary of Russia during the 20th century.

237

in the Urals. Most of the iron produced was used in the manufacture of armaments and agricultural implements. Towards the end of the 18th century Russia was the world's largest producer of iron and was even exporting some to England.

In the 19th century a textile industry, protected by tariff barriers, was built up in the area around Ivanovo, to the northeast of Moscow, and foreign capital, machinery, technicians, and, until late in the century, cotton, were imported. The construction of railways in the 1860s and 70s in the Ukraine made it possible to transport the iron ore of Krivoy Rog to the coking coal of the Donbass (Donets basin), where a large iron and steel industry grew up, also with the help of foreign capital and technicians. In the 1890s, once again with foreign capital, large-scale oil production began in the Baku area, and in 1900 Russia was producing about half of the world's oil. On the eve of the First World War, therefore, Russia was already an industrial country of some importance, although in capacity and efficiency its industries were far behind those in the U.S.A. and the leading industrial nations of Western Europe. The following industrial areas could be distinguished (see fig. 32):

1. The Moscow (or central) region, with light industries (mainly cotton textiles). 2. The Donbass and associated centres of mining and manufacture, producing five-sixths of Russia's coal (about 25 m. tons per year) and most of its iron and steel goods. 3. The moribund iron industry of the Urals, which was still run on charcoal and therefore unable to compete with the Donbass (in 1913, about 20 per cent of Russia's iron came from the Urals, 70 per cent from the Donbass). 4. Individual centres, mostly ports, with special industries: Baku and Batum (oil refining), Odessa, Archangel, and St Petersburg. 5. Poland, with textile and other industries (this part of the Russian Empire was lost during the Second World War).

Industrial development during the Soviet period may be summarized thus:

1. Pre-1928: the rehabilitation of war-damaged industries in the areas already mentioned and the inauguration of a plan (GOELRO) to electrify European Russia. Lenin attached great importance to electricity, and is often quoted as saying: 'Com-

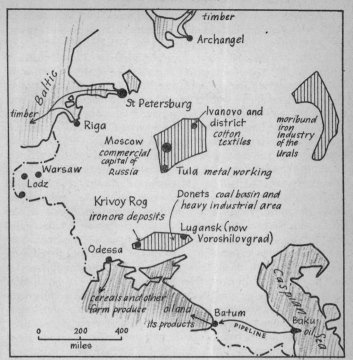

32. Industrial areas and centres in Russia before the First World War.

munism is Soviet rule plus the electrification of the whole country.'

2. 1928–41, the first three 5-Year Plans. During this period Soviet industrial capacity was greatly expanded, new branches of industry introduced (engineering and chemicals, in particular), fresh sources of minerals exploited, and factories constructed in parts of the U.S.S.R. where previously there had been little or no industrial development. The most spectacular achievement of this period was, perhaps, the Urals-Kuzbass *kombinat* (see ch. 7) using Urals iron ore and Kuzbass (and later Karaganda)

coking coal to build up an iron and steel industry which in
capacity now rivals the Donbass industry (itself greatly expanded
since 1928).

3. 1941–50, the war and the postwar rehabilitation of industry.
Much of the Soviet industrial capacity in European U.S.S.R.
was destroyed during the war, but the Volga towns, Urals, and
Kuzbass developed rapidly. The Fourth (postwar) 5-Year Plan
(1946–50) was devoted largely to reconstructing war-damaged
areas. During the war and postwar period, however, attempts
were also made to introduce some degree of industrial self-
sufficiency in the regions most distant from European U.S.S.R.,
including Transcaucasia, Central Asia, and the Soviet Far East.

4. 1951–60, two 5-Year Plan periods (in 1957 the 1956–60
Plan was modified) with the emphasis still on the development
of heavy industry and the production of capital goods at the
expense of the consumer, and with further attempts at decentralization. Decentralization has been encouraged by the formation
(in 1957) of 105 local planning councils to reduce the influence of
centralized management, thus making the planning and management of industry more flexible. Features of the 1950s have been
the training of large numbers of technicians, the first commercial
production of atomic power, the beginnings of automation, and
rapid advances in certain branches of industry, particularly
engineering (no doubt with the help of scientists from East
Europe), to bring the U.S.S.R. up to the level of Western Europe
and the U.S.A. at least in some aspects of industry. Spectacular
achievements have been the completion of the world's largest
hydro-electric power station on the Volga near Kuybyshev, the
expansion of oil production in the Volga-Ural field from about
15 m. tons in 1950 to about 55 m. tons in 1956, and the doubling
of Soviet steel production between 1950 and 1957. One important
long-term undertaking, started in the current 5-Year Plan, is the
project to build up a third heavy industrial base (to rival the
Donbass and Urals) in Eastern Siberia, in the region of Lake
Baykal.

III. AIMS AND METHODS OF THE COMMUNIST REGIME

IN November 1957 the Communist Party of the U.S.S.R. celebrated the 40th anniversary of its accession to (or acquisition of) power in Russia. Although the leadership has changed hands several times during that period and a new generation has almost completely replaced the revolutionaries who gained control in Russia in 1917 and established a communist regime, the Soviet communist leaders have consistently adhered to a number of aims. Firstly, they have pledged themselves continually to raise the material and cultural standards of the Soviet people on the basis of the utmost development of productive forces (1). Secondly, they intend that eventually *per caput* production in all branches of the economy of the U.S.S.R. shall be higher than in any of the leading capitalist countries of the world (2). Thirdly, they await, and encourage wherever they can, the downfall of the capitalist system. A further aim appears to be to ensure that the Soviet Communist Party, as the most experienced, should control or at least guide all other Communist Parties as they are established in other parts of the world.

All this means that the main purpose of the Soviet Communist Party has been to turn the U.S.S.R. into a powerful industrial country. During the interwar years efforts were made to raise total industrial capacity to the level of that of Germany and the U.K., the most powerful nations of Europe. Since the Second World War the U.S.S.R. has passed these in absolute output (*but not in* per caput *output*, for it has four times as many people) and in some branches of production is now challenging the U.S.A. The ultimate aim of the present Soviet leaders appears to be eventually to surpass the U.S.A. in industrial strength (see also ch. 9) and to overtake all capitalist countries in *per caput* output. This has been called by Khrushchev 'our basic economic task'. But it has been pointed out in *Pravda* (3) that the capitalist countries themselves will be expanding.

The Soviet leaders assume that they will be able to catch up and overtake the leading capitalist countries in *per caput* production because of the 'fact' that 'the socialist mode of production possesses decisive advantages over the capitalist mode of production' (4). They show that the tempo of industrial expansion has been more rapid in the U.S.S.R. during the last forty years than in non-communist countries *during the same period*. The claim is discussed later in this section, and in ch. 9, section IV.

Another matter that must be borne in mind in any consideration of the U.S.S.R. is the assumption of the Soviet leaders that sooner or later all countries will turn to communism (5). Only the reader who accepts without any reservations the interpretation of history believed by communists, will be of the opinion that communism must inevitably follow capitalism. A further questionable point is whether present Soviet socialism (for communism has not yet been reached) is in reality Marxist, or even Leninist, or even anything approaching socialism or communism, whatever these are. To what extent is Soviet communism a continuation of Russian nationalism? Is not the Soviet Communist Party merely a group of ruthless individuals maintaining itself in power in Russia, maintaining the Russian hold over the Ukrainian and other national minorities in the Soviet Union, and using the former Russian Empire as an instrument to extend its influence over other parts of the world? At all events, it is essential to distinguish between Communist Parties and communism and, further, to remember that Communist Parties contain only a small and carefully selected minority of the inhabitants of the countries they rule. The other members of the community are *not* therefore Communist Party members.

The communists have attempted to eliminate the idea of Russian superiority and domination in the U.S.S.R. Very soon after the establishment of the communist regime the former colonies of the Russian Empire, as well as other European peoples within the Empire, such as the Ukrainians and Belorussians, were given theoretical independence within the Union. In Soviet publications the term Russian is not used to refer to the whole of the U.S.S.R., yet this policy of keeping the idea of Russian domination in the background has not prevented many heroes of Russian history from being rehabilitated, while Soviet history books teach that in the past the Russians have been more enlightened colonizers than other Europeans. It is difficult to believe, therefore, that the Soviet communists have not inherited some of the traditions of tsarist Russian nationalism and empire building. The Soviet leaders differ from their tsarist predecessors only in that they run the economy of the country more efficiently (at least by Russian standards).

Some of the methods employed to achieve the aims of the Soviet Communist Party have varied from one period to another, but in general there has been little change in Soviet policy. The policy of the country is made by the Communist Party. This has now between seven and eight million full members (6) though most young citizens are for a time Young Communists (*komsomoltsy*). There is therefore only about one party member to thirty ordinary citizens. The Communist Party does not tolerate any political opposition. It maintains itself by means of a strong police force and controls all activities in the country by means of its members, who are distributed throughout the community. It dominates the press and broadcasting, decides what may be published, and has hitherto kept a very strict control on the movement into and out of the Soviet Union of individuals, literature, correspondence, and even goods.

By controlling all means of production the Communist Party of the Soviet Union has been able to plan centrally the economic development of the country over the last forty years. Production targets are used to boost output, and rewards, material as well as non-material, are given to individuals and groups of workers who work outstandingly well or who help to introduce innovations. Although they realize that high standards of living can be achieved only if all branches of the economy are developed harmoniously, the Soviet leaders have so far almost constantly given priority to the expansion of mining and heavy industry. They have greatly increased the output of steel and other metals and have built up an engineering industry almost from nothing. Their obsession with heavy industry has forced them to neglect light industry and to attach less importance than they might have done to achieving greater production in agriculture, which they assumed, perhaps, would automatically result from collectivization in the early 1930s.

The control of economic development and investment by a

central planning authority has led to a form of state capitalism. Instead of the consumer being exploited by a continually diminishing number of large companies or monopolies, as, according to the communists, has been happening in the more advanced capitalist industrial countries, the Soviet consumer is almost completely at the mercy of one monopoly, the State, which decides, at least in industry, what can and what cannot be produced. In other words, it appears merely to have gone a stage further into capitalism than the U.S.A., U.K., and other industrial powers.

To build up their industries, the Soviets have not hesitated to make use of technical innovations and experience from capitalist countries. Khrushchev pointed out (7): 'we must study capitalist economy attentively and not take an over-simplified view of Lenin's thesis on the decay of imperialism, but study the best that the capitalist countries' science and technology have to offer, so as to use the achievements of world technological progress in the interests of socialism'.

As mentioned earlier in this section, a very important method of flattering the achievements of the U.S.S.R. under the Soviet regime has been the publication of changes in output as percentage increases (or very rarely, decreases) on a previous year or period. Very few absolute production figures were published between the 1930s and 1956, when important sources of statistical data began to appear again. Even now no absolute figures are available for the production of many crops, minerals, and manufactures, and surely it is not modesty that prevents their publication but rather considerations of security or fear that they would seem very small if compared with figures from other countries.

Hitherto, Soviet propagandists have taken advantage, when presenting their percentage increases, of the fact that Soviet mining and industry has expanded from modest beginnings in the 1920s. It is significant that they rarely do the same for agriculture, in which there have been decreases as well as increases during the Soviet period. The following fictitious example illustrates the method: in a given year there is only one factory producing cycles. It turns out 10,000 per annum. The next year another cycle factory is opened. It also produces 10,000 per annum. The output of cycles has increased in a year by 100 per cent. If another of the same capacity is opened the next year, however, it means that only 10,000 additional cycles will be produced, against 20,000 already being produced in the two previous factories, an increase of only 50 per cent in that year. As time goes on the same absolute figure (in this example, 10,000) comes to represent a smaller and smaller percentage increase. This trend is illustrated by the following set of figures quoted by Khrushchev (8). The figures refer to the total volume of industrial production in the U.S.S.R. and the U.S.A. The 1929 figure is in each case represented as 100.

	1929	1955
U.S.S.R.	100	2049
U.S.A.	100	234

During 1929–55 Soviet industrial output increased more than 20 times, U.S. output less than 2½ times. To appreciate their true significance, however, these should be reduced to absolute figures. If Soviet production in 1929 was equal to 1 unit, U.S. production was at least equal to 20 units (it is impossible, of course, to compare the volume precisely). The table should thus be shown more fairly as follows:

	1929	1955
U.S.S.R.	1	20½
U.S.A.	20	47

In absolute terms the U.S. increase from 20 to 47 was equal to 27 units, the Soviet increase from 1 to 20½, to 19½ units. Output per worker, which, as Soviet politicians agree, is what really matters, is still between two and three times as great in industry (and more than five times as great in agriculture) in the U.S.A. as in the U.S.S.R.

Now that production is high in absolute terms in many branches of the Soviet economy it is possible to show, by the very methods used up to now by communist propagandists, that industrial output is increasing *more rapidly* in certain other countries than in the U.S.S.R. Take as an example steel production in Brazil and the Soviet Union. The 1938 figure is in each case represented as 100.

	1938	1948	1954	1960
Brazil	100	525	1280	2180
U.S.S.R.	100	103	250	380

Even if we take into account the destruction of Soviet capacity in the war, these figures are not flattering to the Soviet Union unless it is appreciated that 100 for Brazil in 1938 represents a mere 92,000 tons of steel while 100 for the U.S.S.R. in that year is 18,100,000 tons. Yet the Soviet oil industry does come off very badly when compared with that of Venezuela even in absolute terms. There are more than 30 times as many people in the U.S.S.R. as in Venezuela. In table 21 both relative increases and absolute production figures are shown.

TABLE 21

	1935	1945	1954	1956	
Venezuela	100	214	460	586	
U.S.S.R.	100	76	236	336	1935 = 100
Venezuela	22	47	101	129	*millions of*
U.S.S.R.	25	19	59	84	*tons*

An attempt has been made, by means of these examples, to show how easy it is to be misled about the significance of figures. The reader will surely agree that when percentage increases are shown, their absolute value should also be taken into consideration. Soviet propagandists are beginning to appreciate that as time goes on they will not be able to show the high percentage increases that they could in the earlier period of development, and in one number of *Pravda* (9) it was remarked that a 1 per cent increase of Soviet industrial production meant more in absolute terms in 1957 than in any previous year. This method of showing production increases can therefore be misleading, for Soviet leaders have been attempting to deceive not only the whole world, but themselves as well, and the flatteringly high percentages have led them to assume that their methods of production were superior to any others.

IV. ACHIEVEMENTS OF THE SOVIET COMMUNISTS

SINCE the influence of the U.S.S.R. on world affairs has been growing so remarkably in recent years and since opinions differ so much as to the magnitude of material achievements, it is important to have some idea of what has been done there in the Soviet period. When considering what has been achieved in the U.S.S.R. during this period it should be remembered that of 40 years, 18 have been taken up with wars and postwar reconstruction.

The importance attached by Soviet planners to heavy industry is shown in the following words of Khrushchev (10): 'Guided by the behests of the great Lenin, the Communist Party of the Soviet Union has always worked steadfastly to ensure the priority development of heavy industry'. The following relative and absolute figures (11) are sufficient to give the reader an idea of the remarkable expansion in some important branches of mining and heavy industry (even though the 1956 increase is based on a fairly modest 1913 figure):

TABLE 22

Increase in output, 1913–56:

Coal (and lignite to its hard coal equivalent)	12 times
Oil	10 times
Electricity	100 times
Steel	11 times
Cement	13 times
Engineering and metal-working	180 times

During this period population increased from about 160 m. to 200 m.

Increase in output, absolute figures:

	1913	1928	1940	1955
Coal[1,3]	30	33	149	314
Oil[1]	10	12	31	71
Electricity[2]	2	5	48	170
Steel[1]	4	4	18	45
Cement[1]	2	2	6	22

1. Millions of metric tons.
2. Milliards of kwh.
3. And lignite reduced to its hard coal equivalent.

In light industry less has been achieved. According to Soviet figures (12) production of consumer goods has increased nine times between 1928 and 1955. Except in cotton manufacture, however, factory production was so small in 1928 that the increase does not make the present absolute figure high, and recently published data (13) for the production of textiles, household appliances, radios, cycles, and other such articles show that the U.S.S.R. lags far behind the industrial nations of Western Europe and the U.S.A. Khrushchev said in 1956 (14): 'The time is not far distant when in the U.S.S.R. atomic energy and other achievements of modern science and technology will be placed at the service of man on a large scale ... *which will ensure an abundance of foodstuffs and other consumer goods*.' Shortages must still therefore exist. Further, we have the word of Malenkov in 1953 (15) that many Soviet goods are poorly produced and that the Soviet shopper often prefers to buy foreign-made articles when he has the opportunity.

In its policy towards agriculture the Soviet Communist Party has been less successful than in industry. More than half of the total population of the U.S.S.R. (56·6 per cent in 1956) lives in rural types of settlements. There are some 20 m. families or probably about 90 m. individuals in collective farms (*kolkhoz*). In state farms (*sovkhoz*) and all other kinds of agricultural undertaking there are more than 2½ m. workers, and therefore, with dependants, another 10 m. individuals altogether. It is safe to say that at least 100 m. people, out of a total population of 200 m., are connected with farming, and that probably 40–50 m. are full or part-time farm workers. This means that on the average a Soviet farm worker produces food and other agricultural items for himself and three or four other people. Here, rather than in industry, therefore, is the great contrast between the U.S.S.R. and the countries that it hopes eventually to overtake in *per caput* production, for in the U.S.A. there are now only about 7 m. full-time farm workers and another 3 m. part time producing for a population of about 170 m. An average U.S. farmer or farm worker produces for nearly 20 other citizens. In Australia output per farm worker is even higher, since half a million agricultural workers satisfy the needs of 10 m. Australians and, in addition, produce one-third of the world's wool, and export enough wheat, meat, dairy produce, and fruit to feed several million people in Europe and elsewhere. In the U.K. also an average farm worker produces many times more than a Soviet farm worker.

According to recently published Soviet figures (16) little more was being produced in agriculture per inhabitant in 1953 than in 1913. Farming, particularly livestock raising, was adversely affected by the wars and also, contrary no doubt to communist expectations, by the process of collectivization, which took place mainly in the early 1930s. Recently published Soviet figures show (16) for example, that the number of cattle dropped from 60 m. in 1928 to $33\frac{1}{2}$ m. in 1934 and the number of sheep and goats fell over the same period from 107 m. to $36\frac{1}{2}$ m. In 1953 there were still only 57 m. cattle and 110 m. sheep and goats. Collectivization had two main aims, one to increase output per farm worker, the other to increase output per unit of area. In the first it succeeded insofar as it facilitated the widespread introduction of machinery and released workers from the land to move into mining and industry. In the second its success was very limited and the reason, surely, is that the widespread application of fertilizer rather than the introduction of collectivization is the key to higher yields.

Agriculture appears to have been neglected during the Stalin period. After his death, in 1953, however, the new Soviet leaders began to give serious consideration to increasing farm output (see a useful article·in *Pravda*, 12 July 1957, pp. 3–4, on this subject). In 1953 it was pointed out (17) that between 1940 and 1953 the tempo of development in agriculture compared very unfavourably with that in industry. Farm output was up only 10 per cent during that period whereas industrial output had increased by 130 per cent. In 1956, Khrushchev stated (18): 'the central committee (of the Soviet Communist Party) has brought to light serious shortcomings and mistakes in the guidance of agriculture'. In April 1957 *Pravda* (19) announced that it was 'a vitally important task' to try to produce more grain, industrial crops, and livestock (and this, indeed, accounts for almost all the farm production). Recently a campaign has been started (and given prominence in *Pravda* (20)) to raise the production of meat, milk, and fats, so that more of these commodities will be produced per citizen (but not, of course, per farm worker) in the U.S.S.R. than in the U.S.A. It turned out that to do this, meat production would have to be increased three times. What, one might ask, has been happening to Soviet meat production over the last forty years? And what guarantee is there that, at last, after thirty years of mixed failure and success under Soviet planners, agriculture will suddenly improve and that, as suggested in the 1956–60 Five-Year Plan directives, output will be doubled between 1955 and 1960?

One feature of the new Soviet leaders is their willingness to criticize the organization of the Soviet economy (though not the idea of communism itself). Yet when referring to shortcomings in farming they have put most of the blame on bureaucrats who run collective farms inefficiently, speculators who commit such sins as buying foodstuffs destined for human beings to feed to their animals (21), and collective farm workers who devote their energies to cultivating their own small plots of land while neglecting the collective farm itself. They have failed to appreciate (or to admit) that some aspects of collectivization itself may be the cause of the trouble and that the peasant, anywhere in the world, likes nothing better than to own the land he works, rather than to work it either for a private landowner or for the state,[1] via collective and state farms. But education and propaganda can work wonders and it is possible that a new generation of farm workers, accustomed to the present system, may already be replacing its discontented parents and grandparents.

The Soviet attitude to agriculture is summarized in the following statement in *Pravda* (22): 'We salute the union of the working class (*rabochiy klass* = industrial workers) and the collective farm peasantry (*kolkhoznyy khrestyanstvo*) under the leadership of the working class – the unshakeable foundation of the Soviet organization !' For forty years everything has been done to foster industrial development and to get as much as possible out of Soviet agriculture without putting anything back. Soviet leaders appear to be aware of this situation and at last they are attempting to do something about it.

Since 1953, very extensive new lands have been ploughed for wheat cultivation for the first time in Western Siberia and Kazakhstan and the Soviet grain harvest in 1956 was far larger

1. It is ironical that many of the members of Italy's large Communist Party are farm labourers who work for landowners of large estates.

The Soviet Union

than in any previous year, though in 1957 the weather in those regions was not so kind and the grain harvest was much smaller there than in 1956. Conditions in the new areas are far from ideal for wheat growing and in any year a dry growing season could greatly reduce or even completely ruin the harvest.

Another favourite theme of Khrushchev is the expansion of maize cultivation. Impressed, no doubt, by reports of the success of U.S. farmers in the corn (maize) belt of the Middle West of the U.S.A., he has recently been advocating the widespread introduction of maize in the U.S.S.R. (23). An elementary knowledge of conditions necessary for its cultivation would have shown him that in the Soviet Union the relatively small Georgian republic is the only region in which conditions are ideal for its growth. It was being cultivated there long before Khrushchev was born (but during the Soviet period has largely been replaced there by tea).

Surely Soviet planners will one day realize that there is no easy way of increasing agricultural output. Stalin's grandiose plan to transform nature (and particularly the climate) by planting belts of trees in dry steppe and semi-desert country has largely been abandoned. Khrushchev thought that the introduction of maize would being great benefits to Soviet agriculture. In ch. 7 it was shown that only a small part of the U.S.S.R. is good farmland. Elsewhere not even a communist regime can prevent a run of dry summers from completely upsetting farm production targets. Not even a communist farmer can extend cultivation into the arid lands of Central Asia (at least without irrigation) or into the podsol soils of the great zone of coniferous forest, which covers half the of U.S.S.R.

An efficient system of transportation is essential in a country such as the U.S.S.R., in which there is a considerable degree of regional specialization of production. For several reasons it has been extremely difficult to develop an adequate system of transport and communications in the U.S.S.R. Firstly, in such a large country distances between the various centres of production are great. Secondly, climatic conditions, which include heavy snowfalls, frosts, and flooding in many areas, make rail and road construction and maintenance difficult.

About 85 per cent of all the goods carried in the U.S.S.R. are handled by the railways and during the Soviet period efforts have been concentrated on improving and extending the system inherited from the tsarist period. Although important new lines have been built and the railways are used much more heavily than they were, Khrushchev stated recently (24): 'it must be admitted that railway transport is lagging behind technically'. During the Soviet period very little has been done to provide the country with a system of roads, while only the Volga and its tributaries are really significant for inland water transport. The Volga–Don Canal, completed in 1953, is frequently quoted as an outstanding example of communist construction. The Panama Canal, completed almost forty years previously by the Americans, makes the Volga–Don Canal appear a very modest piece of engineering in comparison. So far, relatively little has been done by the Soviets to make use of sea transport, though this form of transport is growing in importance.

The shortage of housing in urban areas is still a serious problem in the U.S.S.R. (25). Although Soviet publications frequently show large new blocks of flats in towns and recently completed dwellings for collective farmers in rural areas, destruction in the war and the priority given to the building of industrial establishments have made it impossible for adequate housing accommodation to be provided for the majority of the population. The number of urban dwellers has increased three times since 1913 and it is therefore understandable that there should be overcrowding in the towns. *Per caput* cement production is still low in the U.S.S.R., being only about one-tenth of a ton per inhabitant per annum against one-quarter of a ton in the U.K. and one-third in the U.S.A. If work has been held up on the construction of such vital enterprises as the Stalingrad dam on the Volga through a shortage of cement (26) it is hardly surprising that housing developments in Soviet urban areas should also be affected by shortages of building materials.

Great progress has been made during the Soviet period in the provision of education and health services (see *Pravda*, 2 July 1957, p. 2, for some recent social statistics). Before the 1917 Revolution about three-quarters of the population of the

Russian Empire was illiterate. Now illiteracy has almost been eliminated. A secondary education will soon be available for every child in the country. Higher educational establishments have been provided in all regions of the country and facilities for technical education have expanded many times. In 1956 there were some 6 m. trained specialists of various kinds, compared with only about 200,000 before the Revolution. A most impressive amount of literature of all kinds is now becoming available at low prices, and (unlike his non-communist counterpart) the Soviet reader, whether he likes it or not, is provided almost entirely with serious reading material. Recent evidence of Soviet progress in science has greatly impressed many people in Western Europe and the U.S.A. precisely at a time when Soviet leaders have been pointing out disadvantages in the Soviet system of education (see *Times Review of Industry*, Jan. 1958, p. 78).

In 1913 there was only one doctor per 10,000 inhabitants in the Russian Empire; now there are 17, though it should be noted that this includes dentists. Then there were only 13 hospital beds per 10,000 people, now there are 70.

One important achievement of the Soviet communist regime has been to change the administrative and economic organization of the Russian Empire. Not much more than half of the total population of the Soviet Union consists of Russians. National minorities (really groups of persons speaking the same language) range in size from the Ukrainians, of which there are more than 40 m., to small groups with only a few thousand members. Soon after gaining power in Russia, the Soviet government created a number of republics within the U.S.S.R. and in this way granted varying degrees of independence to the larger national groups. The question of how much freedom should be given to the republics is still being debated (27) and this is proof that much of the independence granted was theoretical. At all events the term colony (*koloniya*) is no longer used and former tsarist colonies have been encouraged to keep alive or revive features of their own culture. On the other hand, the paucity of published material in minority languages must make it inevitable for members seeking a higher education to read Russian. But educational facilities have been greatly improved in many of the former colonial areas, especially Transcaucasia and Central Asia, and industries have been established in regions where, in tsarist days, the only important activity was farming. It is fair to say that with the exception of certain small minorities the communist regime has treated non-Russian communities no more harshly than it has treated the Russians themselves, and in this connexion it is worth recalling that Stalin was a Georgian[1].

The present relationship between the Russians and the non-Russians in the Soviet Union is conveyed by the following lines from *Pravda*, 24 Feb. 1958, by representatives of the cotton growers of the Central Asian and Transcaucasian republics: 'The great Russian people helped us to free ourselves from the oppression and harsh exploitation of the tsarist regime and the local feudal landlords, with the aid of the Russian people we acquired independence as states and now in the friendly family of all the peoples of our motherland the Uzbek, Turkmen, Tadjik, Azerbaijan, Kazakh, Kirgiz, and Armenian peoples confidently move towards the building of communism in our country. We express from our hearts warm thanks to our elder brother – to the Russian people, for our good fortune to live and unceasingly to work for the happiness of all the peoples of our multi-national state.'

During the last forty years the U.S.S.R. has suffered great material losses at the hands of foreign invaders. Furthermore, hostile propaganda from non-communist countries has helped to create misunderstandings and to keep the Soviet Communist Party constantly alert to the possibility of further attacks. At the same time it has provided a pretext for maintaining what might almost be called a state emergency. Under these circumstances it is hardly surprising that appreciable material progress has been made only in certain branches of the country's economic and cultural life. The remarkable development of the engineering industry contrasts with the very slight progress made in providing an adequate system of roads, while the great advances made in

1. It was as strange for the Russians to have a Georgian premier as it would be for Great Britain to have, for example, a Maltese or Cypriot prime minister.

technical education are offset by the almost complete lack of progress in literature, painting, and architecture.

What have the Russians and the other citizens of the U.S.S.R. gained as a result of forty years of communist domination? Undoubtedly living conditions are better than they were four decades ago for most of the population, and there is the possibility that very soon they will improve appreciably, because the U.S.S.R. is a country with great mineral and forest resources and it now has a basis of heavy industry on which other branches of the economy can be built. On the other hand Soviet citizens have very little freedom in a political sense; they have been discouraged, if not prevented, from practising any religion; and they have had communist propaganda preached to them from early childhood. In spite of this, the citizens of the U.S.S.R. do not appear to have become machines; they certainly have not lost their personalities nor their ability to think and to judge about matters for themselves. In spite of what they have suffered both from the Communist Party inside the U.S.S.R. and from aggressors, particularly the German army, from outside, they do not appear to be bitter. The friendliness shown by ordinary Soviet citizens when visiting non-communist countries and the enthusiastic welcome given by the Russians indiscriminately to all foreign visitors to their own country in recent years must frequently have embarrassed the Communist Party members.

Both Party members and ordinary citizens appear to be extremely sensitive. Khrushchev says (28): 'we are criticized for not always keeping up with the latest Paris fashions and still often wearing padded jackets which are not very flattering to the wearer, but we see this ourselves and admit that it is so'. Naturally no country likes to be told that it has slavery. Khrushchev remarks (29): 'You like to call our socialist organization slavery. We, however, think that slavery for the workers, slavery for the overwhelming majority of the people, is the capitalistic set-up.' A feeling of inferiority among Russians, at least with regard to the backwardness of their country, is evident in 19th-century Russian literature. It takes the form of boasting now, and the following passage from an article in *Pravda* (30) on Air Force day, is just one example: 'In our country were designed and constructed for the first time in the world the aeroplane and glider, the hydroplane and the multi-motor machine, the parachute and radios in aircraft, and a series of other forms of aviation equipment.' To what extent, then, were the Soviet earth satellites a means of showing the world that the Russians are as capable as the other leading industrial nations of the world of making innovations in science?

Finally, one further remarkable achievement of the Soviet period should be mentioned – the new set of social classes. The Soviet picture of pre-Revolutionary Russia is a vast mass of peasantry exploited by a minority of landowning aristocrats and capitalists; a much smaller army of underpaid clerks and downtrodden industrial workers in the towns; and a small body of professional workers. This has changed to the following: the underpaid collective farm peasantry (*khrestyanstvo*); the generally more fortunate industrial workers (*rabochiye*); the office workers (*sluzhashchiye*), frequent targets for Soviet cartoonists; the professional classes (*intelligentsiya*); and, occupying a small section of each of these – the members of the Communist Party – a privileged aristocracy or nobility. Undoubtedly the party members, in general, are better off than their non-party counterparts. Khrushchev indirectly admits this himself in the following significant passage (31): 'Proper distribution of party members in the national economy is of great importance for the successful accomplishment of the tasks confronting the party. It is an abnormal situation when a considerable proportion of the Communists employed in a number of branches of the national economy are engaged in work which is not directly connected with the decisive processes of production. There are some 90,000 Communists in coal industry establishments, for example, but only 38,000 work in the mines, underground. More than 3 million party members and candidate members live in rural localities, but less than half work in the collective farms, machine and tractor stations, and state farms.'

In an interesting article on this subject (Social Differences in Soviet Russia, *Geographical Magazine*, June 1957), Mr Zev Katz concludes thus: '... it will be seen that in the Communist Soviet Union the differences between "rich" and "poor", between "haves" and "have-nots", are by no means abolished. Despite the abolition of private ownership of means of production, the Soviet élite seems to enjoy a standard of life and a series of privileges which stand in contrast to the austere life of the ordinary citizen. What accentuates these differences and privileges is the apparent contradiction between them and the supposed aims of Communism. In the end it is reality that matters and not the slogans professed or the pronouncements about the coming millennium.' The reader will find an even less flattering assessment of the achievements of the Soviet Communists in *Life* (International edition), 18 March 1957, pp. 19–35. The following lines are typical: 'The Kremlin today is like a reckless company board of directors that has been overobsessed with making its firm the biggest in the world. Now it must pause and adjust its ambitions to reality.'

V. SOVIET FOREIGN POLICY

PRESENT Soviet foreign policy can only be appreciated when two facts are borne in mind: firstly that it is the continuation, although largely in different forms, of four centuries of Russian empire building, and secondly that since 1945 Russia has changed from being merely one of a number of world powers of broadly comparable strength to being one of the two great world powers.

Soviet Communist foreign policy is very much affected by two assumptions (the first of which was discussed earlier in this chapter): that the spread of communism (or socialism) throughout the world is inevitable; and that, while this is happening, the leading capitalist countries of the world may, in order to prevent or delay economic collapse, start a war between themselves or with the U.S.S.R. Mr Khrushchev expressed the opinion that the U.S.A. is the only country that could constitute a danger to the U.S.S.R. The following remark, made during a discussion with Mr Turner Catledge, Managing Editor of the *New York Times*, in May 1957 is reported thus for readers of *Pravda* (31): 'The only country, besides the U.S.A., that might be considered a threat to the Soviet Union – says Mr Khrushchev in a joke – is Luxembourg.' Now that Soviet scientists have produced a long range intercontinental ballistic missile, there is little justification even for assuming that the U.S.A. would think of attacking the U.S.S.R.

One of the vital questions in world affairs until 1957 was the problem of whether Soviet leaders were justified in assuming that a capitalist country (and therefore the U.S.A.) would start a war against the Soviet Union. The remarkable boost given to the United States economy by the conflict that began in Korea in 1950 was taken by Soviet leaders as recent evidence that an economic crisis can be avoided by a war, thereby justifying their second assumption.[1] To support their argument that capitalist countries will attack the U.S.S.R. and other communist countries, Soviet leaders can point to the period of foreign intervention in Russia following the 1917 Revolution, and to the Nazi invasion in 1941. Since 1945 some sections of the U.S. public, not least the Russian and East European émigrés now living there, have talked of a crusade to liberate East European countries and the Russians themselves from communist domination. It is easy to have the impression that in the postwar years many Americans regarded a 'showdown' between the U.S.A. and the Soviet Union as inevitable, even if they were vague as to the form it should take and horrified at the thought that a future war might even reach North America.[2] Furthermore, until 1957 the communist leaders of the U.S.S.R. must have been alarmed at the

1. The Soviet assumption that rearmament in the U.S.A. and Western Europe since 1950 was introduced to prevent unemployment appears to have been proved wrong by present moves to reduce manpower in the forces.

2. The following passage, which must have reached tens of millions of readers, is typical of the casual way in which the American press speaks of a matter of life and death: 'One day last December a mysterious piece of hardware was carefully moved from a closely guarded seven-storey shed in California.... Nothing betrayed the presence of the most monstrous potential new weapon in democracy's arsenal – designed to be fired 5,500 miles along a trajectory reaching 500 miles above the earth's surface at speeds up to 16,000 m.p.h. to plunge an H-bomb warhead into an enemy target. Under the shroud was Atlas, a U.S. inter-continental ballistic missile (ICBM)'. See *Reader's Digest*,

vastly superior strategic position held by the U.S.A. in the world (see ch. 9) although they have not stressed this to the Russian public. Even a brief study of the location on a globe of U.S. and Soviet air bases will convince the reader of the advantageous position held by the U.S.A. until the intercontinental rocket era.

The fact remains that the U.S.A. did not exploit its superior position when it could have done, even though the idea that the U.S.A. should fight the U.S.S.R. before it could perfect its atom bomb was not infrequently expressed in the years following the war. One eminent person to point this out was Bertrand Russell: 'Either we must have a war against Russia before she has the atom bomb or we will have to lie down and let them govern us.' (Reported in the *Observer*, 21 Nov. 1948.)

On the other hand, there are many reasons why it seemed improbable that the U.S.A. would start a war against the U.S.S.R. without being provoked, even before the Soviet atom and hydrogen bombs, and rocket, appeared on the scene. The Americans have always been reluctant to become involved in wars outside their own continent and they cannot be blamed for starting or encouraging any major conflict outside what they have considered to be their sphere of influence. It was more than two years after hostilities began in Europe before Japan and Germany (in December 1941) compelled the U.S.A. to enter the Second World War. After the war, between 1945 and 1947, U.S. military expenditure decreased rapidly and from 1947 to 1950 remained very low. It is improbable that this would have happened if U.S. policy had been to build up for a war against the U.S.S.R. Fig. 33 shows U.S. expenditure on 'major national security' over the period 1934–55 (source of figures: *Statistical Abstract of the United States*, 1955, p. 224).

There is another reason why it was unlikely that the U.S. government would deliberately have started a war against the

July 1957, 'The Missiles: Tomorrow's Weapons'. Enough to make any Russian a little apprehensive. Not much more than a month after this was published, the U.S.S.R. announced that it already had an I C B M. Too bad for democracy's arsenal.

U.S.S.R. The complicated machinery that would have had to be set in motion before it could actually embark on a war precluded the possibility of a sudden aerial bombardment, yet this offered the only chance, if a slender one, of ensuring that the opponent would not retaliate.

Finally, there is the Soviet assumption that U.S. capitalists have no other aim in life than to build up for wars, yet the U.S.A. has been passing through a remarkable period of pros-

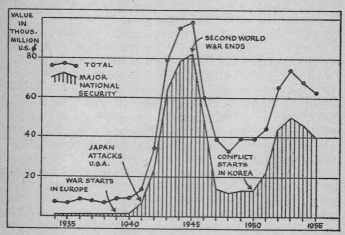

33. U.S. Federal Budget Expenditures, 1934–55. Note, the real value of the dollar tends to diminish over this period.

perity and in Latin America, Southwest Asia, and now Africa, U.S. investments and enterprises are yielding excellent profits and providing cheap raw materials (see ch. 9). Few American capitalists would wish to upset the progress of this unprecedented expansion of U.S. overseas trade and investment. The 1958 picture looks far less bright, however, and the gravity of the current recession should not be underestimated.

Turning now to the question of Soviet policy regarding the assumption that communism will eventually replace capitalism, it is essential to appreciate that a country can extend its influence not merely by annexing territory, that is, by military means, but also by political, economic, and even cultural expansion. Admittedly Russia, like the other European nations that built up empires, relied until the present century mainly on military expansion to enlarge its sphere of influence. During the Soviet period, on the contrary, other means of expansion or penetration have assumed much greater importance. Boundary changes as a result of military expansion have therefore not altered the shape of the U.S.S.R. greatly, though they have been significant (see fig. 31). During and immediately after the First World War Russia lost several small though populous provinces. During the Second World War, it regained part of what was lost and in addition acquired the northern half of East Prussia and a foothold across the Carpathians.[1] It also, of course, has established bases and kept forces in some of the countries of East Europe which it liberated from the Germans in 1944–5. Finally, it was granted bases in Finland (Porkkala) and China (Dalniy) but has now withdrawn its forces from these.

Although the establishment and maintenance of communist regimes in East Europe has depended largely on the presence of strong Soviet forces in the region it is a mistake to think of these countries as being Soviet territorial acquisitions. East Europe fell into Soviet hands somewhat unexpectedly, as a result of the war with Germany, and the Soviet leaders must realize that their control over East Europe can only be temporary. Since 1945 Soviet forces have not taken part in any conflict outside the U.S.S.R. or East Europe, and although arms have been supplied to China and North Korea in the communist bloc and to Egypt, Syria, and the Yemen outside, it seems very unlikely that any military penetration is contemplated. Almost no political boundary could now be crossed without entering a country connected by some kind of treaty with the U.S.A. or the U.K.

Whereas military penetration is difficult and dangerous, political penetration is less likely to involve the U.S.S.R. directly

1. The Transcarpathian Ukraine gives the Soviet Union a common frontier with Hungary. In 1956 this was useful, for it enabled Soviet troops to move directly from the Ukraine into Hungary without crossing Czechoslovak or Romanian territory.

in any conflict. Although most of the citizens of the non-communist world live either in advanced industrial countries, in which Soviet communism has little appeal, or in backward agricultural countries where, according to Marxist-Leninist doctrines the economy has not yet reached a stage when the inhabitants can be introduced to it, the Soviet leaders have endeavoured to spread communist influence wherever possible. They have been careful to distinguish between the oppressive ruling class on the one hand and the exploited masses on the other. They make a distinction, for example, between the German people on the one hand and the Nazi gangsters[1] and their successors, the West German leaders, on the other, or between the mass of the American people and the U.S. monopolies and generals (and might we not, therefore, distinguish between the Russian people on the one hand and the Communist Party members on the other?).

The obvious failure of communist parties to gain any appreciable following in many countries and the danger that national communist movements may break away from Soviet influence anyway may have made present Soviet leaders more ready than their predecessors of the Stalin period to establish relations with non-communist regimes in various countries of the world, rather than with communist parties themselves. The approach has therefore differed according to local circumstances. Firstly, there are countries in which the communist movement is legal and is or has been well supported. These include France, Italy, India, and Mexico. Secondly, there are countries such as the U.K. and the U.S.A. in which it is legal but has never had the sympathy of more than a small part of the population. Thirdly, there are countries in which communism has been banned or not been permitted to develop. These include many of the countries of Southwest Asia, the colonial territories of Africa, and most of the Latin American republics. Some of these have trading and other connexions with the Soviet Union while others, without even Soviet consular representation, have almost no

1. cf. C. Wilmot, *The Struggle for Europe*, p. 794. Stalin made a clear distinction between the Nazis and the German people while the U.S.A. and U.K. called for unconditional surrender.

contact at all. In Appendix 2 the reader will find a list of the countries of the world whose communist parties were represented by a speaker at the gatherings in Moscow early in November 1957 to celebrate the 40th anniversary of the Bolshevik Revolution.

Economic expansion, or the spread of influence by the establishment of trading and financial connexions with other parts of the world, differs from military and political expansion in that it can be to the advantage of both sides concerned. Russia has never been considered one of the great trading nations of the world. Before the Revolution most of the population was engaged in agriculture and each community or group of communities was to a large extent self-supporting, while during the communist period national economic self-sufficiency has almost been achieved, largely, of course, because the country is so extensive and has such a great variety of natural environments as well as every important economic mineral.

Until the Second World War, Russian exports consisted almost entirely of raw materials (timber, grain, oil) while imports were mainly manufactures. In recent years the structure of its foreign trade has for various reasons become more complex and, helped by the recent expansion of the Soviet merchant fleet, has been growing considerably in volume. Soviet foreign trade is at present of three kinds. Firstly, there is trade with other members of the communist bloc. The U.S.S.R. supplies East Europe with some food and raw materials (oil, iron ore, cotton, grain) as well as manufactures, while it receives other manufactures. In the other direction it supplies China mainly with capital goods, including equipment for mines, factories, and railways. Secondly, the U.S.S.R. trades with the non-communist countries in order to import food and raw materials that cannot be produced at home or that are at the moment in short supply. Owing to the fact that the U.S.S.R. lies outside the tropics many plants cannot be cultivated there. These include rubber, beverages such as coffee and cocoa, sugar cane, and tropical fruits. These, therefore, have to be imported if wanted, although none is vital to the Soviet economy, because synthetic rubber can be manufactured and certain latex-bearing plants are grown, while enough sugar beet could be cultivated at home to satisfy Soviet sugar needs. Owing to the difficulties in agriculture already mentioned in this chapter, the U.S.S.R. has been importing large quantities of food from Argentina, Canada, New Zealand, Denmark, and other countries while it has been a large buyer of Australian wool. Thirdly, the Soviet Union carries on trade with some non-communist countries largely for the sake of establishing contact by means of the exchange of goods. This is true of Soviet trade with countries in Southwest, South, and Southeast Asia. Soviet exports to this part of the world have consisted mainly of manufactured goods, and Soviet technicians have accompanied equipment sent to such countries as Egypt, India, and Burma.

Since the war, therefore, the Soviet Union has become a significant exporter of manufactured goods, especially engineering products, while foodstuffs and raw materials are tending to occupy a growing share of its imports. It has also made loans on favourable terms to several non-communist countries recently.

One other aspect of Soviet economic expansion is the visits to the South Atlantic since 1947 of the whaling flotilla Slava, operating from Odessa. Although the various whaling products no doubt make a useful contribution to the Soviet economy it should not be forgotten that Soviet sailors are gaining experience in navigation in sea areas where conditions differ greatly from those in the seas around the U.S.S.R.

Whether the Soviet leaders attach more importance to political or to economic expansion we shall perhaps be able to judge from their approach to the present United States recession. They may use it as a means to stir up political unrest or they may prefer to exploit it as a means of expanding trade with capitalist countries anxious to sell their products, and thus break down the existing ban on many strategic items.

Yet another form of expansion, cultural (which touches such fields as education and sport), has acquired great importance in the world in recent decades. Countries such as the U.S.A., U.K., and U.S.S.R., provide educational facilities for students of poorer countries, spend large sums of money on the dissemination of propaganda by broadcasting and by subsidizing the sale of literature, and take part in competitive sport. The Soviet communist regime has wholeheartedly entered these fields of competition and attaches much importance to their success. In the Olympic Games of 1952 and 1956 the U.S.A. and the U.S.S.R. won a large share of the medals. The Soviet attitude to sport is described by Mr Franz Stampfl in the following lines (*Observer*, 21 July 1957, p. 14): 'The conflict between East and West is not a purely political conflict but a total conflict in which sport, too, plays a big part. Quite clearly their (the Soviet) idea is to use outstanding athletes as a propaganda means and to say: "Look, our athletes prove that our way of life is better".'

Cultural contacts between the U.S.S.R. and the rest of the world in the postwar period have so far been mainly with countries in the communist bloc, with non-communist Europe (where old contacts have been revived) and with many countries of Southwest, South, and Southeast Asia. In Appendix 2 the reader will find a list of the countries outside the communist bloc with which the Soviet Union has diplomatic relations.

Partly through the efforts of the Communist Party to make the Soviet Union a powerful industrial country, partly as a result of the war, which took Soviet troops into Central Europe and into Japanese territories on the mainland of Asia, the U.S.S.R., like the U.S.A., has come to play a leading role in world affairs. The failure of Germany and Japan to retain large areas annexed by them and held only by military force has shown that outright territorial expansion is no longer a means of extending influence. The U.S.S.R. has therefore been experimenting with other means of extending its influence. In the end it may give up the idea of political expansion as well as military expansion and concentrate on economic expansion. Here trade with and the granting of aid to the poorer countries of the world would no doubt become the main field for peaceful competition with the capitalist industrial countries.

So much is written about the Soviet Union that it is difficult to form an unbiased view of the country, its people, and its achievements. Most readers will have formed their opinions about the U.S.S.R. from books and articles in English, by British and U.S. authors. To balance this inevitable one-sidedness in choice of reading matter the references for this chapter (see selected references given on pp. 316-19) have been made largely of Soviet material, some of it available in English. One recent publication of great interest (and available in English) is Mr Khrushchev's speech at the 20th Congress of the Communist Party of the Soviet Union made in February 1956.

REFERENCES IN CH. 8

(See selected references for chs 7 and 8 for details of a, b, and d below and for other publications.)

(a) *The Soviet Union in 1960:* (1) p. 8.

(b) *Report of the Central Committee, 14 Feb. 1956:* (2) p. 34; (4) p. 27; (6) p. 79; (7) p. 11; (8) p. 8; (10) p. 33; (14) p. 9; (18) p. 42; (21) p. 49; (23) p. 45; (24) p. 38; (25) p. 57; (28) p. 94; (31) p. 87.

(c) *Pravda:* (3) 30 March 1957, p. 4; (5) 17 March 1957, p. 1; (9) 7 Feb. 1957, p. 1; (19) 15 April 1957, p. 1; (20) e.g. 25 May 1957, p. 1; (22) 21 April 1957; (26) 31 Aug. 1955; (27) e.g. 24 July 1957, p. 1; (29) 14 May 1957, p. 1; (30) 30 June 1957; (31) 14 May 1957.

(d) *Narodnoye khozyaystvo SSSR, Moscow, 1956:* (11) pp. 62–79; (12) p. 46; (13) pp. 58–61; (16) pp. 96–154.

(e) Koshelev, F. P., *Novyy etap v razvitii narodnovo khozyaystva SSSR, Moscow, 1954:* (15) p. 58; (17) p. 167.

Chapter 9

THE UNITED STATES OF AMERICA

I. TERRITORIAL EXPANSION OF THE U.S.A.

THE U.S.A. has been an independent state for not much more than 150 years. In this respect, then, it contrasts with Russia, which, as the Moscow principality, was emerging as a powerful state almost 500 years ago. Yet since 1783 the U.S.A. has passed Russia in industrial output, rivalled it in agricultural production, and approached it in population. Both have expanded towards the Pacific, Russia eastwards from an original nucleus in Europe, the U.S.A. westwards from a nucleus on the Atlantic coast, facing Europe, its main source of immigrants.

Although the population of North America is now almost entirely English speaking, the continent attracted the interest of several European nations after the discovery of America. Until the 19th century Florida and what is now Southwest U.S.A. were northerly extensions of the Spanish American Empire. England, France, and Holland all approached from the east and annexed territories along the Atlantic side of the continent. In the 18th century the Russians entered across the Bering Strait to occupy Alaska and the Pacific coast as far south as Spanish California. In 1700, after a century of colonization, the English settlements in the lowland between the Atlantic and the Appalachians, with fewer than 300,000 inhabitants, did not look like the nucleus of a state destined to extend across the continent to the Pacific coast, but in 1783, when the English colonies had gained their independence from the mother country, they already had more than 3 m. inhabitants of European origin, almost all of them, however, rural dwellers. There were almost no industries in the colonies, and communications were poor.

The period between 1783 and the Civil War (1861–5) was one of great territorial expansion. Fig. 34 shows the main area of European settlement in the U.S.A. in the 1780s, and the various territorial acquisitions up to the 1850s. The purchase of Louisiana from Napoleon in 1803 and of Florida from Spain in 1819

34. Growth of continental U.S.A. between the War of Independence and the Civil War. The date of acquisition of each new territory is shown.

enlarged the U.S.A. to more than half its present size. Subsequent expansion up to the Rio Grande in 1845 brought it into conflict with its neighbour, Mexico, and as the result of a war and purchases, this country lost about half (though at the time the more thinly peopled part) of its territory.[1] In the north, an agreement was reached with Britain over the U.S.–Canadian boundary, and in 1846 the Oregon territory became part of the U.S.A. Continental U.S.A. has therefore had its present form for

1. If U.S. history books tend to overlook this example of U.S. military expansion in the best European tradition, the Mexicans do not forget it, which serves as a reminder that though there may be two ways of looking at any question, military superiority counts in the end. A Mexican geographer, Jesús Galindo y Villa, writes thus in *Geografía de México*, p. 114 (Barcelona, 1950): '... but as a consequence of the unequal struggle in 1846 and 1847 against the U.S.A., we lost for ever the vast territory of Texas, which today is the most extensive state in that country, while New Mexico and Upper California were snatched from us as well.'

more than a hundred years. As a result of the U.S. Civil War the future unity of the U.S.A. was assured, and the completion of the first transcontinental railway in 1869 might be taken to mark the final consolidation of modern U.S.A.

During the period of its expansion in North America the U.S.A. took only a small part in affairs outside that continent.[1] In the war with Britain in 1812–15, fighting was confined largely to the Canadian frontier of the U.S.A. and to sea battles in the Atlantic. During the following decade, when the Spanish and Portuguese colonies of Latin America were struggling for independence from Europe, the U.S.A. was satisfied merely to show its sympathy with the new republics by the enunciation of the Monroe doctrine. This opposed any further attempts by European powers to colonize the American continent. Only after the Civil War, which ended in 1865, did the U.S.A. begin to take an active interest in areas outside North America – mainly in the North Pacific and Central America.

In 1867 Alaska was purchased from the Russians for $ U.S. 7,200,000 while in the same year Midway Island was acquired (see fig. 35). U.S. interest in the Pacific at this period was partly a result of the rapid growth in importance of the Pacific states (particularly California), and contacts were established with East Asia. As a result of the short war with Spain in 1898 the U.S.A. acquired the Philippine Islands, a foothold and important interest in East Asia itself, while the Hawaiian Islands, annexed in the same year, provided a vital link in the widely scattered, though territorially small, U.S. Pacific empire. Other small islands were subsequently annexed.

In Central America the U.S.A. had been content in the 1850s to extend its frontier only as far as the Rio Grande. The war with Spain in 1898 gave it control over the last Spanish colonies in Latin America – Cuba and Puerto Rico. The former was freed technically, but has always been strongly influenced by the U.S.A. Puerto Rico remained in U.S. hands, becoming a commonwealth in 1952. After 1898, U.S. interest grew in Central America, and

1. It is interesting to recall, however, that as early as 1803–4, a U.S. naval squadron (forerunner of the present 6th Fleet) was sent to the Mediterranean to combat the North African pirates.

when a revolution conveniently occurred in the Colombian province of Panama, the U.S.A. was quick to sign a treaty with the newly formed republic there, thus ending long negotiations with the Colombian government to acquire a concession to build a canal across its territory. The transcontinental canal was opened in Panama in 1914 and at once became vital to the U.S.A. both strategically and economically, which is why this

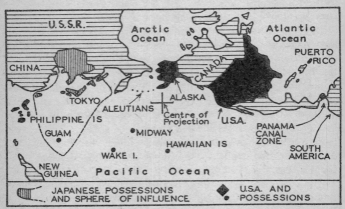

35. United States 'empire' of Central America and the North Pacific. Projection: oblique zenithal equidistant. Centre of projection: 45° N, 160° W.

part of America has on several occasions been the scene of U.S. intervention. Fig. 35 shows the U.S. and Japanese empires on the eve of the Second World War.

Participation in 1917–18 in the war in Europe was followed by a period of isolation, and up to 1941 the U.S.A. attempted to keep out of conflicts in other parts of the world. The Japanese attack on Pearl Harbour in 1941 forced it into the Second World War, and, in spite of some opposition at home, successive postwar governments have committed the U.S.A. by treaty to support, in the event of a war, not only almost all the Latin American republics (Rio Treaty, 1947) but also many of the European and Asian countries in the *inner zone* fringing the communist bloc.

The United States of America

II. DEMOGRAPHIC AND ECONOMIC EXPANSION

THE rise of the U.S.A. to its present position as a leading world power can only be appreciated when the enormous demographic and economic expansion of the country during the last 170 years is taken into account.

In the 1780s the U.S.A. had about 4 m. inhabitants, most of them of European origin. In 1860 it had about 30 m. In 1957 the total passed 171 m. In the last 170 years its population has therefore increased more than 40 times. During the same period the population of the whole world increased about five times, that of Russia about three times, and that of the British Isles not much more than twice. During the whole of its history up to about 1930, with the exception of a few brief periods, the increase of U.S. population has been more the result of immigration than of natural increase. Since then the larger share of the increase has been accounted for by the natural increase.

Before the 1780s there had been very little industrial development in the North American colonies, most of the population being engaged in farming. Between independence and the Civil War the southern states continued to develop their colonial type of economy and benefited from the rapid expansion of cotton manufacturing in Europe and in the New England states of the U.S.A. In 1794, 17,000 bales of cotton were produced, in 1810, 178,000, and in 1859, 5,400,000. During this period the northern states, and the New England states in particular, were endeavouring to set up large-scale modern industrial establishments on the lines of those in Britain at that period. Cotton spinning by machinery was the first branch to become firmly established, but in the early decades of the 19th century the production of iron began on an appreciable scale, and by about 1850 an engineering industry was developing. Already before the Civil War firearms, rails, steam engines, and agricultural implements were being mass produced.

Although great harm was done to the economy of the southern states as a result of the Civil War, and many still unsettled political and social problems were created, the industrial states, and subsequently the whole of the U.S.A., benefited greatly

271

from experience of various kinds gained during what was the first war to be waged with modern forms of transport and machinery.[1]

During the remaining decades of the 19th century U.S. industry expanded rapidly, and new branches of manufacturing were constantly being introduced. During this period it overtook the leading industrial countries of Europe both in absolute production (by 1900 it had more inhabitants than any except Russia) and, in many branches of industry, also in production per industrial worker. Fig. 36 shows population growth and pig iron output during the period 1870–1954 in the U.S.A., the widening gap representing the increasing amount produced per inhabitant.

During the present century the U.S.A. has led all other countries of the world in many branches of manufacturing, and has been the largest producer, in absolute terms, and frequently in *per caput* terms as well, of many types of manufacture. Between 1850 and 1900 the number of people engaged in manufacturing rose from 1 m. to 5 m., the latter producing much more per individual than the former. In 1950 there were 15 m. workers in manufacturing, again producing much more per individual than their 5 m. predecessors did in 1900.

III. THE U.S.A. AS A WORLD POWER

THE Japanese attack on Pearl Harbour in December 1941 might be said to mark the beginning of a third phase in the expansion of U.S. influence, the first two being the growth of the U.S.A.

1. '... the American Civil War of 1861–5, which even in the number of troops involved far surpassed the order of magnitude of the Napoleonic Wars and in which for the first time the railway was used for large troop movements, the telegraph network for messages and a steam fleet, keeping the sea for months on end, for blockade, and in which armoured ships, the torpedo, rifled weapons and monster artillery of extraordinary range were discovered. ... Amongst the wholly new problems was that of rapidly restoring railways and bridges; the bridge at Chattanooga, for the heaviest military trains, 240 metres long and 30 metres high, was built in 4½ days.' Spengler, O. *The Decline of the West*, Vol. 2 (p. 421 in the English translation by C. F. Atkinson, Borzoi Books, New York, 1946).

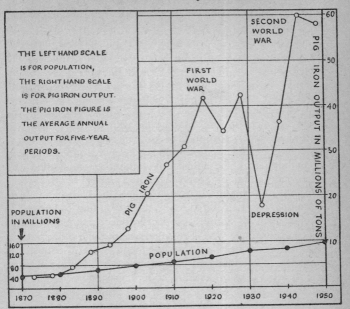

THE LEFT HAND SCALE
IS FOR POPULATION,
THE RIGHT HAND SCALE
IS FOR PIG IRON OUTPUT.
THE PIG IRON FIGURE IS
THE AVERAGE ANNUAL
OUTPUT FOR FIVE-YEAR
PERIODS.

SECOND
WORLD
WAR

FIRST
WORLD
WAR

PIG IRON OUTPUT IN MILLIONS OF TONS

DEPRESSION

PIG IRON

POPULATION
IN MILLIONS

POPULATION

36. Population growth and expansion of pig iron output in the U.S.A.
1870–1950.

in North America following the War of Independence, and the
growth of its North Pacific and Central American empire following the Civil War. Since 1941 U.S. influence, like Soviet influence,
has been extended in various ways.

One form of expansion that has played an important part is
military expansion. During the war U.S. forces fought in Europe,
North Africa, South, Southeast, and East Asia. Since the war
they have stayed in occupation in certain areas in this *inner zone*
including Germany and the Ryukyu Islands near Japan. They
have also remained in, returned to, or come for the first time
to many other countries of Europe and Asia (including Japan,
the U.K., France, and Spain) with the approval of the governments concerned, although the governments in many cases are

273

not formed on U.S. democratic lines and are not necessarily there by the approval of the majority of the population. U.S. financial aid given to allies specifically for military purposes might be included in this form of expansion. U.S. military influence extends therefore to allied countries with (e.g. U.K.) or without (e.g. Pakistan) U.S. bases and to countries (e.g. Saudi Arabia) with U.S. bases but not connected by treaty. It should be noted, however, that the U.S.A. has not permanently annexed any territory as a result of the war. On the contrary, it has granted independence to the Philippines.

A second form of U.S. expansion has been of a political nature. Although opposing the spread of communism and abhorring in theory any form of government not chosen by the whole population, participating in free elections, the U.S.A. has been much less active than the U.S.S.R. in attempting to spread its particular form of political organization. Assuming perhaps that its own example would be sufficient to guide other nations to the most desirable form of government, it has distributed its foreign aid indiscriminately during the last decade. Among recipients are Yugoslavia with a communist regime, Spain with a fascist one, Saudi Arabia with a doubtful monarchy, France and the U.K., which are colonial powers, several Latin American countries with military dictatorships, and Bolivia with (since 1953) what has been described in the U.S.A. as a Marxist government. It therefore appears that more importance has been attached to limiting the spread of Soviet Communist influence than to replacing communist and other non-democratic (in the American sense) regimes by an American type of democracy.

The growing influence of the U.S.A. on the rest of the world has been felt most strongly in the present century in the economic sphere. The economic depression of the early 1930s, originating apparently in the U.S.A., affected the whole world with the exception of the U.S.S.R., then enduring its First 5-Year Plan. During the Second World War, U.S. manufactures, perhaps even more than U.S. forces, played a leading part in the defeat of Germany and Japan. Since 1945, U.S. economic expansion has taken place in three main forms: by investment, by increased trade, and by the distribution of credits (loans) and grants (not to be repaid). Fig. 37 summarizes the direction of U.S. investments, trade, and financial aid in the post-1945 period. U.S. policy in the economic sphere can be summarized by considering the threefold division of the world suggested in ch. 3 – the *outer zone*, *inner zone*, and *communist bloc*.

1. *The outer zone.* Canada, Latin America, Africa, and Australasia, with 15 per cent of the world's population, have more than 70 per cent of U.S. foreign investments and 60 per cent of its foreign trade, but they received only an insignificant amount of aid up to 1954. 2. *The inner zone.* Non-communist Europe, Southwest, South, and Southeast Asia and Japan, Korea, Formosa, with 45 per cent of the world's population, have less than 30 per cent of U.S. foreign investments and 40 per cent of its trade but received more than 90 per cent of its aid. 3. *The communist bloc.* The U.S.S.R., East Europe, and China, with 34 per cent of the world's population, have no U.S. investments, almost no trade with the U.S.A. and received no aid (except, in the immediate postwar period) until 1950, when Yugoslavia was already cut off from the communist bloc.

A number of interesting points are brought out in the table. With regard to U.S. foreign investments, Latin America has some 40 per cent and Canada 30 per cent. But since Latin America has more than ten times as many inhabitants as Canada, U.S. investments are relatively far more significant in the economy of Canada than in Latin America as a whole. In Latin America, however, certain countries, including Venezuela, have much larger U.S. investments than others. Southwest Asia (the oil-producing countries) and European colonies in Africa have considerably larger U.S. investments now than before the war.

Turning to trade, it can be seen that Canada and Latin America are important here, as for investments, though non-communist Europe also has a large share of U.S. trade. The trade with the communist bloc is mostly with Yugoslavia.

The two final columns show the direction of U.S. aid. Non-communist Europe has received by far the largest part of it, and Japan, Korea, and Formosa much of the remainder. The evidence suggests that in the selection of recipients for its non-military aid the U.S. government has so far given little thought to

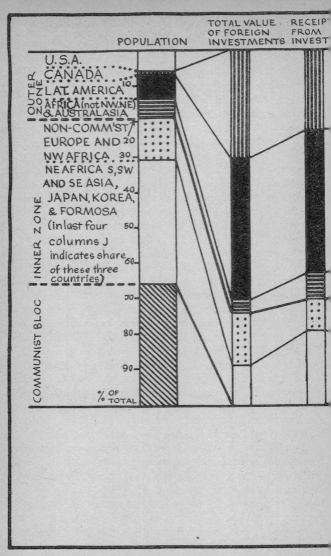

37. Influence of the U.S.A. on the rest of the world. Direct
For explana

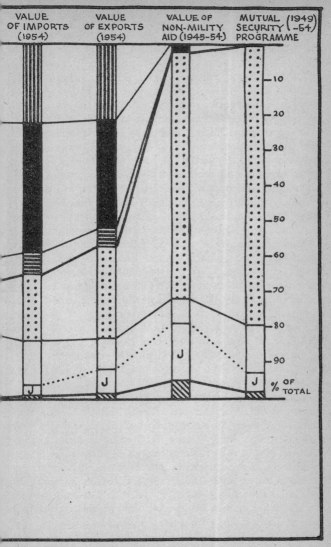

VALUE OF IMPORTS (1954) VALUE OF EXPORTS (1954) VALUE OF NON-MILITY AID (1945-54) MUTUAL SECURITY (1949) PROGRAMME (-54)

— 10
— 20
— 30
— 40
— 50
— 60
— 70
— 80
— 90
% OF TOTAL

U.S. investments, trade and financial aid during 1945–54.
text.

helping the poorer countries of the world or to rewarding countries that have helped it during and since the war or have set up regimes on U.S. lines. In 1951–4, communist Yugoslavia, with 17 m. inhabitants, received $U.S. 325 m. in grants while the whole of Latin America, needing it just as badly, and with ten times as many people, received only $U.S. 101 m. Between 1945 and 1954, West Germany, the former enemy of the U.S.A. and a country with a high standard of living, received $U.S. 3659 m. in grants, while India and Pakistan, allies during the war and poor countries, with nearly ten times as many people as Germany, together only received $U.S. 149 m. in grants.

Only a limited amount of money is, of course, available for foreign aid, and the U.S. government has to decide to which countries the grants and credits can most usefully be sent.[1] On some occasions, however, its choice of recipients must have caused disappointment. What is more, the unsatisfactory use to which much non-military aid has been put has frequently shown that it is not sufficient merely to advance large grants or credits to poor countries. Some knowledge should first be gained of conditions there, and particularly of the stage of technological development, and an appropriate programme of assistance worked out. One of many examples is sufficient to show how misdirected U.S. aid can be. In 1955 $U.S. 14½ m. was given to start five airports in Afghanistan in an attempt to provide the country with a network of airways, yet Afghanistan has no railways, few roads, and almost no motor vehicles.

The reader will appreciate that it is not easy to separate the various forms of U.S. expansion – military, political, and economic. Not surprisingly, however, almost all of the U.S. aid, both military and non-military, has so far gone to countries in some way connected with it by military treaty and at the same time of great strategic importance to it. The result is that communist China has received none, India only a negligible amount, and colonial Africa and Latin America very little. These parts of the world, which are among the poorest, and which together have

1. In 1957, for example, $U.S. 4,500 m. was devoted to foreign aid, some 6 per cent of the total U.S. budget, itself only a modest part of the total national income.

more than half of the world's population, have so far benefited little from U.S. aid.

IV. THE U.S.A. AND THE U.S.S.R.

THERE is a fundamental difference between U.S. and Soviet foreign policy. In the U.S.S.R. every aspect of policy is controlled by the Communist Party, which has its preconceived ideas about the future of world affairs. In the U.S.A., foreign policy is improvised because it is made by different parties and different individuals. Many conflicting interests are represented, and that is why completely opposite views may be expressed simultaneously by influential persons. Differences of view are publicized in the U.S.A. much more than in the Soviet Union. Apart from the isolationists there are those who stress the importance of solidarity within the American continent and regard Latin America as a back garden well worth cultivating, those who regard East Asia or Europe as the key area of American foreign policy, and those who look north across Canada and see the U.S.S.R. just across the Arctic Ocean.

Fig. 38a is an attempt to summarize the world position of the U.S.A. at present. U.S. allies are shown by vertical shading and U.S. and British bases encircling the communist bloc are also indicated. Fig. 38b shows the situation in the form of a diagram related to the twelve regions of the world discussed in ch. 3. Little idea can be gained of the significance or of the success of U.S. policy in encircling the communist bloc with a ring of allies and air bases on any of the maps of the world shown on the more commonly used projections, but a globe, of course, is superior to the projection and diagram in fig. 38. For purposes of comparison, fig. 39 shows the Soviet view of encirclement.

The communist bloc occupies a fairly compact land area, roughly triangular in shape, including about one-quarter of the earth's land surface. It controls or claims a number of sea areas (the largest, the Sea of Okhotsk) and a sector of the Arctic Ocean, but only in one main area, northeast Siberia, does it have direct access to any of the three larger oceans, the Pacific. The U.S.A. has air bases in a zone round the communist bloc within less

than one thousand miles of most of the large industrial centres of
the U.S.S.R. and China. On the other hand, its own main
industrial areas (in Northeast U.S.A.) are at least 3,000 miles
from the nearest Soviet air bases and are protected from an
attack by aircraft based in the closest Soviet territory to the

38a. A United States view of world affairs. Smallness of scale makes it
necessary to omit many important details.

U.S.A. by the radar warning lines in the north of Canada and
Alaska. This early warning radar system would presumably be
of no use against intercontinental rockets.

Table 23 shows distances between the nearest part of the
U.S.S.R. to the U.S.A. (the Chuhkotka peninsula) and the ten
metropolitan areas with the largest population in the U.S.A. It
also shows distances between U.S. bases in Germany and air-
fields in Turkey, a NATO ally of the U.S.A., and ten important
centres in the U.S.S.R. The distances were of course far more

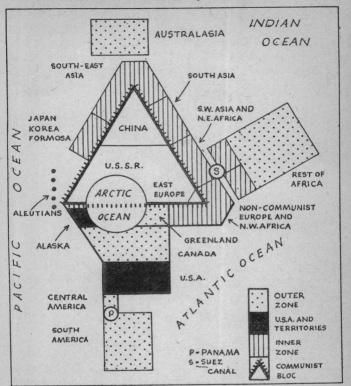

38b. A United States view of world affairs in terms of the three zones suggested in ch. 3, the outer zone, inner zone, and communist bloc.

significant before the evolution of intercontinental rockets, and greatly influenced both U.S. and Soviet policy between 1945 and 1957. The reader will find two articles of remarkable interest on this subject in the *Observer*, Sun. 15 June, and 22 June 1958, by Mr A. Buchan. The list of blood-curdling weapons of destruction now available and their horrible capabilities will be harder to explain away to our children than Father Christmas and the origin of babies.

39. A Soviet view of world affairs. This projection is used for the first
map (entitled The U.S.S.R. on the Map of the World) in *Geographical
Atlas of the U.S.S.R.*, Moscow, 1953 (Geograficheskiy atlas dlya 7-vo
i 8-vo klassov sredney shkoly).

Now that the evolution of intercontinental rockets has made
these distances less significant, certain points in connexion with
the position on the globe of the U.S.A. and the U.S.S.R. deserve
consideration even though at first sight they still appear to be
merely of academic interest. One is that the 'centre' of the

TABLE 23

From Chukhotka To		From W. Germany To		Shorter of two distances	Turkey
New York	3800	Moscow	1000	1000	1000
Chicago	3400	Leningrad	900	900	1300
Los Angeles	2500	Donbass	1100	500	500
Philadelphia	3800	Sverdlovsk	2000	1500	1500
Detroit	3500	Kuzbass	3000	2400	2400
Boston	3800	Kiev	800	600	600
San Francisco	2200	Baku	1900	300	300
Pittsburgh	3700	Kharkov	1100	600	600
St Louis	3500	Gorky	1300	1100	1100
Cleveland	3600	Tashkent	2600	1300	1300
Average	3400			1000	

world's population *on the surface* (one could be found below the surface, of course) is somewhere in the vicinity of the centre of Asia. Most of the world's population is in, or near (in terms of world distances) to, the U.S.S.R. Fig. 40 shows that if lines are drawn at a distance of about 1500 miles from the boundaries and coasts of continental U.S.A. and U.S.S.R., the former includes large stretches of ocean and no more than a few tens of millions of people in Canada and Mexico, while the latter includes about one-half of the world's population (including most of Europe, India, and China). This would mean that, were not its southern frontiers in difficult mountain and desert country, it would be in a better position than the U.S.A. to reach the main concentrations of the world's population.

Fig. 41 gives a more realistic view of economic spheres of interest in the world. The main concentrations of industry are named, the size of the circles representing them being approximately proportional to the consumption of all sources of energy, expressed in terms of coal equivalent. The other parts of the world with which these industrial areas carry on a large part of their trade and have large investments are shown. Four main spheres are suggested. The sphere of U.S.S.R. and East Europe appears to be the one with least chance of participating in the future development of the three main areas in the world in which farmland might appreciably be extended – tropical Latin

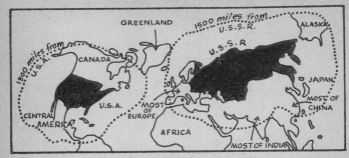

40. Parts of the world within 1,500 miles of the U.S.A. or U.S.S.R.

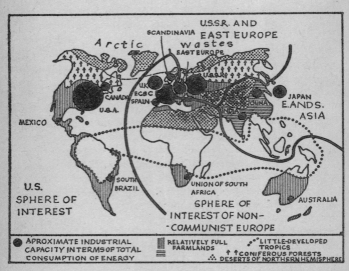

41. Four spheres of interest in the world.

The United States of America

America, Africa, and Southeast Asia. The map is not intended to imply that the limits of the spheres are not crossed. In reality, for example, the U.S.A. has large investments in tropical Africa and Southwest Asia, while Japan trades with countries in Latin America, with Australia, and so on. What the map suggests is that if the U.S.S.R. and East Europe wish to trade more widely with predominantly non-industrial countries they must enter one of the other three spheres. Tropical Latin America and Southeast Asia are both at great distances from the industrial centres of European U.S.S.R. and East Europe. Africa is more promising, but much of this is still in the hands of European colonial powers. Africa is reached from the U.S.S.R. most easily through Southwest Asia (or the Middle East). Perhaps this is why Soviet leaders are showing such an interest in Southwest Asia now and why they are becoming champions of African nationalism (stressing that the U.S.S.R. is the true friend of the peoples of Africa and Asia – see e.g. *Pravda*, 1 Dec. 1957).

Some idea of the comparative economic strength of the U.S.A. and U.S.S.R. is important in the study of world affairs, and Table 24 has been prepared to give the reader an idea of

TABLE 24

U.S.A. AND U.S.S.R. COMPARATIVE FIGURES, 1955

	Absolute numbers		U.S.S.R. as % of U.S.A. U.S.A. = 100	Per Caput U.S.S.R. as % of U.S.A.
	U.S.A.	U.S.S.R.		
Population (millions)	165	198	120	
Area (m. sq. mls)	3	8½	283	
AGRICULTURE				
Farmland (thous. sq. mls)	1800	2000	111	
Cropland (thous. sq. mls)	600	850	140	
Cotton (thous. tons)	3192	1487	46	39
Cattle (millions)	97	65	67	56
Sheep (millions)	32	118	370	326

285   (*Continued overleaf*)

TABLE 24 (*continued*)

	Absolute numbers		U.S.S.R. as % of U.S.A. U.S.A. = 100	Per Caput U.S.S.R. as % of U.S.A.
	U.S.A.	U.S.S.R.		
ENERGY				
Coal and Lignite (m. tons)	448	314	69	58
Oil (m. tons)	336	71	21	18
Electric energy (thous. m. kwh.)	629	170	27	23
Total energy in terms of coal (m. tons)	1364	442	32	27
HEAVY INDUSTRY				
Pig iron (m. tons)	72	33	46	38
Steel (m. tons)	106	45	42	35
Cement (m. tons)	50	22	44	37
Fertilizers (m. tons)	20	10	50	42
LIGHT INDUSTRY				
Cotton cloth (m. metres)	9235	5904	64	54
Footwear (m. pairs)	577	300	52	43
Radio sets (millions)	14	$3\frac{1}{2}$	25	21
Television sets (millions)	8	$\frac{1}{2}$	6	5
TRANSPORT				
Railway route mileage (thous.)	230	70	30	25
Ton kilometres of goods on railways (thous. million)	915	971	106	89
Motor vehicles in circulation (millions)	61	3	5	4
Merchant shipping (millions of gross tons)	24	$2\frac{1}{2}$	10	8

production in the mid-1950s (figures are for the year 1955) in certain branches of the U.S. and Soviet economies. The first and second columns contain absolute figures (e.g. steel in millions of tons, motor vehicles in circulation in millions) for the two countries. In the third column the Soviet figure has been

converted to a percentage of the U.S. figure (which therefore =
100 all through – e.g. 14 m. radio sets produced in the U.S.A. =
100 and 3½ m. produced in the U.S.S.R. thus = 25). The U.S.S.R.
has about 20 per cent more inhabitants than the U.S.A., and the
absolute Soviet production (in the second column) is for 198 m.
people whereas the U.S. production is for only 165 m. This
means that to show production *per inhabitant* in the U.S.S.R.
as a percentage of production per inhabitant in the U.S.A., the
figures in the third column must be reduced by $\frac{165}{198}$ – as has been
done in the fourth column.

An examination of the table brings out many interesting
features of comparison. Although the Soviet Union is almost
three times as extensive as the U.S.A., the total amount of land
used for all farming purposes, and the area used for the cultivation of crops, are not much greater than in the U.S.A. Moreover,
the area of good-quality farm land in the U.S.A. appreciably
exceeds that in the U.S.S.R. and, in general, yields tend to be
higher in the U.S.A. for this reason (as well as for others). It is
difficult to compare the output of different agricultural items in
the two countries, for certain crops and types of livestock (e.g.
rye and sheep in the U.S.S.R., maize and pigs in the U.S.A.)
play a much larger part in the farming economy of one than of the
other. It is worth noting, however, that in spite of restrictions
on acreage, the U.S.A. produces about twice as much cotton
(the principal textile fibre in the two countries) as the U.S.S.R.
In output per farm worker the U.S.A. is far ahead of the Soviet
Union, for its labour force of about 7 m. permanent and 3 m.
seasonal workers produces about as much as perhaps 50 m.
permanent and seasonal farm workers in the U.S.S.R. Although
so much importance is attached by Soviet communist leaders to
overtaking the U.S.A. in output *per worker* in all branches of the
economy it should be appreciated that the 1957 campaign, given
so much publicity in the Soviet press, to overtake the U.S.A. in
the output of meat, milk, and fat, means output *per inhabitant*
of the country, *not* output per farm worker, which would have
been a much more difficult objective.

The basis of modern industry and transport is energy. Remarkable progress has been made in the U.S.S.R. in the production

of coal, oil, and other sources of energy during the last thirty years. Even so, the total in terms of coal equivalent was less than one-third as much as the U.S. production, and the production per inhabitant (taking into account the larger population) was consequently little more than one-quarter that in the U.S.A.

During the Soviet period great importance has been attached to the expansion of heavy industry, yet the total Soviet output of such basic items as pig iron, cement, and fertilizers is less than half the U.S. output, while per inhabitant it is not much more than one-third.

Light industry has inevitably been neglected in the Soviet economy. The output of basic consumer goods such as textiles and footwear is about one-half as great per consumer as in the U.S.A., while the production of items such as television sets and washing machines, which are luxuries in the U.S.S.R., if not in the U.S.A., bears no comparison.

To facilitate the development of specialization in agriculture and industry in large countries like the U.S.A. and the Soviet Union, an efficient system of transportation is necessary. Although the U.S.A. has more than three times as many route miles of railway, the average mile of line is used much more heavily in the Soviet Union, and the total amount of goods transported (in ton-kilometres) is slightly higher there than in the U.S.A. But it should be remembered that while the railways handle about 85 per cent of the goods carried in the U.S.S.R., roads, inland waterways, pipelines, and coastal shipping rival the railways in importance in the U.S.A. (on occasions, of course, competing wastefully with them). There are about 20 times as many motor vehicles in circulation in the U.S.A. as in the Soviet Union, and the U.S. merchant fleet is about ten times as large as the Soviet one (which will have to be greatly expanded before the U.S.S.R. can hope to trade on a large scale with countries outside the communist bloc).

At present, the total industrial capacity of the U.S.A. is far greater than that of the U.S.S.R., although U.S. supremacy in certain branches of industry and science is now being challenged. Even a brief study of Soviet resources and present output shows that to catch up the U.S.A. (even assuming there is no expansion there), further enormous efforts will have to be made. But the Soviet Union is like a runner that has started a race late and made great sacrifices to put on a spurt to catch up the leaders. He has not done so yet and, provided the leaders continue to run, he may have to settle down to run at their pace some way behind.

Since the greatest ambition of Soviet leaders appears to be to overtake their rival in output *per worker* in mining and industry (if not in agriculture) it is important to consider whether they are likely to fulfil this aim. The Soviet theme at present is that in the last four decades production in most branches of heavy industry has increased about ten times in the U.S.S.R. (in spite of conflicts and postwar reconstruction) whereas U.S. industrial output has roughly doubled (in spite of, or as a consequence of, the depression). The broad implication is that if Soviet output again increases ten times in the next forty years and U.S. output only doubles, then in a matter of decades the U.S.S.R. will be ahead of the U.S.A. as an industrial nation. The mistake is to assume that Soviet output will increase ten times in the next few decades. The matter was discussed in ch. 8. The point is that whereas a small industrial capacity can be expanded many times over a short period – e.g. from 1 to 10, it is impossible to expand a considerable capacity the same number of times over the same period – e.g. from 10 to 100. The communists infer that the 'unprecedented' high rate of expansion of industrial capacity in the U.S.S.R. is a result of the superiority of the communist over the capitalist system. Until recently, surprisingly little has been done by non-communist economists to examine and challenge the Soviet claim. Lack of space makes it possible only to mention a few points in connexion with this important question.

Against the communist argument several points should be borne in mind. Large-scale modern industrial development began in several countries long before it began in Russia, and Soviet industries have therefore been able to benefit from the experience gained elsewhere (without now offering much in return, for their own advances are jealously guarded) and to learn from mistakes already made. Moreover, to ensure that a large part of industrial output has gone into the further expansion of capacity, drastic methods have been used to control investment and limit the supply of consumer goods at the expense of the mass of the population. To ensure that resources in remote and inhospitable parts of the Soviet Union would be exploited (e.g. the Vorkuta coal and the Kolyma gold) drastic (and quite arbitrary) methods have been employed to select large numbers of workers and move them to places in which few people would voluntarily settle. Admittedly, destruction in wartime, the growing danger of attack from Germany in the 1930s, and the conviction that the U.S.A. would attack after the Second World War could hardly be expected to make matters easy for Soviet planners. Soviet industry, then, has benefited from experience gained elsewhere, while drastic methods, often sacrificing the comfort of the Soviet population, have enabled great progress to be made in certain branches of industry.

Another matter that ought to be cleared up is the communist assertion that the rate of increase of expansion of their economy is unprecedented. The mistake here is to compare Soviet industrial progress with progress in the U.S.A. (or with that in any of the older industrial countries) *during the same period*. The comparison should be made between the Soviet Union during the communist period and the U.S.A. in the decades following the Civil War. Then the communist assertion is shown to be incorrect, for many branches of industry expanded much more rapidly in the U.S.A. during 1870–1910 than they did in the U.S.S.R. during the last forty years, even though the U.S.A. had only the then relatively limited experience of certain European industrial countries to learn from. In the end, however, it is output per inhabitant that counts, and even if the rapid U.S. expansion between the Civil War and the First World War was partly a consequence of the fact that the total population increased from 40 m. in 1870 to more than 90 m. in 1910, a comparison of output *per inhabitant* of pig iron (one of the industrial products that has always been given priority in the Soviet economy) shows that the rapid increase in output put in the U.S.S.R. of this metal is *not* something unprecedented.

Table 25 shows that in 1858 (on the eve of the U.S. Civil War) the U.S. output of pig iron per inhabitant was almost the same as output per inhabitant in Russia in 1913 (on the eve of the First World War).

TABLE 25

	U.S.A.				U.S.S.R.		
Pop'n in millions	Total pig iron	Year	Per inhabitant output (in kgs)		Year	Total pig iron	Pop'n in millions
29	0·7	1858	24	26	1913	4·3	159
34	0·9	1863	26	4	1918	0·6	160
38	1·6	1868	42	2	1923	0·3	140
43	2·2	1873	43	22	1928	3·3	151
48	2·6	1878	54	44	1933	7·1	162
54	4·3	1883	80	88	1938	14·7	168
59	7·2	1888	122	?	1943	?	?
67	8·2	1893	122	78	1948	13·7	175
73	11·8	1898	162	143	1953	27·4	191
80	18·0	1903	225	218?	1958	45·0?	207?
89	24·0	1908	270		1963		

SOURCES OF FIGURES: U.S.A. – *Historical Statistics of the U.S.A. 1789–1945*, U.S. Department of Commerce, 1949.

U.S.S.R. – *Narodnoye khozyaystvo SSSR, statisticheskiy sbornik*, Moscow, 1956.

After 40 years of development (1858–98 in the U.S.A. and 1913–53 in the U.S.S.R.), output per inhabitant in the U.S.A. had increased more than 6 times, in the U.S.S.R. less than 6 times. Even if the output target originally set in the Soviet Sixth 5-Year Plan for 1958 is reached (which seems unlikely, according to trends in 1956–7), then output per inhabitant will still not have expanded as rapidly in the U.S.S.R. as it did in the U.S.A. over a comparable period of its history. It is worth noting that between about 1840 and 1880 the British output of pig iron per inhabitant also increased about six times – credit, surely, to the pioneers of the modern iron and steel industry, though it should be remembered that this meant the investment of a large share of the national income and sacrifice of the consumer in a way that has been happening in the U.S.S.R. during the communist period. Indeed, the Swedish economist G. Myrdal (*Economic Theory and Under-Developed Regions*, London, 1957) points out: 'There is no

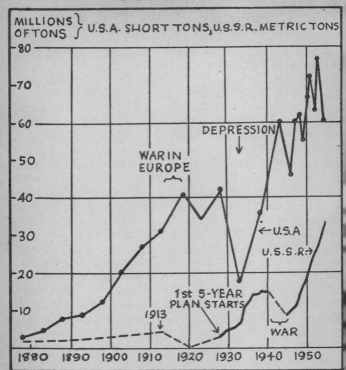

42. Pig iron output in the U.S.A. and U.S.S.R. 1880–1955. Sources of figures: *Statistical Abstract of the U.S.A., 1955*, p. 836, and *Narodnoye khozyaystvo SSSR*, Moscow, 1956, p. 62.

other road to economic development than a compulsory rise in the share of the national income which is witheld from consumption and devoted to investment'. If we criticize the Soviets for the line they are now taking we must also criticize our own predecessors.

Fig. 42 shows pig iron output in absolute terms. The high rate of increase of output in the U.S.S.R. in the 1930s and post Second World War periods should be compared with that in the

U.S.A. in the period 1860–First World War. Rapid progress was made in the U.S.A. in the expansion of this basic industry even though the modern iron and steel industry was only in its infancy and other branches of the economy were not sacrificed, as they have been in the U.S.S.R.

It might be suggested, then, that the Soviet Union will have to spend the next thirty or forty years to bring production up to *present* U.S. levels, but after three or four decades U.S. production could be double what it is at present. That is why Soviet economists are waiting anxiously for a major depression in the U.S.A.

By now the reader will have come to appreciate that whatever U.S. and Soviet politicians say, the two great powers resemble each other in many ways, though there is an inevitable time lag, because the U.S.A. started first. For a start, they are comparable in size, if we consider the extent of useful farmland, in number of inhabitants, and in many aims (e.g. constantly to raise living standards). But, it may be pointed out, one has slave camps, no political and religious freedom, and no scope for individual enterprise. The other, it may also be suggested, has ex-slaves who are still underprivileged in many ways, two main political parties which, to many outsiders (and, recently, to many Americans as well) appear to differ only superficially in basic policy, and plenty of scope for individual enterprise but under the constant threat of unemployment. Certainly general living conditions in the U.S.A. are superior to those in the U.S.S.R. at present, and, technologically speaking, the U.S.A. is still ahead of its rival in many branches of industry, though the gap is closing. But as living standards improve in the U.S.S.R., may not that country be able to afford the luxury of a more liberal political and economic set-up? The two powers resemble one another also in that each is complacent about its superiority over the other. The U.S.A. is complacent about the present (though *sputnik* and Mr Nixon's 1958 visit to Latin America have shaken this), the U.S.S.R. is complacent about the future (though ready to criticise itself at the present).

In order that we may not be misled by U.S. and Soviet propaganda on this subject, let us bear in mind the following idea of another politician, Mr Nehru (*News Chronicle*, 5 July 1957): 'The new Soviet generation is different. They are the most technical people in the world except the Americans. In fact, it's remarkable how closely those peoples resemble each other, when you come to think of it.' Western politicians would tend to group the U.S.A. and India together as members of the free world, the U.S.S.R. and China as communist powers. They might just as usefully be regrouped, with the U.S.A. and U.S.S.R. together as great industrial powers, and India and China as predominantly agricultural countries struggling to build industries on the basis of an almost entirely illiterate rural population.

The attitude of the two great powers to the United Nations deserves some consideration. Since the representation in this organization bears no relationship to the military and industrial strength of its members (and for that reason is very useful, because it enables small nations to voice their opinions on an equal footing with powerful ones) it is unlikely that the leading world powers need ever be much concerned about any particular decision made in the United Nations about them. But what is important is that both the U.S.A. and the U.S.S.R. are very sensitive as to what other countries think and say about them.

How unrepresentative the General Assembly of the United Nations is of the strength of its different members the reader will appreciate from the following examples: the U.S.A. has one vote, Latin America twenty, yet the U.S.A. has a far larger industrial capacity than all its twenty neighbours to the south together, and far more efficient and effective armed forces; communist China, with not much less than one-quarter of the world's population, does not even have one vote; and the members of the communist bloc muster but a few seats out of about eighty, which is why the Soviet leaders stress that the Assembly and the Security Council are both hopelessly unrepresentative of the strength of the U.S.S.R. (*Pravda*, 14 May 1957). Hence Mr Khrushchev's remark that the United Nations is at present not much use for solving international problems and why he called it a 'filial' of the U.S.A.

The attitude of the two great powers to a future war is also a very important matter. Two points are worth bearing in mind this connexion. The first is that the thoughts of people in any continent or any country are very much influenced by the 'last' war. While the Russians have only to think back fifteen years to remember the last war that greatly affected their country, the Americans must go back nearly a hundred years to their Civil War to think of a struggle in which a large part of the population was directly involved, for in 1941–5 not one enemy bomb fell on the U.S.A., not one enemy soldier invaded it, and life was very little changed. The present-day Americans, apart from a few million ex-servicemen who participated in various conflicts over the world, have *no* idea, except from films and books, of what a war really means. That is why they can still talk about the possibility of having another one.[1]

The second point is that a country embarking on a war (as Germany and Japan did in 1939–41) does so on the assumption (however misguided its estimation of its own and of its enemy's strength may be) that it will win, and it goes on fighting as long as enough people running the war think that it will win. Yet we know that neither side can win in a modern nuclear war. The Russians must surely realize this very well, for it will be a long time before they can forget the enormous destruction caused in their country by the Germans. Do the Americans realize this? Surely the thought that intercontinental rockets with atomic warheads can be dropped accurately *on any* of their cities is enough to make them rule out at last the possibility of starting a third world war.

The consequences of a full-scale nuclear war are unthinkable. Towards the end of 1957 the reply of U.S. politicians to the Soviet announcement that their rockets could hit any city in the United States was to boast that two thousand bombers (not armed, one assumes, with mere high explosive or incendiary

1. The following figures, one estimate of the number of military personnel killed in the Second World War, show that the U.S.A., considering its large population, came off better than any of the other main belligerents: U.S.S.R., 7,500,000; Germany, 2,850,000; China, 2,200,000; Japan, 1,506,000; U.K., 306,000; U.S.A., 296,000. These figures do not take into account civilians. It should be remembered that the U.S.S.R. also suffered by far the biggest losses here.

TABLE 26

U.K. (1950)		U.S.A. (1950)		U.S.S.R. (1955)	
London	8	New York	13	Moscow	5
Manchester	2	Chicago	5½	Leningrad	3
Birmingham	2	Los Angeles	4½	Stalino	1
Merseyside	1½	Philadelphia	3½	Gorky	1
Glasgow	1½	Detroit	3	Keiv	1
West Riding	1	Boston	2	Baku	1
Tyneside	1	San Francisco	2	Kharkov	1
Edinburgh	½	Pittsburgh	2	Sverdlovsk	¾
Nottingham	½	St Louis	1½	Chelyabinsk	¾
Bristol	½	Cleveland	1½	Kuybyshev	¾
Total in ten urban areas	18½		38½		15¼
National total	50		/50		200
Per cent of national total	37		26		8

bombs) were constantly on the alert ready to obliterate Russian cities in a matter of a few hours. Fig. 43 shows the areas that would be affected if the ten largest concentrations of urban population in the U.S.S.R., U.S.A. (superimposed on this in the map) and Great Britain (superimposed on both) were hit by hydrogen bombs. The three countries are all on the same scale. Allowing that only one-fifth of the population in each of the thirty towns (see table 26) were killed, then Great Britain would lose 3,500,000 people, the U.S.A. 7,500,000, the U.S.S.R. 3,000,000. Our 3,500,000 would be about fifty times as many as all the civilians killed in air raids on the U.K. during the six years of the Second World War. That the above figures are in fact gross underestimates is suggested by the lesson of a mock hydrogen bomb alert in the U.S.A. in May 1958. This showed that at least 50,000,000 people would have perished over a very short time had a real war started.

It is unfortunate that some people in Britain still look back on the Second World War with a kind of nostalgia, while many appear to lack the small amount of imagination needed to visualize the results of a third one or remain indifferent to the possibility of it occurring. In reply to those who suggest that a war may be the only means of solving certain problems it might be suggested that in addition to causing the death or suffering of tens of millions of people, the two world wars, like all others, have left as many new problems as they have solved old ones.

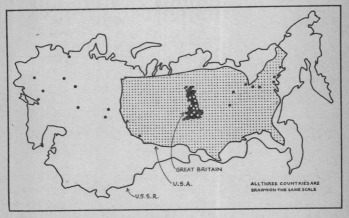

43. Vulnerability in a nuclear war. See text for explanation.

To end this chapter on a lighter note, it should not be forgotten that in the struggle between the two great powers there is a significant linguistic struggle – one between the English- and Russian-speaking worlds. In this connexion, it is worth bearing in mind that English is more widely spoken (by about 250 m. people) than Russian (by 110 m. Russians and by most of the 90 m. non-Russians in the U.S.S.R.) and that it is also more widely studied outside the English- and Russian-speaking worlds, being a kind of *lingua franca* in India, and the most widely studied modern language in most European countries (including the U.S.S.R.) and in Latin America. Those who are anxious to use this cultural means of extending the influence of the English-speaking world into other countries should appreciate that the introduction of a phonetic alphabet for English would make it a much easier language for foreigners to learn well than it is at present (and also an easier language for future generations of English-speaking children to spell).

Chapter 10

THE UNITED KINGDOM

A POINT has for the first time been reached in history when world affairs are largely dominated by no more than two powers. The emergence of the United States and the Soviet Union to their present supremacy as economic and military powers is very recent, although foreseen more than a century ago by Alexis de Tocqueville. The position may change again soon, though in a matter of decades, rather than years. If it does, the challengers will not be any of the former world powers of the 19th and early 20th centuries but perhaps China, and certainly a union of Western European nations, if such a union comes into existence.

There is at present considerable disagreement in the U.K. as to its own importance as a world power. A hundred years ago Britain was the leading industrial and trading nation of the world, producing about half of the world's pig iron, financing projects of all kinds not only in the Empire, but also elsewhere, and still annexing overseas territories:

> Beautiful England – on her island throne, –
> Grandly she rules, – with half the world her own;
> From her vast empire the sun n'er departs:
> She reigns a Queen – Victoria, Queen of Hearts.[1]

Fifty years ago, on the eve of the First World War, Britain was still a leading world power and London the capital of the largest Empire the world had ever known. Is it surprising, then, that opinions differ so widely in the U.K. as to its present significance as a world power? Those who remember the interwar years, and particularly the years before 1914, seem less willing to accept the recent decline in importance of certain powers than their children, born during the last two or three decades, who naturally accept the present position without question. Since British foreign policy is still largely directed by those who remember their country as a powerful nation, it is important that some attempt

1. In *Geographical Fun: Being Humorous Outlines of Various Countries* (London, *c.* 1870).

should be made to assess its real strength. This can be done by comparing its area, population, resources and productive capacity with those of other countries.

Fig. 44 serves as a rough guide to the strength of a number of countries, which, on the grounds of large industrial capacity, large population, or large area, or two or all of these, might claim to exert considerable influence in world affairs. In the three vertical columns each small square represents 1 per cent of the world's total steel output (col. 1), population (col. 2), and area (col. 3). Certain points should be remembered in connexion with the figures used. Steel output is only a rough guide to the industrial capacity of a country, and from the point of view of military strength, of course, it is the use to which the steel is put that counts. With regard to population, col. 2 assumes that all men are equal and does not take into account possible distinctions in mental capacity between different individuals and groups of individuals resulting from differences in physical characteristics. Nor does it take into account that conditions differ greatly from one region to another and that the average Canadian or Swede, for example, is better nourished, clothed, and educated than the average Indonesian or Congo pygmy, and produces far more of everything, except, perhaps, children. Finally, col. 3 flatters territorially extensive countries such as the U.S.S.R., Canada, and Australia, in which large areas are useless or of little use for farming. Although, for example, Australia is fifteen times as large as France, France has a larger area of cropland.

Fig. 44 suggests that at least four types of country could claim to be ranked as world powers. Firstly, the U.S.A. and the U.S.S.R., because they each have an appreciable percentage of the world's total population, area, and industrial capacity. Secondly, certain countries with a considerable industrial capacity. These, however, have relatively few inhabitants and occupy an insignificant area (each one merely a fraction of 1 per cent of the world's land surface). They are the U.K., the ECSC countries (West Germany, France, Benelux, Italy), and Japan. Thirdly, China and India, because they are large both in population and in area. At present, however, their industrial capacity is only small. Lastly, Canada, Brazil, and Australia, because they are

	STEEL OUTPUT	POPU-LATION	AREA
U.S.A.			
U.S.S.R.			
U.K.			—
WEST GERMANY			—
FRANCE			—
BENELUX			—
ITALY			—
JAPAN			—
CHINA			
INDIA			
CANADA			
BRAZIL	—		
AUSTRALIA		—	

44. World powers. Each square represents 1 per cent of the world total. A dash means less than 0·5 per cent.

NOTE 1. Steel output is average 1952–4. 2. U.S.A. includes Alaska.
3. France includes Saar.

very large territorially, though small in population and industrial capacity. Many other countries might also claim to exert a powerful influence on world affairs, whether economic, political, or military. Indonesia and Pakistan have large populations but almost no industrial capacity. Argentina, Mexico, and Iran are extensive but, again, without many industries. Poland, Czechoslovakia, Spain, Sweden, and Switzerland all have important industries but, like their more powerful neighbours in Europe (except the U.S.S.R.), are small in area.

Two points are made clear by fig. 44: the U.K. alone cannot be ranked with the U.S.A. and the U.S.S.R. as a world power, but a union of W. Germany, France, Benelux, and Italy (the nations now embarking on the Common Market project) with the U.K., could be a major world power. These countries together exceed both the U.S.S.R. and the U.S.A. in population, and the U.S.S.R. in industrial capacity as well. The union could be further appreciably strengthened by the inclusion of Scandinavia, Spain, Switzerland, and Austria.

Fig. 44 suggests, then, that alone the U.K. is no longer a leading world power. It occupies a mere one-five-hundredth of the earth's land surface, and has such a large proportion of its population living in urban areas (more than 80 per cent, half of it in no more than seven conurbations) that it would probably be more vulnerable in a nuclear war than any other country in the world with a comparable number of inhabitants. Being so small, also, it is unable to produce more than about one-half of its food and, although fortunate in having good coal reserves (many of the more accessible seams of which have, however, been worked) it lacks almost every important agricultural and mineral raw material except low-grade iron ore. It has only about one-fiftieth of the world's population, and if present world trends continue should have little more than one-hundredth in 50 years' time.

The importance of the U.K. as a world power rests largely upon its industrial capacity. Many of the inventions that led to the development of modern industry were first applied commercially in Britain. The lead gained in the 18th century was kept well into the 19th, and the wars on the continent between 1789 and 1815 contributed to keep Britain ahead, disrupting economic development in the rest of Europe in many ways and hindering the flow of techniques and technicians out of our island until after 1815. The rise of the U.K. to its supremacy as the leading industrial, trading, and financing nation of the world around the middle of the last century might be studied and assessed in many ways. Pig iron output serves as a rough guide to the heavy industrial capacity of a country. During and since the last decades of the 19th century more and more has been used for steel production, but before this little steel was produced. Fig. 45 shows the approximate proportion of the world's iron produced by Britain since 1800. It was in Britain that coke was first widely used instead of charcoal for smelting iron ore, and the British pig iron output rose rapidly in the 19th century. Britain's share of the world total (itself, of course, increasing) also rose appreciably. During the period 1850–70 Britain was producing about 50 per cent of the world's pig iron (yet it had little more than 2 per cent of the world's population). In 1850 it produced 2½ m. tons out of 5 m. and in 1870 the approximate figures for annual output were the following:

TABLE 27

	Output	Per cent of world total
Britain	6 m.	50
U.S.A.	1¾ m.	15
Germany	1¼ m.	11
France	1¼ m.	11
Belgium	½ m.	4
Austria	½ m.	3
Russia	½ m.	3

As the industry expanded on modern lines in other parts of the world, Britain's share diminished. By 1913 it was no more than 12 per cent of the world's total (10 m. tons out of 78 m.). The U.S.A. (31 m. tons) and Germany (17 m.) were both well ahead, Germany having benefited from its acquisition of Lorraine from France in the 1870s. At present the U.K. produces less than 8 per cent of the world's pig iron which, together with scrap, is the principal ingredient for steel production. This does not imply, of course, that Britain's influence as a world power is only eight-fiftieths what it was in 1850–70, but it certainly suggests that both economically and militarily Britain is relatively much less significant than it was a century ago, even if its population is much larger than it was then, its total industrial capacity far greater and the living conditions of most manual workers far superior.

It might be suggested, indeed, that the present influence of the U.K. as a world power is stronger than its industrial capacity alone would justify. There seem to be several reasons for this. A kind of momentum appears to have been imparted by past influence and achievements. Considerable prestige (particularly

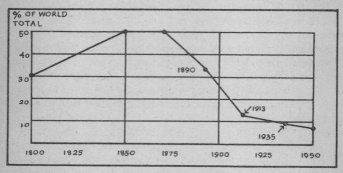

45. British pig iron output as a percentage of the world total, 1800–1950. Figures are only very approximate.

in its own eyes) was gained at the very time when the weakness of the U.K. as a world power was most clearly shown, that is, when it held out alone (with its Commonwealth) against Germany in 1940–1. Then there is the fact that the Commonwealth countries have contributed both in peace and war to strengthen the economic position of the U.K. In addition, it should be remembered that although the industrial capacity of the U.K. is now only a small proportion of the world's total, this country is still among the leaders with regard to the most recent developments of industry and particularly in the production of modern armaments. Its long tradition of manufacturing and the experience gained are perhaps the most important single asset it will have in the future.

The United Kingdom

It is difficult for a former leading world power to accept its reduced importance and to modify its policies at the suggestion of more powerful countries. Sweden, Spain, and Turkey, all the mother countries of former empires, are resigned to their present role as small powers. Even Japan and Germany, overawed, no doubt, by the rise of their great neighbours, China and the U.S.S.R., have accepted their appreciably reduced importance. In May 1957 (*News Chronicle*, Tuesday, 14 May 1957), the West German Foreign Minister said: 'The West German Federal Republic of today and the reunified Germany of tomorrow are not and will not be great powers and even less world powers.'

If opinions differ in Britain as to its importance as a world power, so they do abroad. Most Conservative leaders talk of 'maintaining' Britain's position as a leading world power, yet the press in many foreign countries (and not only communist ones) took the weak attitude of the Labour Government over the Iranian oil dispute in 1951 and, more recently, the half-hearted 'gunboat' action in Suez in 1956, as signs that even insignificant nations could now make a stand against Britain. Mr Muggeridge (*News Chronicle*, Thursday, 17 May 1956) says: 'The days of GREAT Britain are over.' Why then do Turkey, Iraq, Iran, and Pakistan join the Baghdad Pact to enlist the protection of the U.K. (against, presumably, the U.S.S.R.)? Why does the U.S.A. now realize that it can benefit from the closer co-operation of British scientists? Perhaps Britain is not a leading military power any longer, but the following words of a Peruvian politician, Raul Haya de la Torre (*Observer*, 10 Feb. 1957) remind us that there is not merely one way of acquiring influence and bringing benefits to other parts of the world: 'Britain a second-class power? Could the country that can teach the whole world lessons in political freedom *ever* be a second-class power?'

Whatever the world thinks, British politicians of all parties are much more ready than their predecessors were a hundred, or even fifty, years ago to think in terms of close co-operation with other countries or groups of countries in military, economic, and even political fields. The present question is, to what extent and in what ways should co-operation be increased or maintained with the U.S.A., the British Commonwealth, and Western

Europe? For although the U.K. is a member of the United Nations, and participates in the various activities of this body, its main concern at present is to find the most useful ways of collaborating in the three blocs mentioned, while still retaining some degree of independence.

In both military and economic matters the U.K. is now dependent on the U.S.A. Financial aid received since the war has been in the order of $U.S. 6000 m. This helped to put the British economy on its feet again in the immediate postwar years. The re-establishment of U.S. air bases in Britain since the war and the plan to start building rocket bases in 1958, leave no doubt that the U.K. would be one of the first targets for long-range missiles in a future war.

While U.K.-U.S. ties have been strengthened in the last two decades, the cohesion of the British Empire has weakened. Before 1914, Britain's chief overseas concern was the Empire, and, during the interwar period, ties with it were still strong. Since the Second World War the Commonwealth has undoubtedly weakened. With many former colonies remaining members largely for the advantages they can derive from trade with other members, and the dominions becoming less dependent on Britain for manufactures, the Commonwealth appears to be changing, if not dissolving, and Britain is now one of many partners, rather than the leader. Even so, the Commonwealth still has about one-fifth of the world's population and area, is to some extent unified by the English language, and is an important trading community. But there is much less unity than there was fifty years ago. The Un. of S. Africa might soon choose to leave it. India frequently opposes British action, and even Canada did so in 1956 over the Suez attack. The U.S.A. meanwhile is constantly strengthening its financial influence within the British Commonwealth with investments in such vastly different parts of it as Canada, Trinidad, and the Rhodesias.

Concerned at present with its relations with the Commonwealth and the U.S.A., the U.K. has found it difficult to make any decisions with regard to its connexions with Europe. Serious talk of some form of economic and later political union in Western Europe belongs only to the postwar period. Any developments

ere would inevitably concern the U.K. and create another set
of connexions comparable with those already existing with the
Commonwealth and with the U.S.A. As tariff barriers are removed between the members of the European Common Market,
the U.K. will be more and more affected (see *Freer Trade in
Europe*, H.M.S.O., London, 1957). Its share of trade in Europe
might be expected to drop if it remained outside. Yet its trade
with the Commonwealth countries would be affected if it
entered. Although some branches of the British economy would
undoubtedly be affected adversely if the U.K. entered a European
Common Market, the eventual aim of the Union is to raise living
standards throughout by making possible a greater degree of
regional specialization in production (comparable with that in
the U.S.A. at present). Moreover, there are obvious advantages
in a strong Western Europe, the various members of which are
each weak individually. Non-communist Europe, with about
300 m. inhabitants and about one-third of the world's steel-
producing capacity, would rival the U.S.S.R. (even with East
Europe) as a world power. It would help to balance the presence
of communist China as this country grows into a major world
power, which it is bound to do if present trends there continue.
It would also reduce the dependence of non-communist Europe
on U.S. help in defence.

The U.S.S.R. not only opposes the NATO defence alliance
in Western Europe; it frequently publishes articles and cartoons
against West European Union (surely a good reason for bringing
it into existence). Undoubtedly it fears the emergence of a single
strong power in Europe, replacing the present relatively weak
ones, which not infrequently voice their differences among
themselves to the glee of Soviet propagandists. It also fears the
strengthening of the economy which might be expected to result
from the greater regional specialization possible within a common
market of perhaps 250 m. or even 300 m. inhabitants. Furthermore, it realizes that the communist countries of East Europe
might feel themselves in a stronger position to resist Soviet
influence with a powerful West Europe nearby. Again, the
U.S.S.R. no doubt fears that a strong unified Western Europe
would be in a better position than the individual nations to

administer aid to poor countries. It is not unlikely that many countries, and even communist China, would be more ready to co-operate with a group of nations in Europe than with either the U.S.S.R. or the U.S.A. What is more, there is a great scope in colonial Africa for European assistance, while most Latin American countries, largely dependent since 1939 on U.S. trade and investments, would be glad to strengthen their economic ties with Europe.

Whether the U.K. associates itself more closely with Western Europe, further strengthens its connexions with the English-speaking countries of the world to form an Anglo-Saxon bloc with Anglo-America and Australasia, or endeavours to strengthen Commonwealth ties, a time has surely come when some decisive step must be taken.

Meanwhile, either alone, or in collaboration with one or more of the above groups of countries, or even through the United Nations, the U.K. will have to face seriously the problem of devoting an appreciable slice of its national income to providing various forms of aid to poorer countries. The present stalemate in the armaments race (likely to last a long time – until the perfection of guided missiles guaranteed to intercept *every* long-range rocket before it lands) means that competition between the U.S.S.R. and the leading non-communist industrial countries must, for the safety of all concerned, take place largely in the economic field. The time has now come for the more prosperous countries to help the poorer ones, *not* with some political or military motive but for philanthropic reasons.

With regard to future aid from the U.K. to poorer countries, the task of deciding under what auspices and to whom help should be sent is far less formidable than the question of persuading the British taxpayer to finance such a project. It is hard to suggest to people who are planning how they will spend the next increase in their own income, if and when it comes, that they should help to improve living conditions elsewhere. One reason, perhaps, is that many people fail to appreciate how great the gap is between living standards in the U.K. and those shared by about two-thirds of the world's population. Another is that it is difficult to argue against those who feel that the poorer countries themselves should make the necessary efforts to improve their living standards.

If the possibility of helping the poorer countries of the world seems very remote then there is always the chance to offer some immediate help by contributing to the assistance of the many millions of refugees still uprooted somewhere in many parts of Europe and Asia. Even if we disclaim all responsibility for them, and put the blame on whatever nation or political system we deem guilty, they still suffer. The world is one community, and if the millions of refugees in Korea, Viet Nam, or Southwest Asia seem very remote, the least we can do is to find out something about the work of the various bodies that are helping them.

There seem to be three great problems today in world affairs behind the smoke-screen thrown up by the politicians of the world to maintain tension among nations, and themselves in power. They are the possible harmful effects of radiation on the future of the human race; the present rapid increase of population in almost every part of the world, together with the great movement of peoples into cities; and the great gap in living standards between the more prosperous and poorer countries of the world. The first problem is hardly in the field of the geographer. The other two are, though economists, sociologists and others also study them. It is hoped that this book will at least have drawn the attention of the reader to some of the ways in which the study of geography can help in the understanding of world affairs in general and of these two problems in particular.

POSTSCRIPT

In books of this kind the authors usually conclude on a note of optimism by pointing the way to a rosy future, or at least by offering an assurance that if everyone were to follow their advice, whether by becoming a Quaker or a Communist, by taking up World Government or adopting Anarchy, all would be well. In the present author's view there is no more and no less reason at the moment to be pessimistic or optimistic about the future of humanity than there ever has been, unless it is that the human race can now destroy itself over a very short period.

In this world of the second half of the 20th century the affairs of civilized man appear at first sight to be dominated by a lethal combination of politicians, scientists, and journalists. The politicians are mostly in their business for the sake of acquiring power and being leaders. In this game the more sensitive and sincere ones can easily be pushed aside. The scientists have to earn a living, and those who have shared in the invention, design, and production of the various weapons of destruction now available to man may satisfy their consciences by passing the blame on to the politicians and generals who instructed them to do so. Not a few journalists appear to be in search of the spectacular and sensational. But they have to sell their news, and can they be blamed for keeping their readers excited in order to do so? But may we not really be flattering these people or, for that matter, any other people we choose to blame, by exaggerating their influence on the course of history? Perhaps it is sufficient to accept that might is right in world affairs and that the rules in the game are made by the strongest, like, for example, international law created by a club of European nations which have shared the world among themselves.

What is of equal concern to all those who regard this life as a testing ground for another life or for other lives (or even a punishment for a former life) and all those who regard this life as an end in itself (and perhaps the only one) is that man can now choose whether or not he brings about his own destruction,

either immediately in a nuclear war or gradually by radiation.[1]
For those who find that the investigations of geologists and
astronomers prevent them from accepting the idea, required by
many religions, of an anthropocentric universe, it is some con-
solation to remember that, measured against time and space in
the universe, man's presence is something insignificant, and to
think that perhaps it is only by accident that he exists at all. If
humanity does not committ suicide now, it is merely a matter
of time, perhaps a few million, perhaps no more than a few
thousand, years, before some accident occurs to end the career
of *Homo sapiens*.

The time traveller of H. G. Wells recounted how, at the most
distant point he reached in the future: 'I looked about me to
see if any traces of animal life remained. A certain indefinable
apprehension still kept me in the saddle of the machine. But I
saw nothing moving, in earth or sky or sea. The green slime on
the rocks alone testified that life was not extinct. A shallow sand-
bank had appeared in the sea and the water had receded from the
beach. I fancied I saw some black object flopping about on this
bank, but it became motionless as I looked at it, and I judged
that my eye had been deceived, and that the black object was
merely a rock.'

1. In a dramatic speech published in the *Observer*, Sun. 6 July
1958, in connexion with the nuclear disarmament campaign, Bertrand
Russell says: 'We are assembled to consider the most grave and
terrible problem with which mankind has ever been confronted.'

SELECTED REFERENCES

SELECTED REFERENCES

The purpose of this list of publications, most of which are by geographers, is merely to provide the reader with at least one detailed work on each of the main topics and regions dealt with in this book. In addition, there is a list of useful articles appearing in recent numbers of three periodicals which are available in most public libraries – *The Times Review of Industry*, *The Geographical Magazine* (English), and the *National Geographic Magazine* (U.S.). All three are very well illustrated. The reader should not forget that material on most foreign countries can be obtained from the various foreign embassies in London.

CHAPTER 1
GENERAL

Boyd, A. *An Atlas of World Affairs*, London, 1957.

Connell-Smith, G. *Pattern of the Post-War World* (Penguin Special), Harmondsworth, 1957.

East, W. G. *Geography behind History*, London, 1954.

East, W. G., and Moodie, A. E. (Editors). *The Changing World*, London, 1956.

Elliott, F., and Summerskill, M. *A Dictionary of Politics* (Penguin), Harmondsworth, 1957.

Flugel, J. C. *Population, Psychology and Peace*, London, 1947.

Kish, G. *An Introduction to World Geography*, Englewood Cliffs (N.J.), 1956.

Lebon, J. H. C. *An Introduction to Human Geography*, London, 1952.

Moodie, A. E. *Geography behind Politics*, London, 1947.

Pearcy, G. E., Fifield, R. M., and Associates. *World Political Geography*, New York, 1956.

Russell, R. J., and Kniffen, F. B. *Culture Worlds*, New York, 1951.

Wooldridge, S. W., and East, W. G. *The Spirit and Purpose of Geography*, London, 1951.

MAP PROJECTIONS

Steers, J. A. *An Introduction to the Study of Map Projections*, London, 1949.

RACE

Clark, W. E. Le Gros. *History of the Primates*, London, 1956.

Manchip White, J. E. *Anthropology*, London, 1954.

Selected References

Romer, A. S. *Man and the Vertebrates*, Vol. 2 (Pelican), Harmondsworth, 1954.

UNESCO series: The Race Question in Modern Science, Paris 1951–3: *Race and Culture* (M. Leiris), *Race and Psychology* (O. Klineberg), *Race and Biology* (L. C. Dunn), *Race Myths* (J. Comas), *The Roots of Prejudice* (A. M. Rose), *Race and History* (C. Levi-Straus), *Race and Society* (K. L. Little), *The Significance of Racial Differences* (G. M. Morant), *The Race Concept: Results of an Inquiry*, *Race Mixture* (H. L. Shapiro).

CHAPTER 2

Forde, C. D. *Habitat, Economy and Society*, London, 1953. On simple societies in various environments in different parts of the non-European world.

Goodall, G., and Treharne, R. F. *Muir's Historical Atlas*, London, 1956.

Madariaga, S. De. *The Rise of the Spanish American Empire* and *The Fall of the Spanish American Empire*, London, 1947. A study of the impact of European empire builders on part of the non-European world. A brilliant work, in which fascinating detail does not obscure the broad view taken by the author.

Pounds, N. *An Historical and Political Geography of Europe*, London, 1949. Deals not only with changes in Europe itself, but also with European empire building elsewhere in the world.

Spengler, O. *The Decline of the West* (translation of *Der Untergang des Abendlandes*) English translation by Atkinson, C. F., New York, 1946. Includes many ideas about the influence of European culture on the rest of the world.

Toynbee, A. J. *A Study of History*, in ten volumes, London 1935–54. An abridgement is available by Somervell, D. C., in two volumes (of Vols I–VI, London, 1946 and of Vols VII–X, London, 1957).

Toynbee, A. J. *Civilization on Trial*, Oxford, 1948.

Toynbee, A. J. *The World and the West*, in B.B.C. Reith Lectures, *The Listener*, 20 Nov.–25 Dec. 1952, and published in book form, 1953.

Wilmot, C. *The Struggle for Europe*, London, 1952. The events leading up to the emergence of the U.S.S.R. as the strongest single power in Europe in 1945.

CHAPTER 4

Barnett, A. *The Human Species* (Pelican), Harmondsworth, 1957. The outlook of a biologist on some of the problems discussed in this chapter.

Selected References

Dicken, S. N. *Economic Geography*, Boston, 1955.

Humlum, J. *Atlas of Economic Geography*, London, 1955. An excellently prepared and very reasonably priced work of reference.

Mumford, L. *Technics and Civilization*, London, 1934. A useful study of inventions and their application up to the 1930s.

Mumford, L. *The Culture of Cities*, London, 1953. An entertaining account of urban development and problems.

Myrdal, G. *Economic Theory and Under-Developed Regions*, London, 1957.

Oxford Economic Atlas of the World, Oxford, 1954. Very good world and regional maps showing the distribution of resources and production.

Petroleum Information Bureau (29, New Bond St., London, W.1.), for up-to-date pamphlets on all aspects of the oil industry, including regional output.

Statesman's Year Book, for notes on the main features of every country in the world. This work of reference is published annually and can be found in most public libraries.

Times Review of Industry, a monthly publication, undoubtedly the most valuable of its kind for enabling the general as well as the specialist reader to keep in touch with progress in industry and with important developments in all parts of the world. Obtainable from The Times Publishing Co., Ltd., Printing House Square, London, E.C.4.

United Nations *Statistical Yearbook* and *Demographic Yearbook*, two of the many works produced by the United Nations with the latest available demographic, economic, and social data for the whole world. Obtainable from H. M. Stationery Office, P.O. Box 569, London, S.E.1.

Woytinsky, W. S., and E. S. *World Population and Production, Trends and Outlook*, New York, 1953. A remarkable work, some 1250 pages in length, profusely illustrated with maps and tables.

Zimmerman, E. W. *World Resources and Industries*, New York, 1951.

CHAPTER 5

ANGLO-AMERICA

Duckham, A. N. *American Agriculture, its Background and its Lessons*, London, 1952.

Kimble, G. H. T., and Good, D. *Geography of the Northlands*, London, 1955. A study of the colder regions of Anglo-America and the U.S.S.R.

Selected References

Pounds, N. *North America*, London, 1956.

Statistical Abstract of the United States, a yearly publication of the U.S. Department of Commerce, Bureau of the Census.

Taylor, G. *Canada*, London, 1957.

White, C. L., and Foscue, E. J. *Regional Geography of Anglo-America*, London, 1956. A well illustrated and most interesting geographical study of Anglo-America, one of the few to be brought up to date since the 1930s.

LATIN AMERICA

James, P. E. *Latin America*, New York, 1950. A very readable account of Latin America as a whole and of each of the republics and colonies.

Royal Institute of International Affairs: series on South American republics, 1951–4: *Argentina* (G. Pendle), *Bolivia* (H. Osborne), *Brazil* (J. A. Comacho), *Chile* (G. J. Butland), *Colombia* (W. O. Galbraith), *Ecuador* (L. Linke), *Paraguay* (G. Pendle), *Uruguay* (G. Pendle).

The South American Handbook, a yearly publication. A useful work of reference for Latin American countries. Obtainable from Trade and Travel Publications, Ltd., 14, Leadenhall Street, London, E.C.3.

AFRICA

Fitzgerald, W. *Africa. A Social, Economic and Political Geography of its Major Regions*, London, 1955.

Stamp, L. D. *Africa – A Study in Tropical Development*, New York, 1953.

Wellington, J. H. *Southern Africa. A Geographical Study*, Cambridge, 1955. Vol. 1. *Physical Geography*, Vol. 2. *Economic and Human Geography*. Mainly on the Union of South Africa.

AUSTRALASIA

Australia and New Zealand Bank Limited. *Australia's Continuing Development*, London, 1954, and *New Zealand's Continuing Development*, London, 1957.

Commonwealth Scientific and Industrial Research Organization. *The Australian Environment*, Melbourne, 1950, an important work assessing the possibilities of Australia for future farming development.

Cumberland, K. *Southwest Pacific*, London, 1956. An account of the geography of New Zealand, Australia (in less detail) and the islands of the Southwest Pacific.

Selected References

Department of National Development. *Atlas of Australian Resources*, Canberra, 1953 and years since then, a series of maps with commentaries, dealing with topics ranging from rainfall to railways.

CHAPTER 6

EUROPE

Hoffman, G. W. (Editor). *A Geography of Europe*, London, 1954.
Shackleton, M. R. *Europe*, London, 1956.

ASIA

Cressey, G. B. *Asia's Lands and Peoples*, London, 1955.
Stamp, L. D. *Asia*, London, 1957.

SOUTHWEST ASIA

Fisher, W. B. *The Middle East*, London, 1956.
Lenczowski, G. *The Middle East in World Affairs*, Ithaca (N.Y.), 1957.
Wint, G., and Calvocoressi, P. *Middle East Crisis* (Penguin Special), Harmondsworth, 1957.

SOUTH ASIA

(for Burma, see Southeast Asia)

India News, a weekly publication of the Information Service of India, India House, London, W.C.2.
Spate, O. K. M. *India and Pakistan*, London, 1957.
India and Pakistan, 1947–57 in *The Geographical Magazine*, August 1957, a number devoted to these two countries.

SOUTHEAST ASIA

Dobby, H. G. *Southeast Asia*, London, 1954.

JAPAN

Trewartha, G. T. *Japan, a Physical, Cultural and Regional Geography*, University of Wisconsin, 1945.

CHAPTER 7

U.S.S.R.

Baransky, N. *Economic Geography of the U.S.S.R.* Moscow, 1956, an English translation (made in the U.S.S.R.) of a standard textbook for use in Soviet schools.
Cressey, G. B. *How Strong is Russia? A Geographical Appraisal*, Syracuse, 1954, A stimulating book, putting the views of an American on the U.S.S.R.

Selected References

Geographical Atlas for Teachers in Middle Schools, Moscow, 1954 (Geograficheskiy atlas dlya uchiteley sredney shkoly) and

Geographical Atlas of the U.S.S.R., Moscow, 1953 (Geograficheskiy atlas SSSR dlya 7- vo i 8- vo klassov sredney shkoly), two excellent Soviet atlases, for which English translations of the keys have been prepared and are available, together with the atlases, from Collet's Foreign Bookshop, 44–45 Museum St., London, W.C.1.

Oxford Regional Economic Atlas of the U.S.S.R. and Eastern Europe, Oxford, 1956.

Shabad, T. *Geography of the U.S.S.R.*, New York, 1954. A general introduction to the geography of the Soviet Union, followed by a detailed account of its regions.

See under ch. 8 for further references.

EAST EUROPE

The geography of the eight communist states of East Europe has not been dealt with in any one book. The reader will find material on it in textbooks on the whole of Europe and in the *Oxford Regional Atlas of the U.S.S.R. and Eastern Europe*, Oxford, 1956.

CHINA

(Material in English on China can be obtained from Collet's Chinese Bookshop, Great Russell St., London, W.C.1).

China Reconstructs, an illustrated monthly periodical in English on developments in communist China. A book, *China in Transition*, has been published with selected articles from *China Reconstructs*.

Chou-En-Lai. *Proposals of the Eighth National Congress of the Communist Party of China for the Second Five- Year Plan for Development of the National Economy (1958–1962)*, in English, Peking, 1956.

Cressey, G. B. *Land of the 500 Million, a Geography of China*, New York, 1955. Well illustrated with maps and photographs.

Foreign Trade of the People's Republic of China, a yearly publication in English, Peking.

Latourette, K. S. *A History of Modern China* (Pelican), Harmondsworth, 1954.

Li Fu-Chun. *Report on the First Five- Year Plan for Development of the National Economy of the People's Republic of China in 1953–1957*, in English, Peking, 1955.

Shabad, T. *China's Changing Map*, London, 1956.

Selected References

CHAPTER 8

(see also references for ch. 7)

Material in English on the U.S.S.R. can be obtained from Collet's Foreign Bookshop, 44–45, Museum St., London, W.C.1.)

TERRITORIAL EXPANSION AND INDUSTRIAL DEVELOPMENT

Atlas of the History of the U.S.S.R. (Atlas istorii SSSR), part 1, pre-1689; part 2, 1689–1900; part 3, post-1900. Moscow: part 1, 1950; part 2, 1949; part 3, 1952.

REMAINING SECTIONS OF CH. 8

Soviet News Booklets (in English): No. 1, *The Soviet Union in 1960*; No. 3, The U.S.S.R. – *A Hundred Questions Answered*; No. 4, N. S. Krushchov, *20th Congress of the Communist Party of the Soviet Union, Feb. 14th, 1956, Report of the Central Committee*; No. 5, *Directives of the Sixth Five-Year Plan of the U.S.S.R. 1956–1960*; No. 17, *Planning in the Soviet Union.*

Miscellaneous: Roitburd, L. *Soviet Iron and Steel Industry, Development and Prospects*, Moscow, 1956. Krzhizhanovsky, G., and Veits, V. *A Single Power Grid for the U.S.S.R.*, Moscow, 1957.

Statistical material: *The U.S.S.R. Economy. A Statistical Abstract*, a translation (published by Lawrence and Wishart, 1957) of the first postwar statistical handbook of the Soviet Union, with figures up to 1955 (*Narodnoye khozyaystvo SSSR*, Moscow, 1956). Other important sources of statistics (but in Russian) include: *The Industries of the U.S.S.R.* (*Promyshlennost SSSR*, Moscow, 1957) and *The Economy of the R.S.F.S.R.* (*Narodnoye khozyaystvo RSFSR*, Moscow, 1957).

Periodicals in English: *Soviet Union*, a well-illustrated monthly publication; *News. A Soviet Review of World Events*, a fortnightly publication.

Pravda. A brief list follows with the dates of numbers of *Pravda* in which important recent developments in the U.S.S.R. are discussed: Feb. 6, 1957, revision of the Sixth 5-Year Plan; June 18, 1957, list of 105 new economic planning regions (*sovnarkhoz*) replacing the dozen existing ones; Sept. 26, 1957, notice of the extension of the Sixth 5-Year Plan; Oct. 13, 1957, achievements of the U.S.S.R. during the last 40 years; Nov. 9, 1957, proposed production figures for 15 years hence; Nov. 12, 1957, chief tasks of the *perspectivnyy* plan for 1958–65; Dec. 4, 1957, mineral wealth of the U.S.S.R.; Jan. 27, 1958, Soviet production figures for 1957; Feb. 28, 1958, further development of the organization of collective farms and reorganization of the machine – tractor stations.

CHAPTER 9

(see also references for ch. 5)

Brown, R. H. *Historical Geography of the United States*, New York, 1948. An interesting account of the filling up of continental U.S.A.

Dean, V. M. *The United States and Russia*, Oxford, 1948.

Kennan, G. F. *Russia, the Atom and the West*, B.B.C. Reith Lectures in *The Listener*, Nov. 14, 1957 – Dec. 19, 1957. Published in book form, 1958.

Roberts, H. L. (Editor). *Russia and America, Dangers and Prospects*, New York, 1956.

Soule, G. *Economic Forces in American History*, Bennington (Vt), 1952.

Statistical Abstract of the United States, a yearly publication of the U.S. Department of Commerce, Bureau of the Census.

Williamson, H. F. (Editor). *The Growth of the American Economy*, New York, 1951, with contributions on this subject by many experts.

SELECTED ARTICLES FROM
THREE PERIODICALS

GM = The Geographical Magazine (English)
NG = The National Geographic Magazine (U.S.A.)
TR = The Times Review of Industry (almost all are
        Reports from Overseas at end)

ANGLO-AMERICA AND ARCTIC

Canada: oil crisis (TR Jan. 58); *U.S.A.:* a European in America (GM Dec. 57); *Canada:* Br. Columbia (TR Dec. 57); *Canada:* uranium (TR Oct. 57); *Canada:* U.K. exports to (TR July 57); *U.S.A.:* railways (TR July 57); *Canada:* Newfoundland minerals (TR June 57); *Canada:* early warning radar (GM Apr. 57); *Arctic:* airlines over (GM Mar. 57); *Canada:* steel (TR Nov. 56); *Canada:* St Lawrence seaway (TR Oct 56); *Canada:* Kitimat aluminium (NG Sept. 56); *Alaska* (NG June 56); *Greenland:* (NG Jan. 56); *Canada:* atomic energy (TR Jan. 56); *Canada:* Eskimos (GM Dec. 55); *Greenland:* ice-cap (NG Jan. 56).

Selected References

LATIN AMERICA

Argentina (NG Mar. 58); *Argentina:* energy (TR Feb. 58); *Brazil:* Amazonia (TR Feb. 58); *Br. Guiana:* Indians (NG June 57); *Mexico:* mining (TR June 57); *Haiti* (TR Apr. 57); *Brazil:* foreign investment (TR Mar. 57); *Panama:* canal (GM Feb. 57); *Venezuela* (TR Feb. 57); *Brazil:* farming in south (GM Jan. 57); *Brazil* (TR Oct. 56); *Peru:* extending cultivation (TR Sept. 56); *Bolivia* (TR Aug. 56); *Venezuela* (GM July 56); *Argentina:* last 10 years (TR Mar. 56); *Bolivia* (GM Aug. 55); *Peru:* oil (TR Aug. 55); *Colombia* (TR Mar. 55); *West Indies* (GM Feb. 55); *Mexico:* social experiment (GM Jan. 55); *Brazil:* São Paulo (GM Nov. 54); *Ecuador* (TR Sept. 54); *Jamaica* (NG Mar. 54); *Brazil:* jungle (GM Mar. 53); *Trinidad* (NG Jan. 53); *Amazon* (NG Sept. 52); *Puerto Rico* (NG Apr. 51); *Peru and Bolivia* (NG Oct. 50); *Uruguay* (NG Nov. 48).

AFRICA EXCEPT NORTHWEST AND NORTHEAST

Un. S. Africa: coal (TR Mar. 58); *Un. S. Africa:* metals (TR Feb. 58); *Swaziland* (GM Nov. 57); *Un. S. Africa:* communications (TR Oct. 57); *C. Africa* (NG July 57); *Ghana* (GM June 57); *Portuguese Guinea* (GM Mar. 57); *Senegal* (GM Feb. 57); *Un. S. Africa:* steel (TR Jan. 57); *Un. S. Africa:* industries (TR Oct. 56); *N. Rhodesia:* copper (GM Sept. 56); *Nigeria* (GM Feb. 56); *Mauritius* (NG Jan. 56); *Portuguese Africa* (GM Nov. 55); *Kenya* (GM Jan.–Feb. 55); *Kenya* (NG Oct. 54); *Uganda* (GM May 54); *Bechuanaland* (GM Aug. 53); *Basutoland* (GM July 53); *Swaziland* (GM June 53); *Fr. Equat. Africa* (GM Jan. 53); *Un. S. Africa:* shanty towns (GM Nov. 52); *Belgian Congo* (NG Mar. 52); *Liberia* (NG Feb. 48).

AUSTRALASIA

Australia: good coverage in TR each month since Jan. 57. *New Zealand:* projects (TR Nov. 55); general (GM June 53 and NG Apr. 52). *New Guinea, etc.:* northeast (NG Oct. 55); *Papua* (GM Aug. 55). *Australian tropics:* northwest (GM June 53); *Arnhem land* (NG Mar. 48, Sept. and Dec. 49).

NON-COMMUNIST EUROPE AND NORTHWEST AFRICA

European economic union, etc.: (TR Dec. 56, Jan. 57, Apr. 57, Oct. 57 and Jan. 58). *Denmark* (GM Mar. 58); *France:* railways (TR Nov. 57); *Italy:* Fiat (TR June 57); *Netherlands:* reclamation (GM May 57); *Spain* (TR May 57); *N.W. Africa:* Sahara oil (TR Mar. 57);

Selected References

Germany (TR Feb. 57); *Netherlands* (TR Oct. 56); *N.W. Africa:* Sahara resources (TR Sept. 56); *Germany:* steel (TR Aug. 56); *Greece:* lignite (TR June 56); *France:* Rhone (GM Mar. 56); *Scandinavia* (GM Mar. 56); *Italy:* oil (TR Mar. 56); *Morocco* (NG Feb. 55); *Libya* (GM Sept. 54); *West Germany* (GM Sept. 54); *Italy:* South Italian fund (GM Apr. 54); *Iceland* (NG Nov. 51).

SOUTHWEST ASIA AND NORTHEAST AFRICA

Kuwait (TR Mar. 58); *Sudan* (TR Nov. 57); *Ethiopia* (GM Sept. 57); *Aden* (NG Feb. 57); *Egypt* (GM Oct.–Nov. 56); *Afghanistan* (GM June 56); *Turkey:* trade (TR June 56); *Turkey:* economic expansion (TR Apr. 56); *Lebanon* (GM Aug. 55); *Iraq:* prospects (GM Sept. 53); *Afghanistan* (NG Sept. 53); *Sudan* (NG Feb. 53); *Kuwait* (NG Dec. 52); *Yemen* (NG Feb. 52); *Iran* (NG Oct. 51); *Turkey* (NG Aug. 51).

SOUTH ASIA

India: oil (TR Mar. 58); *Burma:* Buddhism (GM Jan. 58); *India:* Malabar fishermen (GM Dec. 57); *India:* Damodar scheme (TR Dec. 57); *India:* industries (TR Nov. 57); *India:* various articles (GM Aug. 57); *Pakistan:* gas (GM Aug. 57); *Nepal* (NG July 57); *India:* northeast (GM Dec. 56); *Nepal* (GM Oct. 56); *India:* industries (TR July 56); *India:* villagers (NG Apr. 56); *India:* minerals (TR Apr. 56) *India* (GM Nov. 53); *Ceylon:* rural development (GM June 53); *Pakistan:* prospects (GM June 53); *Kashmir* (GM Feb. 53); *Bhutan* (NG Dec. 52); *Pakistan* (NG Nov. 52); *Kashmir* (NG Apr. 48).

SOUTHEAST ASIA

North Vietnam (TR Oct. 57); *Indonesia* (TR Apr. 57); *Sarawak* (NG May 56); *North Borneo* (TR Jan. 56); *Indonesia* (NG Sept. 55) *Malaya:* new villages (GM Apr. 55); *Malaya* (NG Feb. 53); *Indo-China* (NG Sept. 52); *Indonesia* (NG Jan. 51).

JAPAN, KOREA, FORMOSA

Formosa (NG Mar. 57); *Formosa* (GM Apr. 56); *Japan:* Hokkaido (GM Oct. 55); *Hong Kong* (NG Feb. 54); *Japan* (GM Nov. 53) *Japan* (GM Jan. 53); *South Korea* (NG June 50); *Japan* (NG May 50) *Formosa* (NG Feb. 50).

Selected References

U.S.S.R. AND MONGOLIAN PEOPLE'S REPUBLIC

U.S.S.R.: education (TR Jan. 58); Europe–Asia rail links (TR Dec. 57); 40 years after Revolution (GM Oct. 57); gold (TR Sept. 57); power transmission, diamonds (TR Aug. 57); social differences (GM June 57); light industry (TR Mar. 57); coal (TR Feb. 57); Trans-Siberian (GM Jan. 57); new economic figures (TR Oct. 56); Baykal industrial area (TR July 56); Asiatic U.S.S.R. (TR May 56); power transmission (TR Apr. 56); industry (TR Nov. 55); *Mongolian People's Republic:* economic advances (TR Aug. 56); general (GM July 55).

COMMUNIST EAST EUROPE

Poland: impressions (GM Feb. 58); *Hungary* (TR Oct. 57); *Hungary:* endurance of (GM Feb. 57); *Yugoslavia:* mining (TR Oct. 56); *Poland:* minerals (TR Sept. 56); *Poland:* shortfalls in production (TR Aug. 56). *Yugoslavia:* re-settlement (GM Nov. 55); *Danube:* traffic (TR June 55).

CHINA

Yangtse bridge (TR Dec. 57); investment (TR Sept. 57); West China (GM July 57); surmounting late start (TR Jan. 57); Lhasa, Tibet (GM July 55).

ANTARCTICA

In NG Sept. 57, July 57, Aug. 56, and in GM Sept. 57.

APPENDIXES

APPENDIX 1

THE POSITION OF RUSSIA IN RELATION TO EUROPE

The important question of whether or not Russia is part of Europe and part of the West seems largely a matter of opinion. Prof. A. J. Toynbee does not include Russia in the West, for he is no doubt thinking of West and East in terms of the Roman Empire and its successor states and churches. In *The World and the West*,[1] for example, he says: 'Russia has managed to hold her own against the west by adopting western weapons.' It is unfortunate that many people think of the West as being Western Europe and the U.S.A. and the East as being India, China, and other countries of Asia, and they therefore tend to put Russia with the East in this broader sense, thus excluding it from Europe. O. Spengler would not even include Russia in Europe, as, for example, in this passage in *The Decline of the West*:[2] 'every non-European tries and will try to fathom the secret of this terrible weapon (the machine). Nevertheless, inwardly he abhors it, be he Indian or Japanese, Russian or Arab.' The contrary idea that Russia is part of the West is expressed by Lord Bertrand Russell in the *Observer*, Sun. 6 July 1958, where, quoting President Sukharno of Indonesia, he talks of 'the Western countries, including Russia'. The important question of Russia's position in Europe is ably reviewed by B. H. Sumner in a paper, *Russia and Europe*.[3]

The question seems to be a matter of classification. Toynbee appears to distinguish between eastern and western Europe: e.g. 1a England, France, Spain, Italy, Germany, etc.; 1b Russia. Spengler's classification would be : 1 England, France, U.S.A., etc.; 2 Russia, Arab world, China, Japan, etc. These classifications are vague, and, of course, any more precise classification depends on the basis chosen. If the grouping is by language, then since the Russian language is Slavonic, a branch of the Indo-European family, Russian belongs to Europe. A classification on a linguistic basis would be 1a Spain, France, Italy, etc. (Romance languages); 1b Germany, Sweden, England, etc. (Teutonic); 1c Poland, Russia, etc. (Slavonic); 2 Chinese; 3 Turco-Tatar; 4 Arabic, etc. If the classification is made according to religion, then Russia is in the Christian world and likewise part of Europe even if the Russian church has its origins in the Orthodox

1 See The *Listener*, Nov. 20–Dec. 25, 1952.
2 Translation by C. F. Atkinson, New York, 1928, vol. 2, p. 504, footnote.
3 In *Oxford Slavonic Papers*, vol. 2, ed. S. Konovalov. Oxford, 1951.

Church. A classification by religions might be 1a Orthodox countries; 1b (i) Catholic countries; 1b (ii) Protestant countries; 2 Muslim countries; 3 Hindu countries, etc. Racially, too, the Russians are Europeans, for they belong to the Caucasiform group, and in physical characteristics they closely resemble the inhabitants of Central and North Europe.

One of the main reasons for suggesting that Russia is not part of Europe is the fact that for several centuries most of it was controlled by Mongol and Tatar invaders from Asia. But Portugal and most of Spain and Sicily (by the Moors), and the whole of the Balkans (by the Turks) would also have to be excluded from Europe on these grounds, for they, like Russia, have been conquered and held by non-European powers and, in some ways, influenced by them more strongly than Russia was.

Another possible reason for excluding Russia from Europe is the fact that until recently it lagged far behind the leading industrial nations of the continent, and the exchange of cultural and technical knowledge has therefore been one-sided. But what Russia has borrowed is mainly European rather than Asian, for there have long been important cultural connexions with the rest of Europe. Italian architects were working in the Principality of Moscow as early as the 15th century, while numerous Dutch and French terms in the Russian language bear witness to the influence of these countries in such different matters as navigation and dress. Marxism and Communism originated in Western Europe, and Lenin spent much of his life here. The contemporary Soviet technical language is full of terms borrowed from German and English and merely used in transliterated form.

In spite of this borrowing we should not underestimate the pre-Revolutionary Russian contribution to European science and art in the regional classification of soils, in agronomy, in the ballet and the novel. In many branches of science, Soviet scientists are now on a level with their counterparts in Western Europe and the U.S.A., and the launching by the Russians of the first earth satellite appears finally to have convinced even the Americans of the ability of the Russians not only to *imitate* but also to *innovate* in technical matters (something the Japanese have not done). Indeed, it is becoming increasingly important that as much Soviet scientific material as possible should be made available in the English-speaking world.

Finally, what seems most important of all, the Russians (and Ukrainians and other peoples as well) consider themselves to be Europeans, for they live in the *European part of the U.S.S.R.* (as opposed to the Asiatic part). For this and other reasons already men-

Appendix 1

tioned, the author considers that Russia can be included with the maritime empire builders of Western Europe as a carrier of European conquest and culture to the non-European world.

Turkey's position in Europe is also debatable, but there appear to be good reasons for not considering Turkey as a European nation, although for several centuries the Ottoman Empire held an appreciable part of Europe. The Turkish language belongs to the Turco-Tatar family, other languages of which are spoken by various peoples in Central Asia. The religion practised by almost the whole of the Turkish nation is Islam. There was only a limited connexion between the Ottoman Empire and the nations of Western Europe until, in the 1920s, Turkey voluntarily adopted many features of European culture, including the Latin alphabet.

APPENDIX 2

SOVIET FOREIGN CONNEXIONS

The following list (from *Pravda*, 7 and 9 Nov. 1957) includes all the countries of the world whose communist parties (or sympathetic parties) were represented by a speaker at the gatherings in Moscow early in November 1957. The order of countries is the order in which the speeches are arranged in the above numbers of *Pravda*. U.S.S.R., communist China, Poland, Czechoslovakia, E. Germany, Romania, Bulgaria, Yugoslavia, Hungary, N. Viet-Nam, N. Korea, Albania, Mongolian People's Republic, France, Italy, Great Britain, India, Spain, W. Germany, Indonesia, Austria, Finland, Argentina, Italy (socialist), Denmark, Sweden, Norway, Syria and Lebanon, Japan, Belgium, Netherlands, Canada (progressive), Israel, Australia.

A useful idea of the extent of Soviet influence in cultural and economic matters is given by the following list of countries in which the Soviet Union has an embassy, a legation (L), or diplomatic relations but no representative (R). In addition to all the members of the communist bloc, the list includes: in *non-communist Europe:* all countries except Spain and Portugal; in *Africa:* Egypt, Ethiopia Libya, Sudan; in *Southwest Asia:* Afghanistan, Iran, Israel, Lebanon (L), Saudi-Arabia (R), Syria, Turkey, Yemen (R); *South and Southeast Asia:* Burma, India, Indonesia, Nepal, Pakistan, Thailand (L); *America:* Canada, U.S.A., Argentina, Bolivia (R), Costa Rica (R), Dominican Rep. (R), Ecuador (R), Guatemala (R), Mexico, Nicaragua (R), Uruguay (R); *Australasia:* Australia, New Zealand.

(N.B. The list is, of course, constantly changing)

APPENDIX 3

Events in mid-1958 in Southwest Asia have once again shown how this part of the world can easily become a trouble area at very short notice. Our mistake is to expect answers to appear to Middle East questions, including Cyprus, as quickly as crises come.

France, too, has held a prominent place in the news since summer 1958. Now that it has emerged from a long period of political chaos, present leaders appear to be trying to catch up by turning the former French colonies overnight into a kind of British Commonwealth. Success has come from the appeal to the colonial peoples, for only one, French Guinea, has chosen immediate independence from France. Algeria remains a difficult area and surely must continue to do so until an appreciable part, if not all, of the Muslim population achieves living standards close to those at present enjoyed by the French colonists, or at least can foresee prospects of achieving them in the future.

Formosa (p. 200) has also come into the news again. Since the Chinese communists have committed themselves to taking Formosa eventually, it seems unlikely that they will ever recognize Chinese nationalist possession of it, and surely it is only a matter of time before they become powerful enough to take it, with or without U.S. opposition. Meanwhile, a more immediate problem for the communists is to clear the way for their shipping to pass between ports of North and South China. At present movement is prevented by the Chinese nationalist blockade of the Strait of Formosa. The capture of Quemoy and other offshore islands held by the nationalists would certainly help to open the way for coastal shipping.

In China itself (pp. 223–5), remarkable economic developments are claimed. *Pravda* (1 Oct. 1958) announces that 1958 steel output will be 10·7 m. tons, compared with 5 m. in 1957, coal 210 m. tons (117 m. in 1957), electricity 27½ thousand m. kwh (19 in 1957) and grain 350 m. tons. Undoubtedly industrial expansion is taking place more rapidly in China than in almost any of the other so-called underdeveloped regions of the world. Will China become another, but much more powerful version of Japan? This may be evident quite soon, for China is already putting cheap manufactured goods on the market, and is showing great interest in its boundaries and in the lands beyond them. Must all non-European peoples at some stage during their career of europeanization show resentment against the Europeans with whom they have come in contact? If China does so, where does the U.S.S.R. stand?

The so-called recession in the U.S.A. (see p. 260) appears to have passed its worst stage. Even if this recession and the slowing down of industrial expansion in Western Europe have not caused much hardship in the industrial countries themselves, one unfortunate consequence has been a general drop in the prices of mineral and agricultural raw materials (not matched by a drop in manufactured goods) at the expense of economic progress in the many countries that depend on the export of one or a small number of these raw materials for their economic survival. It is ironical that industrial capacity remains idle in the U.S.A. and other non-communist industrial countries, when so many other parts of the world are short of both capital and consumer goods. The non-communist world will have this problem to deal with as long as world productive capacity is very unevenly distributed, as it is at present.

The U.S.S.R. has not come off too well in the last few months in its competition with the capitalist world. In mid-1958, it issued its usual threats and warnings about U.S. and British intervention in Southwest Asia, but showed, as has so often been pointed out, that it respects strength, in this case the arrival of U.S. bombers in Turkey. As usual, too, it was quick to write off a situation once it saw that nothing could be gained. In the field of competitive sport (see p. 265), the decisive defeat of the Soviet football team in the World Cup in Sweden by the Brazilian team has shown once and for all that there is nothing special about Soviet sportsmen. In the sphere of technology, the partial success of the U.S. moon rocket in October 1958 before any announced Soviet success of this kind should bring to an end the Soviet cartoonists' paradise of U.S. failures.

INDEX

INDEX

Index

*Other recently published Penguin
Specials are described on
the following pages*

CHINA: NEW AGE AND NEW OUTLOOK

Ping-chia Kuo

S179

One of the world's most pressing issues is the rise of a new Colossus in the Far East. Professor Kuo gives in this book a stimulating and challenging analysis of the Chinese revolution and of the first decade of the Communist régime.

He treats with detachment, insight, and understanding the culmination of an economic and social revolution, the failures of the Kuomintang, and the rise of Communist leadership. He also describes the establishment of a strong central government after 1949, and the important issues of 'socialist transformation' and 'socialist construction' which have filled the last decade. Equally authoritative and penetrating are his chapters on the new social milieu and on foreign policy changes.

For this Penguin edition Dr Kuo has brought the book up to date with new material. On its first publication in 1956 it was widely praised in England and America:

Spectator: 'A notable book which no student of Eastern politics can afford to overlook'

New Statesman: 'Dr Kuo . . . writes as an historian. His is a deeply reflective and courageous book' (David Hawkes)

Reynolds News: 'He brings to his task both erudition and notable fairness of outlook . . . eminently readable, and has the balanced view of a well-informed onlooker' (Earl Attlee)

New York Times: 'Every thoughtful American should read *China: New Age and New Outlook*' (Arthur M. Schlesinger)

Saturday Review: 'A refreshing and unique contribution. . . . For all concerned with China and East Asia as they are today, it is "must" reading' (Kenneth S. Latourette)

KHRUSHCHEV'S RUSSIA

Edward Crankshaw

S182

This book deals neither with the Russia of the tourist, nor with that much discussed enigma, the Russia of the conference room. There is a third country, Khrushchev's Russia, too seldom seen for what it is, too often confused with the mask it wears in the world arena.

The author does not discuss Russian foreign policy, nor (except in a brief account of the war and of the re-shuffling after Stalin's death) Russian history. He is concerned with the material progress and internal aims that have established themselves under Khrushchev, with the targets set to bring the country level with America in both *per capita* and total production, with Khrushchev the man (whom the author sees primarily as a superb practical administrator), with the new young Russians and their mental climate, and with the inside story of the Pasternak affair, of which a fascinating account is given.

The result is a book not about an international symbol, but about a reality. It will thus appeal to those who are interested in what Russia is today, and not with what it has come to represent.